Book Buddies

Book Buddies

A Tutoring Framework for Struggling Readers

THIRD EDITION

Marcia Invernizzi
Donna Lewis-Wagner
Francine R. Johnston
Connie Juel

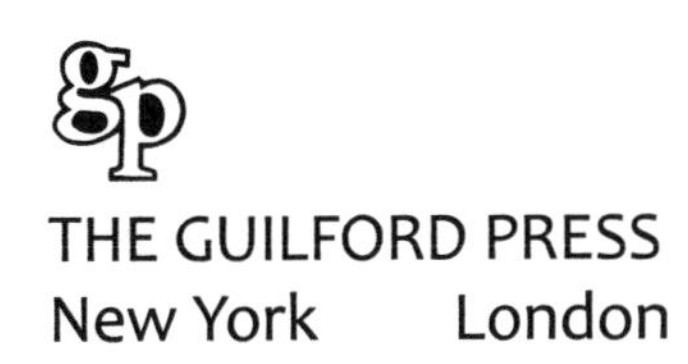

THE GUILFORD PRESS
New York London

A Division of Guilford Publications, Inc.
370 Seventh Avenue, Suite 1200, New York, NY 10001
www.guilford.com

Printed in the United States of America

This book is printed on acid-free paper.

Last digit is print number: 9 8 7 6 5 4 3 2 1

Library of Congress Cataloging-in-Publication Data is available from the publisher.

ISBN 978-1-4625-4549-0 (paperback) – ISBN 978-1-4625-4550-6 (hardcover)

About the Authors

Marcia Invernizzi, PhD, is the Edmund H. Henderson Professor Emerita of Reading Education at the University of Virginia (UVA). As cofounder of Book Buddies and PALS, an early literacy screening and diagnostic tool for PreK through the elementary grades, she has a strong interest in evidence-based practices to ensure early language and literacy success. These practices were honed at UVA's McGuffey Reading Center, a reading clinic that Dr. Invernizzi directed for many years, and are described in several of her coauthored books, including *Words Their Way: Word Study for Phonics, Vocabulary, and Spelling Instruction.* A former classroom teacher and reading specialist, Dr. Invernizzi continues to engage with preschools, elementary schools, and educational organizations seeking to ensure that *all* children learn to read.

Donna Lewis-Wagner, MEd, is a reading specialist and coordinator of UVA's America Reads federal work–study program. She has served in elementary schools as a Book Buddies coordinator, Title I reading teacher, and intervention coordinator. A former journalist and publicist, Ms. Lewis-Wagner was inspired by her 4 years as a Book Buddies volunteer tutor to pursue a career in reading education, earning her master's degree in reading from UVA.

Francine R. Johnston, EdD, taught courses in literacy and coordinated the Reading Master's Program at the University of North Carolina at Greensboro until her retirement in 2012. After teaching first grade for 12 years, she later worked as a Book Buddies coordinator while pursuing her doctorate in reading education. Dr. Johnston has a special interest in how children learn to read and spell and is the illustrator and coauthor of *Words Their Way: Word Study for Phonics, Vocabulary, and Spelling Instruction.*

Connie Juel, PhD, is Professor Emerita of Education at Stanford University. Her research focuses on literacy acquisition, with a particular interest in how classroom instruction affects the development of children with different reading and linguistic profiles. A former elementary school teacher, Dr. Juel is noted for her longitudinal research on models of reading development and her work on interventions to help struggling readers. She is a recipient of the Oscar S. Causey Award for outstanding contributions to reading research from the Literacy Research Association and was inducted into the Reading Hall of Fame.

Preface

As the Book Buddies tutoring framework nears a fourth decade of effective reading intervention, we present the third edition of *Book Buddies: A Tutoring Framework for Struggling Readers*. In this edition we offer examples of additional instructional activities, including FastRead reproducibles. These and our other reproducible materials appear in the appendices and can also be accessed online through the book's companion website (for more information, see the box at the end of the table of contents). The training videos are now also available online for convenient screening at the companion site. In addition, we have added a simple phonemic awareness task to the assessment activities presented in Chapter 3.

We have also updated the reading research and established Book Buddies' seat at the table of reading intervention programs that meet the International Dyslexia Association's basic components and teaching principles for instructional effectiveness. Along with our focus on English language learners at the end of each developmental lesson-plan chapter (emergent, beginning, and transitional), we have added a focus on learners with reading challenges, including dyslexia.

In a recent elementary school intervention team review of a student's dyslexia diagnosis by a private educational psychologist, Donna discovered the psychologist had included *Book Buddies* in the report's list of recommended resources for the student's parents and educators. The Book Buddies framework does, in fact, offer an excellent tutoring model for students with a wide range of reading intervention needs, from those who require a little boost to those exhibiting more pronounced reading challenges, including dyslexia.

Simply said, amid the growing reading research revealing and reaffirming what works, Book Buddies remains relevant. It is an evergreen.

For nearly 30 years Book Buddies has helped thousands of children learn to read. Now and again we hear how some of those children are doing years after they leave the program. We celebrate a former Book Buddy now succeeding in her middle school honors language arts class and another former Book Buddy now attending a prestigious British university. We celebrate one of Marcia's Book Buddies, Mariam (a pseudonym), a refugee from Afghanistan who came to the United States before first grade. Mariam spoke no English prior to starting school. At the same time she was learning English, she was learning how to read. Mariam recently graduated from a top U.S. university and is now pursuing a master's degree in global affairs. She wants to work with refugees, just like her—and she is fulfilling her dream. Perhaps someday she will end up as a Book Buddies tutor!

We know solid reading ability is a critical tool for our children's success in school and for achieving their own future dreams. And we know early intervention is key for struggling and challenged readers to attain the reading ability they need. The third edition of *Book Buddies* is a resource for educators, university students, educational psychologists, and parents and caregivers. We wish you well as you use it to help young readers reach for the stars.

Acknowledgments

We are grateful to Tisha Hayes, director of the McGuffey Reading Center at the University of Virginia, for her help with this edition, and to Amy Waddell, who provided valuable feedback. Thanks to Mary Fowler for the FastRead activity that has become an integral part of Book Buddies instruction, and to Laura Lindemann and Susan Thacker-Gwaltney for their early input and consistent support of the program.

Special thanks go to Jeanette Rosenberg, a Book Buddies coordinator for 20 years and a generous and gracious ambassador for the program.

Book Buddies is an adaptation and expansion of Darrell Morris's Howard Street Tutoring Project (Morris, Shaw, & Perney, 1990). We are indebted to Darrell for his inspiration and leadership.

Over nearly 30 years, a number of foundations and organizations have provided generous grants to the Charlottesville Book Buddies program to buy books for the children to keep. They include the Charlottesville Area Community Foundation; Congregation Beth Israel of Charlottesville, Virginia; the Dollar General Literacy Foundation and Book Baskets; the Hershey Foundation of Cleveland, Ohio; the Inez D. Bishop Foundation of Charlottesville, Virginia; the Arnold F. Baggins Foundation of New Canaan, Connecticut; the Dammann Fund, Inc.; the Gerald and Paula McNichols Family Foundation; the State Farm Companies Foundation; the Wish You Well Foundation; Kiwanis of the Piedmont; Crestar Charlottesville 10-Miler; and VACRAO—the Virginia Association of Collegiate Registrars and Admission Officers. Thanks go to each of them for helping to inspire the love of reading in many children.

We also want to acknowledge with thanks the agencies responsible for funding important Book Buddies research: the U.S. Department of Education, the Office of Educational Research and Improvement, the Center for the Improvement of Early Reading Achievement, the National Institute for Literacy, and the Educational Research and Development Centers Program.

Last, but certainly not least, we want to thank the coordinators, teachers, paraprofessionals, university students, and volunteers who have shared their time, energy, patience, and passion for reading with Book Buddies children in Virginia and beyond. You have helped so many children to reach for the stars.

Contents

Purchasers of this book can download select practical tools and video files at *www.guilford.com/invernizzi-materials* for personal use or use with students (see copyright page for details).

Book Buddies

Chapter 1

The Book Buddies Tutoring Framework

Book Buddies is a one-on-one tutoring framework for primary-grade struggling readers featuring individualized, structured lesson plans based on ongoing assessment. It can be employed in school and university clinic settings, by individual tutors, and by parents or caregivers who wish to give a child a boost. In a school or university clinic, lesson plans are written by experienced reading teachers, usually reading specialists, who train tutors and supervise them during each lesson. Tutors are primarily volunteers; university students; and school personnel, including teachers, administrators and paraprofessionals (teacher assistants). Tutoring sessions are scheduled for 45 minutes, generally twice a week. For those children facing serious reading challenges, including *dyslexia,* or English language learners who are learning to speak English at the same time they are learning to read, we recommend daily lessons. (We italicize glossary terms throughout the book where we think a definition could be helpful.)

In this chapter we offer an overview of the Book Buddies framework and address its history, along with supporting research.

Early Intervention and One-on-One Tutoring Programs

Children who struggle in learning to read in the primary grades continue to do poorly in subsequent grades if additional literacy interventions are not implemented immediately (Clay, 1985; Elliott & Grigorenko, 2014; Juel, 1988; Vellutino, Fletcher, Snowling, & Scanlon, 2004). In fact, research shows that children who are not reading on grade level by the end of third grade usually fail to meet grade-level expectations for reading skills in future years (Francis, Shaywitz, Stuebing, Shaywitz, & Fletcher, 1996; McNamara, Scissons, & Gutknetch, 2011).

This grim reality has led to additional efforts to provide structured, research-based interventions to supplement classroom instruction. Many of these efforts have involved one-on-one tutoring largely because of the positive results obtained from longitudinal research (Vellutino & Scanlon, 2002; Vellutino et al., 1996; Vellutino, Scanlon, Small, & Fanuele, 2006) and the demonstrated effectiveness of one-on-one instruction as part of a multi-tiered approach to early intervention (Wanzek et al., 2018; Wanzek & Vaughn, 2007). The instruction in these evidence-based interventions targets language components that are fundamental to reading development:

- *Phonological awareness,* or awareness of speech sounds, especially *phonemic awareness* (or *phoneme awareness*), which is the conscious awareness of individual *phonemes* within words. A phoneme is the smallest unit of speech in a language system (e.g., the /c/ in *cat* and the /sh/ in *ship*).
- Sound–symbol associations and the *alphabetic principle* (how alphabet letters map to speech sounds)
- Word identification and *decoding* strategies that build on the sound structure of spoken words and their spelling
- *Phonics* and spelling (letter patterns within and across *syllables*)
- *Morphology* (base words and affixes)
- *Semantics* (word meanings)
- *Syntax* (word order, parts of speech, grammar, and sentence mechanics)

These components align with the criteria spelled out in the International Dyslexia Association's primer on Structured Literacy (Cowen, 2016). Importantly, in addition to teaching these elements directly, the evidence-based interventions provide ample opportunity for students to apply the skills while engaged in meaningful reading and writing activities.

While there is no evidence to support one specific structured intervention program over another (Shaywitz, Morris, & Shaywitz, 2008), there is evidence to suggest that interventions including these language components are superior to non-language-based interventions, such as those based on visual perception or motor skills (Aaron, 2012; Joshi, Treiman, Carreker, & Moats, 2008; Post & Carreker, 2002). Interventions that are structured explicitly to teach word identification and decoding strategies within a comprehensive, language-based curriculum benefit all students, especially those who struggle with reading, including those with dyslexia (Elliott & Grigorenko, 2014).

Different reading interventions package these language-based components within broader categories for ease of planning and implementation. The Book Buddies lesson plan is organized into four general categories: *rereading, word study, writing,* and *new reading.*

Book Buddies

Book Buddies addresses the language components in three lesson plans—for emergent, beginning, and transitional readers—that are arranged into four basic areas:

1. *Rereading* involves rereading previously read texts or reading easy text to increase confidence and fluency, to build a firm concept of word in text, and to solidify automatic word reading skills.
2. *Word study* includes phonological/phonemic awareness instruction, alphabet

and sound–symbol association, and phonics/spelling. Foundational language concepts like *phonology,* or the study of speech sounds, and the alphabetic principle are built upon and expanded as we teach children how the English spelling system represents various speech sounds in basic syllable structures, or spelling patterns like CVC (consonant–vowel–consonant) and CVCe (consonant–vowel–consonant plus silent *e*). Word study also includes instruction in morphology—for example, how meaning is represented through the spelling of *inflectional morphemes* such as the *s* for plural endings and the *-ed* for past tense.

3. *Writing* involves the application of foundational reading skills in writing along with instruction in syntax, including sentence structure, grammar, and mechanics. Writing can also enhance and extend reading comprehension.
4. *New reading* on the child's reading level is introduced at the end of each lesson. Reading new material provides practice in the application of word recognition, decoding, and phonics knowledge. It also provides the context for instruction in semantics, including word meanings and word usage, as well as the building of concepts and vocabulary. Over time, new reading selections increase in difficulty, adhering to a systematic, logical progression.

Explicit, Systematic and Cumulative, and Diagnostic

Cowen (2016) states the teaching principles that guide Structured Literacy instruction as *explicit, systematic and cumulative,* and *diagnostic.* The Book Buddies framework fundamentally embraces all these principles.

Explicit

Specific instructional activities within each of the Book Buddies lesson plan components are designed to explicitly, or directly, teach the foundational concepts through continuous student–tutor interaction. These explicit activities include *multi-sensory* teaching. Children see written letters and words while simultaneously saying and writing them to enhance memory and learning. They also engage in manipulating phonemes and letters as they learn sound–symbol associations through direct instruction in phonics and spelling. Teachers have long recognized the power of "see, say, write" because learning to read and spell requires making associations between speech sounds and visually distinct letters. The Book Buddies lesson plan provides lots of opportunities for students to have, in the words of Margaret Byrd Rawson, their "writing hands, eyes, ears, and voices working together for the conscious organization and retention of their learning" (International Dyslexia Association, 2000).

Systematic and Cumulative

Book Buddies lessons are built around the logical progression of written language and presented in a systematic and cumulative fashion. The scope and sequence of the curriculum begin with the easiest, most foundational concepts and build to more difficult concepts, with each learned concept informing the next. This instructional procedure can only work if there is a diagnostic component to the intervention, as only careful and ongoing assessment can indicate what students already know, understand, and can do—and what they need to learn next.

Diagnostic

At the start, the diagnostic component of Book Buddies allows tutors to decide on the best "point of entry," based on assessed needs. Book Buddies offers three different lesson plans: the emergent, beginner, and transitional plans. While all three lesson plans are structured, they are adaptable to individual needs demonstrated by performance on the Book Buddies literacy assessment.

Table 1.1 shows how the Book Buddies lesson plans' instructional components correspond to the Structured Literacy components described by the International Dyslexia Association's primer "What Is Structured Literacy?" (Cowen, 2016).

As shown in Table 1.1, instruction of these language-based components, as appropriate for the reader, is fluid throughout the Book Buddies lesson plan. For example, syntax instruction happens in the reading, writing, and word study sections of the lesson plans; sound–symbol association instruction happens throughout the plans. This is because the parts of each plan work together as a structured whole.

A Note about Phonics Instruction

Research studies have consistently demonstrated the effectiveness of systematic phonics instruction for beginning readers (Brady, 2011; de Graaff, Bosman, Hasselman, & Verhoeven, 2009; National Reading Panel, 2000; Spear-Swerling, 2019). Superior results come from phonics programs with a planned sequence of instruction that moves logically from easier to more difficult skills, as presented in the Book Buddies framework. While there is no question about the superiority of systematic phonics instruction, there is still confusion (and controversy) at the granular level of sound–symbol instruction. Should systematic phonics instruction emphasize individual grapheme–phoneme correspondences only? Or should the instruction also include attention to larger phonological units such as *onsets* (beginning consonants, consonant blends, and consonant digraphs) and *rimes* (the spelling pattern constituted by the vowel and the letters that follow). In other words, should decoding of the word *top* be taught only as *t–o–p,* or is there a time and place for teaching it as *t–op*?

Some studies conducted since the publication of the National Reading Panel report (2000) have shown results in favor of phonics instruction that emphasizes individual grapheme–phoneme correspondences (e.g., Johnston, Watson, & Logan, 2009).

Others have reported outcomes showing that instruction of larger spelling chunks within the onset and rime is equally as effective (Christensen & Bowey, 2005; Walton & Walton, 2002). Missing from this debate is what we know about the development of phonological awareness and children's parallel understanding of how the spelling of words represents the sounds of speech.

We know, for example, that very young children grasp larger units of speech sounds, such as syllables and rhymes, more easily than individual phonemes. This is why phonological awareness instruction for emergent readers typically progresses from becoming aware of larger speech sound units before progressing to smaller ones such as phonemes (Invernizzi & Tortorelli, 2013). And we know that before children even understand what a printed word is (as opposed to a syllable or phrase), and

TABLE 1.1 **How Book Buddies Aligns with Structured Literacy Components**

Structured Literacy components	Book Buddies components
Phonology: The study of speech sounds. *Phonological awareness* includes the conscious awareness of the sound structures within spoken words, including syllables, rhyme, and phonemes (the smallest unit of speech sounds). *Phonemic awareness* is the ability to consciously identify individual phonemes.	Addressed in the alphabet, language play (emergent plan), and word study (all plans) sections of the Book Buddies lesson plans. Includes multisensory activities in rhyme, syllables, beginning sounds, and individual phonemes within words.
Sound–symbol association: Mapping individual phonemes to letters (graphemes) and vice versa. Includes the *alphabetic principle:* the ability to segment individual sounds within spoken words and match letters to each one while spelling.	Addressed in all areas of the Book Buddies lesson plans with a heavy emphasis on the application of the alphabetic principle in both reading and writing.
Syllables: Units of spoken language that consist of a vowel that may be preceded and/or followed by several consonants. Syllable awareness helps readers decode and spell unfamiliar words. There are predictable spelling patterns within syllables such as CV, CVC, CVCe, CVVC, and others, such as *r*-influenced patterns.	The scope and sequence of Book Buddies word study systematically addresses the spelling patterns of the most common syllable types, including CV, CVC, CVCe, CVVC, and *r*-influenced patterns. Syllable awareness is taught within the language play piece of the emergent lesson plan; the spelling of syllable types is taught in the word study sections of the beginning and transitional plans.
Morphology: The study of morphemes, the smallest unit of meaning in a language. Morphemes in written English include base words and affixes. Morphological knowledge helps learners read and understand the meaning of words.	Book Buddies addresses the spelling of singular and plural nouns (a form of inflectional morphology), words with multiple meanings, homophones, and the spelling of present and past tenses of irregular verbs. Morphology is taught in the word study sections of all the lesson plans and applied in the reading and writing sections.
Syntax: The structure of sentences including word order, parts of speech and grammar, and other mechanics of written language. Knowledge of syntax helps learners make sense of reading and writing.	Book Buddies addresses syntax through the reading and writing sections of all three lesson plans. Syntax is also addressed in the word study section of the lesson plans where students are asked to compare and contrast words by parts of speech and to construct sentences with word-bank words.
Semantics: Knowledge of the meaning underlying words and how words are related to each other and to overarching concepts.	Book Buddies addresses word meanings in the word study, writing, and new reading sections of all three lesson plans through such activities as concept sorts, vocabulary instruction, the study of homophones, and completion of various graphic organizers.

where printed words begin and end, they have trouble segmenting the individual phonemes within words (Flanigan, 2007; Mesmer & Williams, 2015; Morris, Bloodgood, Lomax, & Perney, 2003). Berninger's Multiple Connections Model (Berninger, 2008; Berninger, Lester, Sohlberg, & Mateer, 1991) has demonstrated how children connect the phonological attributes of words, syllables, and phonemes to the representation of those attributes in spelling as their word knowledge grows in response to instruction.

So, while learning to read in an alphabetic writing system like English absolutely requires an awareness of individual phonemes and how these phonemes map onto letters and letter combinations, there is also evidence to support the teaching of larger spelling chunks at certain points in development as well.

Book Buddies builds on this developmental perspective and offers three distinct lesson plans depending on children's degree of phonemic awareness, their attainment of the alphabetic principle, and their spelling development. The emergent reader plan focuses on foundational print skills, including how words are made up of syllables, onsets, and rimes, and how letters mark the beginning sounds of syllables and words. The beginning reader plan focuses on individual phonemes, letter–sound correspondences, *and* letter clusters within closed-syllable types (e.g., CVC and CVCC), and the transitional reader plan focuses on spelling patterns within additional syllable types (e.g., CVCe, CVVC, and *r*-influenced), base words, and simple inflectional morphology.

Book Buddies and Multi-Tiered Systems of Support

A multi-tiered reading intervention framework involves evidence-based instruction based on assessment and regular progress monitoring of students, beginning with how well they succeed in regular education classrooms—the first tier in a multi-tiered approach. The approach may be referred to as a multi-tiered system of support (MTSS), response to intervention (RTI), or positive behavioral interventions and supports (PBIS; National Center on Intensive Intervention, 2020). The most common model offers three tiers, with instruction becoming more intensive at each level. Across tiers, groups become smaller and duration and frequency of instruction increases.

An individualized program using diagnostic assessment to plan instruction, Book Buddies takes a problem-solving approach to literacy instruction. It is flexible enough to support an expanded lesson plan and scheduling beyond 2 days a week. As such, the Book Buddies instructional process fits with the data-based individualization that guides a multi-tiered intervention framework, and it can be employed in both a second- and third-tier intervention. As a twice-weekly, 45-minute, one-on-one intervention, Book Buddies works ideally in the Tier 2 model but can be used at Tier 3 depending on who is doing the tutoring and how often. As a more intensive Tier 3 intervention Book Buddies would be increased to daily lessons. Here a professional teacher, usually a reading specialist or special educator, would likely act as tutor. The lesson plans can also be extended to include additional activities as suggested in Chapters 4, 5, and 6.

Book Buddies Background and Research

Volunteer and Paraprofessional Tutorials

Over the last few decades, given the growing number of children who have needed additional literacy support and the reality of budget constraints, many school districts have been forced to consider less expensive means of providing early intervention (Invernizzi, Rosemary, Juel, & Richards, 1997; Wasik, 1997). Programs using community volunteers as tutors, including university students and paraprofessionals or teacher assistants, have provided one source of help. There is a long history of research conducted on such programs, starting in the 1990s.

Studies reported significant gains for children in the Howard Street Program, in which the tutors were volunteers (Morris, Shaw, & Perney, 1990) and Next Steps, a program using teacher assistants to implement the Howard Street model (Brown, Morris, & Fields, 2005). Students tutored by teacher assistants in another program, Partners in Reading, also showed significant gains (Miller, 2003). Juel's cross-age tutoring program using university student athletes as tutors yielded positive results as well (Juel, 1991, 1996).

The Book Buddies Tutorial

Book Buddies was the first large-scale model to mobilize hundreds of community volunteers in an alternative one-on-one intervention. Book Buddies was developed as a joint effort by the Charlottesville City Schools, the University of Virginia, and the community of Charlottesville, and was adopted in 1992 as part of the school division's long-range plan that all children read independently by third grade (Invernizzi, Juel, & Rosemary, 1996).

The community volunteers teach from a lesson plan prepared by reading specialists and are trained and supported on-site throughout the year. Analyses of the program have revealed the growing efficacy of the program. Children with more than 40 sessions have significantly outperformed children with fewer than 40 tutoring sessions on most pre- and posttest gain scores, and on both outcome measures of text reading and word recognition. Effect sizes for gains in word recognition have been considerably higher than effect sizes reported for other tutorials using paraprofessionals and volunteers (Invernizzi et al., 1997).

The gains over the years have demonstrated that a tutorial featuring two 45-minute sessions of one-on-one tutoring per week for a minimum of 20 weeks, conducted by a trained community or student volunteer under the supervision of an experienced reading teacher, can be an effective and affordable alternative intervention for children at risk for reading failure.

Further Book Buddies Research

In 1997 Book Buddies was replicated in four schools in New York City's South Bronx. Volunteer tutors recruited by the Experience Corps were trained by University of Virginia researchers. In a year-long study conducted at one of the schools, Book Buddies students showed significant gains at midyear, significantly surpassing students in an untutored group on measures of alphabet knowledge, word reading, and passage reading. A second group, tutored during the second half of the year, showed dramatic gains at the end of the year. End-of-year testing on both groups indicated no distinguishable differences between the two groups (Meier & Invernizzi, 2001).

Nearly 10 years later, in 2006–2007, independent researchers at Washington University in St. Louis and Mathematica Policy Research in Princeton conducted a study of the effectiveness of Experience Corps' New York City Book Buddies model. By this time the program had spread to 16 elementary schools in four boroughs. First and second graders in six of those schools became the basis of the study. Nearly all the students were minorities, and 15% were English language learners. Study results showed Book Buddies students scored significantly higher on the posttest measures than the control group did (Gattis et al., 2010).

Keys to Success for Book Buddies Tutorials

One key to the successful efforts using paraprofessionals, university students, and volunteers is likely the training and close supervision given to the tutors. In his analysis of five studies of one-on-one tutoring programs using noncertified tutors, Morris (2006) found the programs' effectiveness to depend largely on the "amount and quality of guidance" from the supervisor (p. 351). In all the programs referenced here, the tutors were trained and carefully supervised, with the volunteers in both Howard Street and Book Buddies supervised on-site during every lesson. Juel's tutors were students in her reading course.

Wasik (1998), in her review of effective volunteer tutoring programs, cites the importance of training and supervising tutors whose lesson plans are prepared by knowledgeable reading teachers. Wasik also stresses the critical importance of a structured lesson plan that includes rereading familiar material to build fluency; word analysis in both isolation and context; writing; and reading a new, slightly more difficult text. These elements are all essential components of the three Book Buddies lesson plans (found in Appendices A.1, A.2, and A.3).

A volunteer tutorial offers one model of an affordable, alternative form of early intervention that can help meet the needs of struggling readers. Book Buddies started as such and has proven highly effective. But the framework is not limited to school-based volunteer and paraprofessional tutorials. It is also appropriate in university clinic settings, for tutoring by trained individual tutors outside schools, and at home by parents and caregivers.

In whichever setting Book Buddies is employed, a key requirement is a point person, or *coordinator,* who is knowledgeable about reading instruction and can oversee organizational and instructional aspects of the tutorial. Another key requirement is collaboration between the people who interact with the child to be tutored. Teachers should collaborate with other teachers, the tutor, and parents. University clinic providers should collaborate with teachers, the tutor, and parents. Parents should collaborate with teachers and, if appropriate, university clinic providers.

In the next chapter we get into the nuts and bolts with a how-to guide for building a Book Buddies tutoring program.

Chapter 2

Getting Started with Book Buddies

We devote this chapter to "setting up shop": coordinator (or point person) and tutor responsibilities, determining whom to tutor, scheduling, gathering and organizing materials, and lesson planning. Finally, we outline recommended practices for tutor training and feedback.

Roles and Responsibilities

While Book Buddies is a reading intervention appropriate for use in multiple settings, we will generally address its implementation in schools and university clinics, where coordinators supervise tutor–child pairs. Trained tutors outside these settings will note that they fill both the coordinator and the tutor roles. Parent/caregiver tutors who are not trained in reading education will want to collaborate with their children's teachers, sharing the coordinator role.

Coordinators

In a school or university clinic setting, the heart of the Book Buddies tutorial is a triad composed of the coordinator, the tutor, and the child. At a school, coordinators may be reading specialists, instructional coaches, Title I reading teachers, and classroom teachers. In a university reading clinic, professors, doctoral students, and staff reading specialists serve as Book Buddies coordinators.

Coordinator responsibilities include:

- Assessing students individually at least three times a year to design an appropriate instructional program and to monitor children's progress;
- Administering ongoing assessments in the form of *spell checks, running records,* and observation;
- Training and providing continual support for tutors;

- Coordinating the instructional program with the classroom teacher and Title I reading teacher, reading specialist, or instructional coach;
- Writing individualized lesson plans to ensure that the needs of each student are being met;
- Documenting time, testing data, and anecdotal information regarding the program;
- Reporting children's progress to parents and teachers through conferences and written correspondence; and
- Recruiting tutors.

If Book Buddies is implemented across a school division, the school-based site coordinators meet regularly with one another and communicate with central office personnel. A child who moves to another school in the division is not lost in the shuffle but is instead picked up by the coordinator at the new school and assigned a tutor. Occasionally, a tutor will even move to the new school with the child.

Tutors

In a school program, coordinators recruit tutors who are available during the school day or after school. Tutors may be community volunteers; school personnel; and university students, including federal work-study/America Reads students. Tutors in university clinics tend to be university students.

Tutors have a number of responsibilities:

- Attend training sessions.
- Arrive for the tutorial ahead of time to review the lesson plan and to ask questions if necessary.
- Follow the instructional plan developed for their child by the site coordinator.
- Provide written feedback following each tutorial.

After the tutorial, tutors ideally meet with their site coordinator to give and receive oral feedback on their lesson. Regular communication is usually maintained through personal contacts and email.

Identifying Children for Book Buddies

If you are a university tutoring program, a parent, or an individual tutor, you know whom you are tutoring. Schools must decide whom to tutor.

Identifying which children would best be served through a reading tutorial is a complex process that varies from school to school. One thing is certain: *This is a decision that cannot be made alone.* The Book Buddies coordinator must collaborate with other school personnel to make these important decisions. Ideally, the Book Buddies tutorial should fit into a school's overall plan for ensuring that all children learn to read.

While Book Buddies has primarily been implemented with first and second graders, the framework laid out in this book can be used to tutor kindergartners and third graders as well. In Chapters 4, 5, and 6 we review in depth how Book Buddies differs for emergent, beginning, and transitional readers.

Title I Schools

Schools and school districts served by Title I, a federally funded program for remedial readers, have procedures for identifying children performing below grade-level expectations in reading. In these schools the Book Buddies coordinator will likely sit down in the fall with whoever oversees the Title I referrals and go over the referral list together. Generally, these lists are rank-ordered by need based on the previous spring's reading assessment results.

In most situations, there will be more children on the referral list than the Title I teacher or teachers can serve. If the Book Buddies tutorial occurs during the school day, a decision can be made as to which children would best be served directly by a Title I teacher or reading specialist, and which children would best be served by a volunteer, student, or paraprofessional tutor. If the tutorial occurs as an after-school program, some children might receive both Title I intervention *and* one-on-one assistance from an after-school tutor. More current fall assessments will help inform any decisions.

School Assessment Results

In schools that are not Title I schools, Book Buddies tutorial candidates may be determined from the previous spring's reading assessment results. Or if the school district conducts a reading assessment in the fall, schools may wait to use fall results. Teachers may also weigh in with concerns about individual students. All in all, the process of determining which students may be candidates for Book Buddies is a team decision.

English Language Learners

When selecting children to be served by Book Buddies, English language learners should not be excluded. English learners benefit greatly from the extra, intensive instruction in reading and the one-on-one nature of the tutorials. It is important when planning Book Buddies lessons for English learners that the coordinator compare the sounds of English to those of the child's primary language and be aware of the child's language and literacy experiences (Helman, Bear, Templeton, Invernizzi, & Johnston, 2012).

Determining Coordinator Caseload

When identifying children for Book Buddies, the coordinator and other school personnel will need to know how many children the coordinator can serve. The total number of tutor–tutee pairs a Book Buddies coordinator can supervise depends on how many hours a week the coordinator can work in that capacity. Time for the tutoring sessions must be considered together with planning, which consumes the bulk of the coordinator's time. Individualized lesson plans are based on ongoing assessment, including observation and tutor comments from each previous lesson plan, and they take time to prepare. They shouldn't be written during tutorials, when the coordinator is supervising and lending a hand when warranted.

For a rough calculation of weekly planning time, divide the total number of tutoring hours per week (for all children) in half. For example, if 15 children are to be tutored for 45 minutes two times per week, the total number of tutoring hours would be about 22. It would take the coordinator about half of that, 11 hours, to prepare for those 30 tutorials.

Assessment

If a reading assessment similar to the Book Buddies assessment has not been recently administered, the coordinator will need to assess each child identified for the program using the assessment outlined in Chapter 3. Even if a similar assessment has been recently conducted, the coordinator may want to administer the Book Buddies assessment to obtain further information. The coordinator must thoroughly familiarize himself with the results for each child in order to write appropriate, individualized lesson plans. The coordinator must be aware of what each child knows about literacy in order to propel the child forward as a reader and a writer.

Permissions

Every school division has rules and regulations for screening volunteers and for obtaining parental permission for children to participate in a tutorial like Book Buddies. A sample parent letter and permission form are found in Appendix B.

Scheduling Tutorials

School-Based Tutorials

The tutorial scheduling process is much easier if the tutorial is set up to be an after-school program. If it is designed as an in-school intervention, the first step is to get each teacher's schedule and then find out when each child is available. Take into account any other interventions, such as speech-language, special education, or English language instruction. The third step is to find out when tutors can come and to match up the two sets of schedules.

There are two important variables to keep in mind in scheduling tutorials. First is the number of tutorials per week. Research has determined that two times per week is the minimum number of tutoring sessions that will actually make a difference. Second is the number of tutors to be supervised at one time. The coordinator's feedback and guidance are essential to the success of a tutorial. To make that feedback possible, the number of simultaneous sessions must be kept small—no more than five or six. For this reason, it is helpful to schedule one group of tutors for a Monday–Wednesday tutorial and another group of tutors for a Tuesday–Thursday tutorial. Also, to maximize the number of students served, tutoring blocks instructing five to six children can be scheduled back to back on those days. Fridays are good for making up missed sessions due to student or tutor absence.

The number of tutorials per week would be increased for students with serious reading challenges or those learning to speak English at the same time they are learning to read. We recommend that these students be tutored daily by professional teachers.

Home-Based Tutorials

We have said that Book Buddies is appropriate for parents who wish to give a child a boost. That may be a small boost or a bigger one. Whichever it is, in order for your child to make progress, it is important to schedule at least two tutoring sessions per week (approximately 45–60 minutes each) at times when your child is not too tired. A location with limited distractions is recommended. The further behind your child is, the more sessions you will need to schedule. Regardless of the number of tutoring sessions you schedule each week, your child will need to practice reading appropriate material every day.

It is also important to use the diagnostic assessment described in Chapter 3. It will tell you what your child knows and what the child needs to learn to move forward. You may want to ask a teacher or tutor to administer the assessment. Regardless of whether you ask a professional to give the assessment, it is essential for parents to work in partnership with someone who is trained in teaching reading to children, especially if a child has already struggled with learning to read. If your child is significantly behind, you should not be the only provider of additional reading instruction unless you are a reading specialist or special educator. Even if you are homeschooling, it is important to collaborate with the teacher resources and expertise available in your school and/or community, particularly if your child is lagging behind in reading.

Acquiring and Organizing Books and Other Texts

Access to lots of text is essential to the success of the tutorial. One emergent or beginning reader who gets tutored twice per week for 7 or 8 months reads anywhere from 50 to 100 books in the tutorial setting alone. If other children are being tutored simultaneously, multiple copies of the same books are a must. There are two major sources of books for emergent, beginning, and transitional readers:

- *Series books that already come leveled by the publisher.* Most of these *leveled texts* can be purchased from educational publishers. However, some are also trade books and can be found in bookstores, in libraries, and online.
- *Trade books that the coordinator must level.* These books may be found in libraries or purchased from bookstores and online vendors.

Texts for Emergent, Beginning, and Transitional Readers

Readers at different stages read different kinds of text, as described below.

Emergent Readers

Emergent readers cannot read in the conventional sense because they know few, if any, words by sight and do not know how to sound out unfamiliar words using phonics. They need materials that offer a lot of support: short, predictable, patterned, and easy to memorize. Reading materials may include nursery rhymes, songs, jump-rope jingles, and easy poetry found in anthologies and online. Reproducible copies of nursery rhymes can also be found at the Webbing into Literacy website (*https://webbingintoliteracy.com*).

"Little books" are books specifically written by publishers for emergent and beginning readers. They include the Little Red Readers by Sundance/Newbridge and the PM Plus Starters series by Rigby. Most of the little books available from publishers come already labeled with the level of difficulty, or the publisher provides a leveling guide.

Other reading material for emergent readers can be created by the tutors and coordinators themselves. Children can tell about experiences they have had, and the tutors can write these down verbatim as the children speak. These "dictated experience stories" can be made into little books.

Beginning Readers

Beginning readers benefit from reading a wide range of text types. These include text in which the phonics elements they are studying are featured. Known as *decodable books,* these books are written with a controlled vocabulary of words that are phonetically regular (*can, pan, man*) and are usually leveled by the publisher. A list of phonics-featured book sets appears in Appendix C.

Beginning readers are also developing a sight vocabulary. They can read little books, but they also benefit from books with controlled vocabulary in which *high-frequency words* (*was, want, look*) repeat. These books are most often leveled too. The PM Plus Starters series from Rigby is popular for this purpose.

A number of publishers offer easy informational books, usually sold in leveled sets. These publishers include National Geographic and Sundance/Newbridge.

Beginning readers will also enjoy nursery rhymes, jump-rope jingles, and other rhymes and ditties. These can be found in books and online.

Trade Books for Emergent and Beginning Readers

Trade books for emergent and beginning readers include simple books written by popular children's authors like Sandra Boynton, Raffi, Nancy Tafuri, Brian Wildsmith, and Pat Hutchins. These books may be found in school and public libraries, in children's bookstores, and online. Information about their level of difficulty is not available on the books themselves, but a leveled list of trade books written by well-known children's authors may be found in Appendix D. Various websites, easily located with the term *leveled books,* provide other sources of leveled books.

Several publishers offer leveled series books that are trade books available in bookstores, in libraries, and online. Some of the books in these series are appropriate for beginning readers (primarily later beginners). These series include the Hello Reader series and are further addressed next, under Transitional Readers.

Transitional Readers

Transitional readers can read from a greater variety of books. Leveled series books are available from educational publishers, including the informational series National Geographic Windows on Literacy, TIME for Kids, Scholastic News Nonfiction Reader, and HarperCollins's Let's-Read-and-Find-Out Science (you can get some of these from online vendors too).

A number of leveled series books for transitional readers are trade books and can be found in bookstores, in libraries, and online. These include the easy-to-read books from the series I Can Read!, Hello Reader, DK Readers, Ready-to-Read, Scholastic's Just for You!, Penguin Young Readers, and Step into Reading. As mentioned earlier, some of these books are appropriate for beginning readers too. While these series are leveled, be aware that the leveling criteria may vary among publishers. A list of leveled trade series for transitional readers appears in Appendix E.

Transitional readers can read many other, unleveled trade books, including picture books by such authors as Jacqueline Woodson, David McPhail, Gary Soto, Doreen Cronin, Yolanda King, and Christopher Meyers. Children's poetry collections by Shel Silverstein, Jack Prelutsky, Lee Bennett Hopkins, and Eloise Greenfield provide delightful, easy reading. As children progress in their reading, they will also enjoy authors like Derrick Barnes, Cynthia Rylant, Arnold Lobel, and Ann Cameron; popular trade series such as Keena Ford, Fly Guy, Cam Jansen, and Magic Tree House; and informational materials such as *Your Big Backyard,* a magazine published by the National Wildlife Federation, and the *National Geographic Kids* magazine. A list of trade books by individual authors for transitional readers can be found in Appendix D, and a list of trade series by individual authors can be found in Appendix E.

Organizing Books for Instruction

In order to give children books they can read successfully, the books must be leveled using resources described earlier. These might be numbered levels or lettered levels or both, depending on the system you use. Because publishers use different systems for book leveling, Table 2.1 cross-references several of the more common methods for your convenience. Phonics-featured books, or decodable books, should be grouped by feature as well as the reading level.

Organizing by Level and Phonics Features

Book Buddies coordinators often stick adhesive colored dots on books to color-code reading level, or simply as labels on which to write the reading level. They usually organize their books in tubs that they keep on a table or cart in the tutoring room (see Figure 2.1). The books inside the tubs can be separated by tall cardboard dividers labeled by reading level.

Decodable books are organized by the phonics elements recurring in all the books. For example, books that feature beginning single consonant sounds are grouped alphabetically by the consonant and separated from books in which a particular vowel chunk, or *word family* (e.g., *at* or *in*), repeats. Within each phonics feature grouping we suggest keeping the books in order of reading level. A "phonics ladder" showing the developmental progression of phonics categories is shown in Table 2.2.

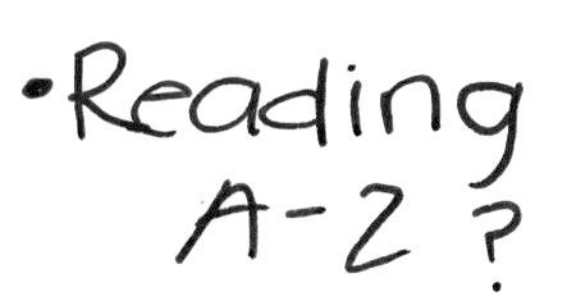

TABLE 2.1. Concordance of Spelling and Reading Development and Text Levels

Grade level Reading levels *Reading stages*	Spelling stages for planning word study **Chapter in *Book Buddies* text**	Lettered (Guided Reading) level	Numbered (Reading Recovery) level
K Readiness *Early emergent–middle emergent*	Early–middle emergent **Chapter 4**	A	1
K–1 Readiness *Middle emergent–late emergent*	Middle–late emergent **Chapter 4**	B	2
K–1 Preprimer 1 *Late emergent–early beginning*	Late emergent–early letter name **Chapters 4–5**	C	3–4
1 Preprimer 2 *Early–middle beginning*	Early–middle letter name–alphabetic **Chapter 5**	D	5–6
1 Preprimer 3 *Middle beginning*	Middle letter name–alphabetic **Chapter 5**	E	7–8
1 Primer (1.1) *Late beginning*	Late letter name–alphabetic **Chapter 5**	F and G	9–12
1–2 First (1.2) *Early transitional*	Early within word pattern **Chapter 6**	H and I	13–17
2 Second (2.1) *Middle transitional*	Middle within word pattern **Chapter 6**	J and K	18–19
2–3 Second (2.2–3.1) *Late transitional*	Late within word pattern **Chapter 6**	L, M, N	20–22

Benefits of Efficient Organization

Organizing your books in this way serves two important purposes. First, the books are organized for instruction in both phonics and reading. The organization forms a curriculum for phonics instruction and, at the same time, a developmental progression of reading difficulty. When students are paced systematically through this scope and sequence, they will be exposed to the phonics features they need to know and, at the same time, get lots of practice reading at appropriate levels of difficulty.

Second, the book organization lends itself to efficient planning. The coordinator must write many individualized lesson plans each week, and the materials must be preselected before the tutor arrives. Organizing the books by phonics elements and by gradations of difficulty makes this process much more efficient. The books are at

FIGURE 2.1. Tutoring Supply Center

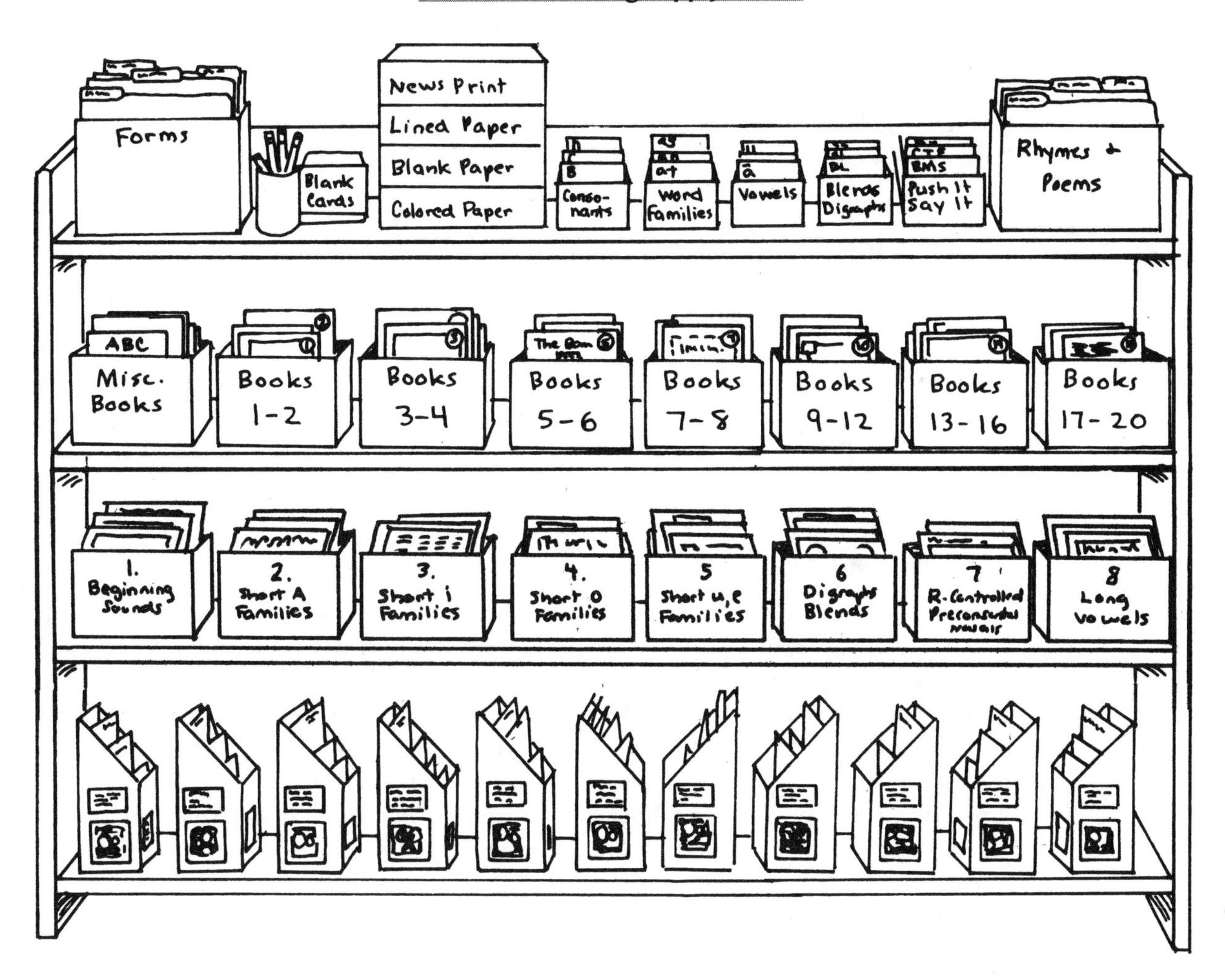

TABLE 2.2. Phonics Ladder

Beginning consonant sounds
Beginning consonant digraphs and blends—pictures
Short vowels—same-vowel rhyming word families
Beginning digraphs
Beginning *s*-blends
Short vowels—mixed-vowel word families
Beginning *l*- and *r*-blends
Short vowels—nonrhyming (outside word families)
Affricate blends and digraphs
Final digraphs and blends
r-influenced vowels
Preconsonantal nasals
Short vowels and long vowels (VCe)
Final *k* (*-ck*, *-ke*, *-k*)
Short, long, and *r*-influenced vowel sounds and patterns (CVVC, other)

the coordinator's fingertips, ready to be matched to the needs of each child. How to determine exactly what level book a child should read is described in Chapter 3. Once the initial level is determined, children should have plenty of opportunity to read many books on that level before advancing to the next. How fast the child advances through the levels is determined by the ease or difficulty with which the child is able to read the book.

Organizing Materials for Word Study and Phonics

Word Banks

A word bank is a collection of known words written on small cards to use for phonics and word study. Word-bank work is an important part of the emergent and beginning reader lesson plans, and some advance planning and preparation can make developing word banks go more smoothly.

Gathering Words for the Word Bank

Word-bank words come from the books the children have read and reread. Only words a child recognizes immediately, out of context, are appropriate for inclusion in the child's word bank. The challenge for the coordinator is how to facilitate this process. One way to plan ahead for gathering word-bank words is to place adhesive library book pockets in the back of each book. We recommend the short kind of book pocket so the word cards can easily be stored and retrieved without getting stuck down inside the pocket. The book pocket can be ordered online from school and library supply companies like DEMCO® (*www.demco.com*) or Vernon Library Supplies (*www.vernonlibrarysupplies.com*). Figure 2.2 illustrates the placement of the pocket in the back of the book.

Once the library pockets have been attached to the backs of the books, the coordinator can pick 6 to 10 words from each book, print them clearly on blank flashcards, and place the cards inside the book pockets. The words to be chosen include

FIGURE 2.2. Book with Pocket of Words

concrete nouns, adjectives, and verbs that evoke strong imagery (e.g., *dog, red, jump*), high-frequency words (e.g., *like, of, with, from*), and words that exemplify the phonics feature being taught (e.g., *mouse, mug,* and *mat* all start with the /m/ sound associated with the letter *m*). After a child has reread a book several times, the tutor can lay out the word cards from the back of the book and ask the child to name and pick up the words the child knows. A record of these words can be made on the alphabetized word-bank record form (see Appendix F) and then copied by the tutor onto blank word cards (about 1″ × 2½″) for the child's personal word bank. We suggest that the tutors complete this after the lesson, as it can take a few minutes. The book's word cards are returned to the book pocket in the back of the book for use by other students who will read that book at a different time.

Organizing the Words in the Word Bank

After planning ahead for the process of gathering word-bank words, coordinators can begin to think about where word cards will be kept and how best to organize them for instructional purposes. While there are different ways to store word-bank cards, we recommend small plastic baggies or rings. The word bank and word-bank activities are discussed in greater detail in Chapters 4 and 5.

Picture and Word Cards for Phonics Sorts

A routine part of the lesson plan for emergent, beginning, and transitional readers involves sorting picture and word cards for phonics instruction. These cards must be organized ahead of time so tutors may have easy access to the cards they need. Coordinators may wish to use ready-made phonics sorts, or they may choose to build sorts with word and picture cards organized and stored according to phonics feature.

Prepared Picture and Word Sorts

A complete curriculum of ready-made phonics sorts can be found in the Words Their Way supplemental sort books, listed under professional books in the back of this book. These paper sorts can be made available to the tutoring pair in two different ways. We recommend that they be photocopied, cut apart, and stored in labeled book pockets, envelopes, or baggies so they are ready to be used and reused by the tutors. An alternative is to supply the tutor with a copy of the sort that he or she cuts apart prior to tutoring. We do not recommend that children spend tutoring time cutting the sorts apart.

Prepared sorts can also be found at the website for the book *Words Their Way: Word Study for Phonics, Vocabulary, and Spelling Instruction* (Bear, Invernizzi, Templeton, & Johnston, 2020). These sorts are available to do electronically or with downloads.

Building Your Own Sorts

For those who are not using ready-made sorts, words for sorts can be written on individual word cards or on the template provided in Appendix G. Word lists of common word families can be found in Appendix H. Photocopying these cards onto card stock makes them easier to pick up and move, and they last a long time when used by different tutors.

Picture cards may be bought from most teacher supply stores or photocopied from *Words Their Way* (Bear et al., 2020) or the Words Their Way supplemental sort books. You can also create your own sorts digitally at the Words Their Way website.

Organizing the Sorts

Once the picture and word cards are copied, laminated (optional), and cut, they can be organized by the scope and sequence of phonics features to be taught as categorized in the phonics ladder (Table 2.2). A particularly efficient method for organizing the picture and word cards within phonics features uses nonadhesive book pockets. The pockets can be labeled with the phonics feature (e.g., the beginning consonant *Bb,* representing the beginning sound /b/, or the word family *an*). Coordinators might store the pockets in empty flashcard boxes, separating them by a piece of cardboard inserted between categories. This piece of cardboard can serve as a label for each phonics category.

Organized in this fashion, a tutor can simply grab the book pockets labeled by the phonics features to be taught, shuffle the enclosed cards all together, and then have the child sort the cards under the labeled pockets, which serve as headers. After the sort, the cards are returned to their respective pockets and placed in the box. Of course, it is the coordinator's job to tell the tutor which phonics features to compare and contrast, and this is determined by the assessment described in the next chapter.

Picture cards will be used in the emergent reader's sorts of initial sounds along with some word-bank words (cards) that start with the targeted sounds. So envelopes for initial sound sorts will contain only pictures representing individual beginning sounds. Many more word cards are used for the beginning reader's phonics sorts. In sorts for later beginning and transitional readers, fewer pictures are used. If both picture cards and word cards are to be used for sorting, it is easiest to store them together by feature. With beginning readers, additional words for sorting should come from the child's word bank.

Letter Cards for Push It Say It Activities

Phonics instruction for the beginning reader includes a brief Push It Say It activity designed to provide concrete, explicit practice in both phonemic awareness and phonics:

- *Phonemic awareness* by dividing a word into individual sounds and
- *Phonics* by matching letters to each sound and blending the sounds into a word.

Push It Say It is described in the word study component of the beginning reader lesson plan in Chapter 5.

Letter cards for Push It Say It can be copied from Appendix I or written on small cards. Coordinators can store the beginning consonant cards together with the word family cards in library pockets, organizing them by feature and labeling them with the words the letter cards will make, in the order they are to be made (see Figure 2.3). The appropriate pocket can simply be placed in the tutoring box as needed.

Alternatively, coordinators might stick a library pocket on one side of the two-

FIGURE 2.3. Push It Say It Cards

pocket folder kept in each tutoring box (see Figure 2.4). Push It Say It letter cards can be tucked inside this pocket and exchanged on a lesson-by-lesson basis (the words to make, in the order in which they are to be made, can be written on a sticky note placed directly on the pocket or written on the lesson plan).

Or each tutoring table can get its own set of Push It Say It pockets filled with letter cards and organized by feature. The book pockets, stored in empty flashcard boxes or small baskets, are numbered and labeled with words to be made. The coordinator has a key indicating each pocket's number and feature, along with the words to be made, and simply writes the number on the lesson plan. The tutor then pulls the envelope with that number. For example, Push It Say It pocket 1 may contain letter cards for comparing the word families *-at* and *-an*. If the coordinator wants to include this particular activity in a session, she or he simply writes "1" beside "Push It Say It" on the

FIGURE 2.4. Two-Pocket Folder for Lesson Plans and Materials

lesson plan, referring to the numbered book pocket. It takes some time to make a set of pockets for each table, but it is worth it for the ease of future planning.

Organizing General Supplies and Record Forms

Books, library book pockets, and word, picture, and letter cards are the most critical instructional materials to organize. Other supplies and materials should also be organized in advance, although the method for organizing these depends on the time and space available for tutoring. It might be prudent to organize one spot for communal supplies that all tutors will have to dip into on a daily basis. Among these, the ones used most would be general supplies and record forms (see the tutoring supply center in Figure 2.1).

General supplies that might go into the communal area include a variety of papers, pencils, scissors, sticky notes, highlighters, crayons or markers, glue sticks, and other desk supplies. Boxes of blank flashcards can be purchased through most teacher supply online catalogs and at teacher supply stores, or cut from index cards. Simply place a box of these cards in the communal supply area for tutors to make word-bank cards. Alphabet letters (magnetic letters, tiles, link letters, foam letters, or paper letter cards) are especially useful for teaching emergent readers who have incomplete knowledge of the alphabet.

Record forms must also be readily available, organized in folders in a box. Word-bank record forms and forms listing books that have been read (which are updated at each lesson by the tutor) are heavily used. A book list form is provided in Appendix J. Other helpful forms include sound charts (picture clues for letter sounds) and handwriting guides that contain arrows for letter formation. Sound charts can be found in Appendices K–L. A handwriting guide for lowercase letters can be found in Appendix M. If books are sent home for practice, a checkout-and-return form must be created. A take-home book form is provided in Appendix N.

If you have the space, it's very convenient to keep pencils, highlighters, crayons, scissors, handwriting guides, and blank flashcards at each tutoring table, along with a set of word- and picture-sort pockets and a set of Push It Say It pockets.

Writing Lesson Plans

The most important job of the Book Buddies coordinator is to write the daily lesson plans for individual children. In addition, the coordinator needs to gather the books and materials to go with the plan. Tutors appreciate being able to arrive shortly before a session, pick up a prepared box of materials, quickly read through the lesson plan, and then sit down and work with their children.

The lesson plans described in Chapters 4, 5, and 6 are multipart plans representing a structured literacy lesson. Copies of the lesson plan forms can be found in Appendices A.1–A.3.

- *The emergent reader plan* includes (1) rereading familiar texts and concept of word practice; (2) alphabet, word study (word-bank work and phonics), and writing; (3) language play (phonological awareness practice); and (4) reading new texts.

- *The beginning reader lesson plan* is composed of (1) rereading familiar texts for fluency, (2) word study (word-bank work, phonics, and spelling), (3) writing, and (4) reading new texts.
- *The transitional reader plan* includes three parts: (1) reading familiar or easy texts for fluency, (2) word study (phonics and spelling), and (3) a lengthier amount of time reading new text with a focus on comprehension strategies, vocabulary, and writing.

Using Assessment

The multipart lesson plan entails critical decision-making by the coordinator based on assessment results for each child. To plan effective instruction for each section, the coordinator must know where the child is and the best way to move forward.

For reference when making plans, coordinators keep assessment information for each child close at hand. The information can be stored in folders or kept in a file box of index cards, one card for each child and arranged alphabetically. Coordinators should also file continuing assessments such as running records, or records of oral reading accuracy taken as the child reads aloud (see the "Recording and Scoring Text Reading" section in Chapter 3), and results from spell checks, or brief assessments of spelling features that have been taught and practiced. Armed with assessment knowledge, the coordinator can plan, using the activities described in Chapters 4, 5, and 6, to meet individual needs.

Take-Home Reading

If possible, it is very beneficial for Book Buddies students to take a book home after each lesson. The reading practice builds not only fluency but also ownership of and pride in the child's increasing skill, which is highly motivating. The take-home book should not be the new book introduced in the current lesson but one that has been read during at least two lessons. The child should be instructed to read the book to an adult or older sibling at least once, and then twice more to her- or himself.

The book can be sent home in a personalized baggie, folder, or envelope along with a take-home sheet with the name of the book, the date, and a place for a signature, so the coordinator and tutor can see whether the child is reading at home. You'll find a take-home sheet in Appendix N. If you cannot send the actual books home for fear of losing them, consider making text-only copies (where the text is typed on a single sheet of paper with no illustrations). Loss is certainly a potential problem, but we find if the Book Buddies children are consistently made aware of their responsibility in protecting and returning books, very few books are lost over the course of a year.

Organizing the Tutoring Box

A simple means of organizing a child's tutoring lesson is to gather all the books and materials and put them in a box labeled with the child's and tutor's names. We recommend using cardboard or plastic file boxes available from office supply stores and online from most teacher-supply companies (see Figure 2.5). Lesson plans and other loose sheets of paper, such as the word-bank record form and the book list form, can

FIGURE 2.5. Individual Tutoring Box

be easily kept in a two-pocket folder, with lesson plans in one pocket and record forms in the other.

The outside of the tutoring box will require some preparation as well. Sound charts and alphabet strips or charts can be glued to the outside of the box for ready reference. Emergent and early beginning readers will frequently need to consult an alphabet chart to remember how to write a particular letter. Which sound chart you glue onto the outside of the box will depend on where each child is on the phonics ladder (see Table 2.2). If a child is learning beginning sounds, glue a beginning sound chart to the outside of the box. If a child is learning consonant blends, glue a consonant blend sound chart to the box. Alphabet charts are provided in Appendices K and O. Sound charts may be found in Appendices K and L.

The Tutoring Box

Before each lesson, the following items should be available in each tutoring box.

1. A two-pocket folder (see Figure 2.4) containing the following:
   a. The completed lesson plan
   b. A book list form. This record, updated at each lesson by the tutor with new book titles and the number of times each book is read, guides the coordinator to know when to rotate a book out of the box (Appendix J).
   c. A laminated handwriting guide (Appendix M)
   d. The word study sequence glued to the fronts of the inside pockets. Features studied will be checked off by the coordinator, providing a record of instruction for both the coordinator and the tutor (Appendix P).
   e. *For emergent readers:* An alphabet chart (Appendices K and O)
   f. *For emergent and beginning readers:* An alphabetized word-bank list (Appendix F) for the tutor to record known words and a word-bank "Rocket" or "Mountain Path" to track the number of word-bank words (Appendix Q)
   g. *For transitional readers:* Timed repeated reading forms (Appendix R)

2. A student notebook (e.g., composition book or stapled booklet of lined paper) *and* a notebook for the tutor (stapled booklet)
3. Pencils, blank word cards, highlighter, glue stick, scissors (unless available on each tutoring table)
4. Familiar texts, easy texts, poems for Part 1 of the lesson plan
5. *For emergent and beginning readers:* Plastic baggie or ring for organizing word-bank words
6. *For beginning readers:* Push It Say It pocket
7. Picture and word cards for sorting. These may be placed in small plastic bags, secured with rubber bands, or transported in their book pockets as described earlier.
8. *For emergent readers:* Materials for concept of word practice, alphabet study, and language play
9. *For beginning readers:* A FastRead sheet (sample FastRead sheets can be found in Appendix S)
10. A new book on the child's reading level

Occasionally the coordinator will want to include word study games to review features.

The finishing touch in preparing tutoring boxes is to personalize each box with the name of the tutor and the name of the child on the side. A picture of the two of them at work can be added. It also helps to put the days and times the tutor comes to work with the child on the side of the box. Thus equipped, the tutors can come in, grab their boxes, read through the lesson plan, and easily tell what materials go with what part of the lesson. Of course, the tutor must also know *how* to conduct each part of the plan. Recommendations for teaching tutors how to tutor and for modeling and providing ongoing support and guidance are outlined below.

Book Buddies Tutor Training

The training of volunteer, student, and paraprofessional tutors is an ongoing process. But at the start, a group training session can set the tone for the tutoring program and outline goals and expectations. If whole-group training is too difficult to plan, the coordinator might schedule smaller group sessions. Tutors will often be overwhelmed at this initial meeting. Reassure them! And make sure they know they're not finished. The tutors, like the children they will tutor, learn best on the job, one-on-one. Recommended practices for training tutors on the job, throughout the year, will be described after a discussion of group training.

Group Training Sessions

The best way to give tutors an idea of what is involved in a Book Buddies lesson is to show them the videotaped tutoring sessions available on the companion website for this book (for more information, see the box at the end of the table of contents). The videos offer two Book Buddies lessons: a beginning reader lesson and a late beginning reader lesson. The lesson plans appear in Chapter 5 *with* tutor comments and in Appendix T *without* tutor comments so they can be used for training. In Appendix T you'll also find, for the coordinator, background notes on the lesson plans as well as notes on each lesson, including tutor behaviors that the tutors-in-training can watch for as they view the videotaped lessons.

Tutors should follow the videos using a written lesson plan as a roadmap for viewing. It is a good idea to have a leader who pauses the video and facilitates a discussion of what's going on in each part of the lesson. As the lesson is divided into several parts, it is logical to pause the video at the end of each part to summarize what was done and why. The leader may ask tutors to look for certain behaviors, thus giving them a purpose for viewing. The more interactive the video viewing, the more the tutors will get out of the training session. Other ideas for interactive video training follow.

Ideas for Video Training

1. Tutors can fill in the comments section of a lesson plan after viewing each part on the video. These comments can be shared and compared.
2. Tutors can practice each part of the lesson plan with a partner sitting next to them. Coordinators can circulate to model and provide feedback as they observe the tutors teaching each other.
3. Tutors can be shown the "Concordance of Spelling and Reading Development and Text Levels" chart in Table 2.1 and representative books along the continuum of difficulty. It is important for tutors to know the terrain they will be traveling.
4. Tutors can be shown the phonics ladder in Table 2.2, representing the sequence of phonics features to be learned. They can also be shown a more detailed word study sequence glued to the pockets of the folder. The suggested word study sequence in Appendix P can be cut in half and glued onto each pocket inside the tutoring folder. Explain to the tutors that the coordinator will check off features on the sequence sheet as the features are taught so both the tutor and coordinator will have a record of instruction. Again, it is important for tutors to know the domain of what is to be learned and to know there is an orderly progression for instruction.
5. It might also be helpful to lay out specific goals related to both reading and phonics instruction. The goals for students starting the year as early beginning readers might include the following:
   a. To read approximately 60–80 books and poems
   b. To recognize all 26 letters of the alphabet, uppercase and lowercase, and to write each letter
   c. To know the sounds letters represent and to apply that knowledge in decoding new words and in writing
   d. To finger-point accurately while reading a known story

e. To spell accurately when writing
   (1) all consonants,
   (2) short vowels,
   (3) consonant blends and consonant digraphs, and
   (4) simple r-influenced vowel sounds (e.g., the *ar* in *far*) and most preconsonantal nasals (e.g., the *ng* in *sting*).

f. To recognize immediately 100-plus words from the word bank

For your group training session, you might wish to include in your handout the Guidelines for Effective Tutor Behaviors included in Appendix U. Tutors may wish to keep these guidelines in the tutoring box for quick reference.

Addressing Issues and Questions

Another purpose for providing a group training session before the tutoring begins is to address educational issues about which tutors might have questions. One question we often get from tutors is why we allow children to make spelling errors in their writing.

Once tutors have seen the ladder of phonics and spelling features to be learned, it is easier for them to understand that these features progress developmentally from easier ones (beginning consonant sounds) to harder ones (e.g., silent letters marking the long vowel sound). The answer to the question "When do we start holding them accountable for correct spelling?" is this: right from the start. We hold children accountable for what they've been taught, but we don't correct their mistakes on features further along on the phonics ladder. This rule of thumb means we *do* correct children when they make an error on a phonics or spelling feature they have been taught (the word study sequence sheet, attached to the folder, helps here), but we do *not* penalize them for what they haven't yet been taught.

Procedures and Rules for Tutors

Group training sessions might also provide information on procedures for checking into the school building; rules for making up missed tutoring sessions due to illness, vacation, or other interference; and general tips for tutoring. It is useful to stress the following points:

Rules for Tutors

- **Regular attendance is critical.** Children look forward to seeing their tutors and are disappointed when they do not appear. Advance notice of absences, if possible, is important. Missed sessions should be made up.
- **Come prepared.** Tutors should come a few minutes before the time they are scheduled to begin working with their children in order to go over the day's plan. The tutoring session should be paced so that little time is wasted.

- **Be friendly but firm.** Children must abide by school rules, such as no running and no gum chewing. Tutors should model attention to the rules as well.
- **Be patient.** Budding readers need time to figure things out and master them. Tutors should not be too quick to correct a mistake. Children should be given a chance to discover their mistakes first—they will learn much more from the experience.
- **Reward hard work and success with praise.** Tutors should encourage their children and maintain a positive atmosphere. However, tutors should avoid treats such as candy or presents unless it is a special occasion, and then they should notify the coordinator first.
- **Seek help.** Working with young children is not always easy. Tutors should ask the coordinator for help when they have questions and problems, including behavior problems.
- **Communicate.** Tutors must communicate with the coordinator about their children verbally or by email *and* through comments on the lesson plan. The importance of communication cannot be stressed too strongly.

Further Training

Group training sessions can provide a general orientation, but they are no substitute for lessons learned on the job. Ongoing tutor training must happen on-site, continuously, throughout the year. Practices for modeling and providing feedback throughout the tutorial are described below.

The First Sessions

The coordinator should model the first lesson each fall even for experienced tutors, who often forget the routine over the summer months. Most new and experienced tutors welcome the opportunity to observe at least once.

During most sessions, tutors are encouraged to maintain a steady pace and to keep the child's attention on the tasks to be accomplished, but the very first session that the tutor works alone may be more relaxed–an opportunity for the tutor to get to know his or her child and vice versa. Here are some suggestions for that first meeting:

Suggestions for the First Tutor-Led Session

- Tutors might share something about themselves—a favorite hobby, family pets, and so on. Children are asked to share something about their families as well. Some tutoring programs take pictures of the tutors and their children, and later put them up on the bulletin board with "All about Me" blurbs under each photograph.
- Tutors might bring something from home that reveals their interests and engages the children, such as photographs, a collection, or a memento from a trip.
- Tutors should talk to their children about why they will be coming to work with them. Tutors should be clear that the goal of their time together is to learn to read better, but they should be cautioned not to make promises they can't keep.

On-Site Modeling and Feedback

Once a tutor is up and running, it is essential that the coordinator observe at least part of each tutorial to stay in touch. Only by observing how things are going can the coordinator jump in and model where needed, or coach the tutor after the tutorial session. Of course, this is impossible if too many tutorials are scheduled simultaneously. The number of tutor–tutee pairs a coordinator can effectively supervise in one session *should not exceed* six (see "School-Based Tutorials" earlier in this chapter).

Even with optimal scheduling, however, it is not humanly possible to observe six tutorials simultaneously. The coordinator's attention will shift from pair to pair during different parts of the lesson. Because of this, the coordinator must rely on the tutor's comments written in the comments section of the lesson plan. These comments provide feedback to the coordinator regarding how things went and help to fill in the gaps of what was not observed. These comments are essential in planning the next lesson. Taken together, the coordinator's observations and the tutor's comments will begin to shape the direction of the tutorial.

Book Buddies Tutors' Common Concerns

Some issues that require the coordinator's feedback and guidance are common to many tutorials using volunteers, students, and paraprofessionals. Tutors frequently worry about their child's reluctance to read or write. Some may be working with an uncooperative child, and this can be a frustrating experience for everyone. Tutors may feel strongly about reading to children, even if "reading to" had not been a planned part of the tutorial. Coordinators can anticipate these issues and be prepared to give helpful feedback. Some common concerns and suggested words of wisdom for tutors are discussed below.

"My Child Is Reluctant to Read!" Reluctance to read may be due to several different things: lack of ownership, lack of confidence, boredom, or frustration. We often suggest that tutors try the following:

- *Offer choices.* Tutors should offer their children a structured choice among a limited number of alternatives. In the lesson plan's rereading section, asking "What would you like to read first?" might be all that is needed to give the child a sense of ownership and control.
- *Provide support.* It may be that the child still lacks confidence in his or her own ability. With emergent and early beginning readers, the tutor can provide more support for new reading by reading every other page ("I'll read a page, and then you read a page"), or echo reading ("I'll read this first and then you read it after me"). However, this should be done only as long as it seems absolutely necessary. Rereading familiar material should be done independently, without support.
- *Try varying the routine.* The child may be bored with the same routine or a text that is being reread. Try varying the order of the lesson plan, and try switching roles. The tutor becomes the "child," and the child becomes the "teacher." The tutor reads slowly, asks the child for help, and makes mistakes the child can cor-

rect. In this role, the tutor can sound out words for the child, who must figure out what the words may be.

- *Notify the coordinator if the text appears too difficult.* It may also be that the child is frustrated by text that is too difficult. If a child is missing more than 1 word in 10, the book is probably too hard, and easier material is in order. Tutor feedback is vital.

"My Child Is Not Cooperating!" Tutors sometimes have difficulty keeping their child's attention. We have found the following techniques to be helpful:

- *Offer a choice.* The tutor must decide what is to be done during the tutoring, but she or he can give the child choices within each component of the lesson plan. Never ask the child a question to which the child can answer "No!" Rather than saying, "Do you want to read now?" say, "Now we will read. Which book do you want to read first?"
- *Keep up the pace.* A forward momentum helps keep the child engaged in the lesson. To keep moving along, however, tutors must review the lesson plan in advance and have materials ready. In addition, tutors should avoid getting sidetracked. Interesting but irrelevant conversations should be saved for the end of the tutorial. The coordinator may need to model another lesson to assist a tutor struggling with pacing.
- *Routines can help.* While there will be exceptions to maintaining the exact routine, as stated earlier, routines do provide the structure and security many young children need. Try keeping the tutoring sequence the same, so the child knows what to expect during each session. Tutors can prepare their children for what comes next in the lesson by making comments such as "This will be the last book we will read, and then we will look at your word-bank words."
- *Ask for the child's assistance.* Involve the child in the management of the lesson. Tutors should include the child in clerical tasks such as coloring in the word-bank rocket or path, laying out Push It Say It cards, helping put word cards away, and other housekeeping details. Allow the child to check off the tasks on the lesson plan as they're completed. This makes the child feel in control of his or her own learning.
- *Be positive!* Avoid negative feedback. When a child makes a mistake, rather than saying no, ask questions that lead the child to the correct answer (e.g., "Let's look at that again"; "Let's look at the letters in that word"; or "What would make sense?"). Avoid criticizing the child. If a child engages in annoying behavior, criticize the action specifically, not the child. For example, if the child is whining, the tutor might say, "No whining allowed! I'm not a fan of whining!" Specific comments such as this indicate it's the behavior that is disliked, not the child.
- *Be in charge.* Establish and maintain boundaries. Children need to know what is expected (i.e., that they will be following the lesson plan and what constitutes acceptable behavior). Children need to know who is in charge.

"What about Reading to My Child?" Reading books aloud to children is a very important part of any reading program. It has not been included in the lesson plans

described in Chapters 4, 5, and 6 because the time allotted for tutoring is short. We are assuming the classroom teacher or parent provides this experience regularly. However, if the coordinator senses a student has had few experiences with books, then it may be worthwhile to read aloud at the end of some lessons. If there is time to read aloud, select books that can be read in a short amount of time (about 5 minutes). Include information books to expand the child's vocabulary and world knowledge.

Here are a few suggestions to give to tutors for reading aloud:

1. Look at the cover, point out and read the title, and ask the child to make some predictions about what the book will be about. Discuss the book's author and illustrator.
2. Encourage the child to respond to the text and pictures with questions and comments during the reading.
3. Ask questions to monitor comprehension. Explain a few unfamiliar words.
4. After the reading, talk briefly about the book. You might ask the child what surprised him or her about the book, whether the child has had a related experience, or other questions he or she might have about the topic.

These are some of the concerns we have heard from tutors over the years. As coordinators model the tutoring process and provide feedback throughout the year, other problems and concerns are bound to appear. These must be handled on a case-by-case basis.

Kudos for Book Buddies Tutors

On-the-job praise and encouragement of our tutors go a long way. But their real reward is their children's *progress*. The best way to give kudos to our valuable tutors is to share the assessment data. Coordinators conduct ongoing assessments to determine what each child has learned and what he or she needs to learn (see Chapter 3). These assessments must be shared with the tutors so they can proceed fully informed about where they are and where they're headed. The going can be long and tough. But if a tutor can see that a child who knew only 2 letters in September knows 24 letters in November, that tutor can see progress. Even if the child does not make it all the way to grade level by the end of the year, the tutor can see and celebrate the child's growth.

The assessments described in the next chapter provide the coordinator and the tutor with information about what the child already knows. Chapters 4, 5, and 6 explain how to move the child forward and extend what he or she knows.

Chapter 3

Book Buddies Assessment

This chapter describes how to assess and then how to interpret results in order to evaluate and plan instruction for beginning readers. The assessment described in this chapter is adapted from the Phonological Awareness Literacy Screening (PALS™) developed at the University of Virginia (Invernizzi, Juel, Swank, & Meier, 2007; Invernizzi, Meier, & Juel, 2007). This assessment is designed to be used with emergent to transitional readers in kindergarten through third grade. The total assessment takes 30 to 40 minutes and is sometimes administered in two sessions with younger children.

These testing materials can be used for the initial assessment, to assess ongoing progress, and as a final assessment for measuring growth at the end of the year. There is space on the Assessment Summary Sheet (Form A, p. 50) for all three sets of scores. *Do not use any of these assessment materials for instruction* or they cannot be used for later testing. An overview of the assessment tasks is offered below. Detailed directions for administering the tasks follow the overview, and the necessary forms and record sheets are included at the end of this chapter. The initial assessment is a critical aspect of an effective tutoring program and is best done by the Book Buddies coordinator or the child's classroom teacher. Parents may choose to have a teacher or tutor administer the assessment. If giving it on their own, parents will want to consult with their child's teacher regarding any leveled (by difficulty) text to be used in the text reading assessment.

An Overview of the Assessment

Before tutoring begins, it is absolutely essential to discover what children already know about reading and how print works. This information will enable you to find reading materials and plan activities that are at the right level of difficulty. This chapter describes assessment tasks that will test knowledge of the alphabet, phoneme awareness, letter-sound knowledge (including phonics/spelling), and identification of words in lists and in text. Note that reading comprehension is not assessed with the materials we provide since we are focused here on measuring the skills that enable children to read in the first place. However, reading for meaning is absolutely essential, even for beginners, and is part of all the instructional plans covered in later chapters.

Letters and Sounds

Familiarity with the letters of the alphabet and the ability to isolate sounds within words is essential for learning to read and spell the English language. If children are unable to read at least 50% of the words on the preprimer word list (as described below), they should be assessed for these skills.

Letter Identification, Letter Production, and Letter-Sound Knowledge

Letter identification is tested as children name lowercase letters presented in random order. The letter production assessment is optional and is tested as children write letters called out in random order. Letter-sound knowledge is assessed when children are asked to provide the sound associated with each uppercase alphabet letter and three consonant *digraphs* (*sh, th,* and *ch*).

Initial Phoneme Awareness

The ability to isolate and identify sounds within words is known as *phonological awareness* and is necessary to master *phonics*. One aspect of phonological awareness involves isolating and identifying initial sounds or *phonemes*. Initial phoneme awareness is assessed by asking children to name two pictures that begin with the same sound. Phoneme awareness is also assessed in the spelling task described next.

Phonics/Spelling

In the spelling assessment, children are asked to spell 10 words as best they can without studying them in advance. The scoring of the spelling task offers information about how completely children are able to separate and attend to the sounds in a word (phoneme awareness) as well as their ability to match those sounds to letters (phonics).

Word Reading

There are three parts to the word reading assessment: (1) concept of word, (2) word list reading, and (3) text reading.

Concept of Word

Children will have a difficult time learning to read if they cannot locate the words on the page and match their oral speech to the printed words. This skill, known as *concept of word in text,* includes the understanding that print moves from left to right and top to bottom, as well as an understanding of where words begin and end, and how the spaces between words establish word boundaries. Although those words and spaces are very obvious to us, they are not obvious to emergent readers. Concept of word is assessed by asking children to point to the words of a short, illustrated story (*Sand Castle*) that has been read to them and they've memorized. Children repeat the story sentence by sentence, pointing to the words as they say them. In addition, children are asked to identify selected words within the sentences.

Word List Reading

The first word reading task is simply to have children read from a list of words organized by increasing difficulty. These lists are a sample of the kinds of words found in reading materials in the early grades. In the Book Buddies assessment, we have included six graded word lists (preprimer, primer, first grade, second grade, third grade, and fourth grade).

Text Reading

To assess word reading in text, children read aloud simple books or passages as you keep a record of the errors they make. The information from the two word reading tasks will enable you to get a fairly good estimate of a child's ability to read with success at a particular level or range of levels.

We include two preprimer text passages: *Sam* (early to middle preprimer) and *My Huge Dog Max* (middle to late preprimer). The passages we provide are meant to give a rough estimate of where to start instruction. You may be able to determine more precise levels using the texts and leveling system of your school. This will be necessary if children meet the criteria for reading the two texts we provide. Note that if you do not have other texts available, the word list reading task offers an approximate guide to the level of text to be used for instruction as outlined in Table 3.1 on page 41. Note that the levels of text difficulty we refer to are those commonly used in public schools: basal reading levels (e.g., preprimer, primer, first grade, second grade), the lettered reading levels of Guided Reading (e.g., A, B, C), and the numbered reading levels of Reading Recovery® (e.g., 1, 2, 3). Find out which system is used in the school children attend.

Administering the Assessment

Before you begin the assessment, you should be thoroughly familiar with the procedures described below and get your materials in order. Step-by-step directions for before, during, and after testing are summarized in the box. Keep handy the assessment flow chart in Figure 3.1 (p. 37) to guide you on where to begin and where to go next.

Before Testing

1. Carefully read these directions and those on the individual assessment forms.
2. You will need this book, a pencil for recording, and paper and pencil for the child to use.
3. Make a copy of the Assessment Summary Sheet (p. 50), the Word List Reading checklists (pp. 53–54), and the Spelling Assessment (p. 58) for each child to be assessed.

4. Children can be asked to read the word lists (pp. 51 and 52) or identify the letters (on p. 55) directly from the book, but if you are assessing more than one child, you may find it easier to work with copies.

5. Copies of other materials will be needed depending on how the child does on the word list reading task. You may want to make the texts into little books by copying them, cutting apart the pages, and stapling them together.

During Testing

1. Set young children at ease by chatting with them briefly and then explain that you are going to do some reading and writing with them. At all points in the assessment, assure the children that they are doing well and that you do not expect them to know how to do everything perfectly.

2. Start with the preprimer word list. If the child is unable to read at least 10 words (50%) on the preprimer word list, go to the Letters and Sounds Assessments and Concept of Word Assessment.

3. If the child can read at least 10 words on the preprimer list, continue on to subsequent word lists, advancing to the next higher level if the child correctly reads 15 words or more. Stop when the child does not achieve a score of at least 15 on a list. If the child's highest score is between 10 and 17 on the preprimer list, the child reads *Sam* and also completes the Letter-Sound Production task.

4. Use the flow chart in Figure 3.1 (p. 37) to determine where to start text reading.

5. Text reading might be saved for a second session, which will enable you to make copies of the stories that you need or to find other texts to use, based on the word list reading.

6. All children are given the Spelling Assessment. This can be done in small groups at another time before or after the other assessments. Call out the spelling words as directed and score at a later time.

After Testing

1. Score the spelling test and any other assessments.

2. Compile all the results on the one-page Assessment Summary Sheet that will be used to estimate the child's reading level and plan instruction.

3. Record observations about children's general demeanor and reactions to testing in the space at the bottom of the Assessment Summary Sheet.

Word List Reading Assessment

The first step is to ask children to read from the leveled word lists. The results are then used to decide about the next step in the assessment (see Figure 3.1 on p. 37).

The results will also give you a rough estimate of your child's reading level as shown in Table 3.1 on page 41.

- Make a copy of Form B (pp. 51–52), where the words are listed, or have the child read from the book. Record his or her responses on Form C, Word List Reading (pp. 53–54). Cover or fold back all but one list at a time to focus the child's attention and reduce anxiety. Begin with the preprimer list.

- Say the following:

"Here is a list of words. Put your finger on the first word. I want you to read each word you know. If you do not know a word, skip it and go to the next one. Some of these words will be difficult, so don't worry if you do not know every word."

- Allow 2 or 3 seconds for each word, and ask children to move on to the next one if they seem to stall. Word list reading is meant to progress fairly quickly; do not force children to sound out unknown words.

- Record responses on Form C, checking those that are known and writing in incorrect responses. If a child corrects herself immediately, put a check beside the word and give credit for that response. If the child offers no attempt, write NA or make a dash (–) beside the word. Record the total number of words read correctly at the bottom of each column, and transfer to the Assessment Summary Sheet later.

- Move to the next higher level each time children read 15 or more words correctly. For example, move from the primer to the first-grade word list if children can read 15 primer words correctly; move from the first-grade list to the second-grade list if they can read 15 first-grade words correctly. Stop when children read fewer than 15 words on a word list.

- If children are unable to read at least 10 words on the preprimer list, go to the Letters and Sounds Assessments and the Concept of Word Assessment described next. Otherwise go to the Text Reading Assessment (p. 40). Use Figure 3.1 to determine what text to use.

Letters and Sounds Assessments

This part of the assessment contains four parts: letter identification, letter production, letter-sound production, and initial phoneme awareness. These tasks are typically given to children who do not have a concept of word, but you might also choose to use them to assess children who are reading at the preprimer level. Note that the Phonics/Spelling Assessment is also a way to assess letters and sounds. It is often administered after the other assessments have been administered because it can be done in a small group. For this reason, we describe the Phonics/Spelling Assessment later in this chapter (p. 42).

To administer the four tasks of the Letters and Sounds Assessments, you will need a copy of both uppercase and lowercase letters in random order (Form D, p. 55) and the Assessment Recording Forms (Forms E.1–E.3, pp. 56–58). You will need a pencil and paper for the optional letter production task.

FIGURE 3.1. Assessment Flow Chart

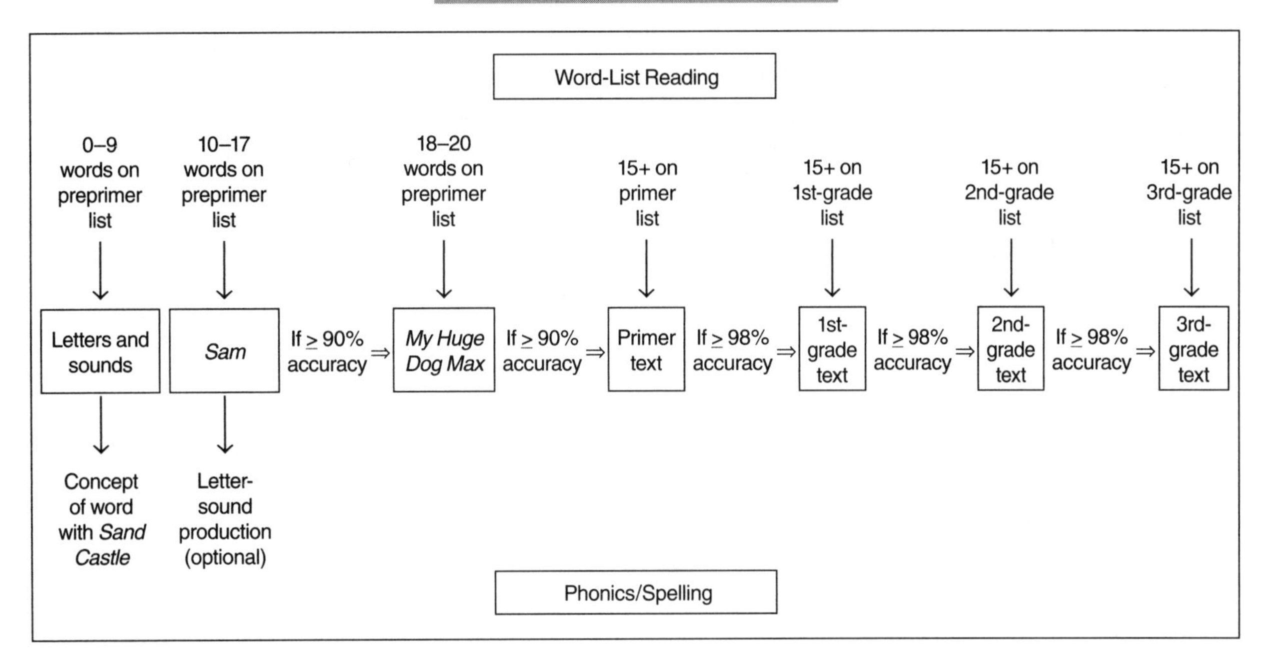

Letter Identification

- Show your child the lowercase letters on the top of Form D (p. 55) or on a copy of the page with the bottom folded under. Say, "See these letters? Put your finger on each letter and name it. If you don't know the name of a letter, skip it and go to the next."
- On Recording Form E.1, circle any incorrect responses. If the child corrects him- or herself immediately, check the circle and count the response as correct. Reversals (such as *b* for *d*) are errors. If the child takes more than 3 seconds to name a letter, count it as an error. The child may be reciting the alphabet or using some other means of coming up with a good guess, but he does not really know that letter by heart.
- Count up the number of errors, subtract it from 26, and record this number on the total line on Form E.1.

Letter Production (Optional)

Children are asked to produce or write the letters of the alphabet, either in random order or in alphabetical order. This can be done in a small group.

- Provide lined or unlined paper and a pencil, and be sure there is no alphabet strip available to copy from. Accept either the uppercase or the lowercase letter as correct. This time, *reversals are scored as correct* (e.g., *b* for *d*). Reversals are common for emergent and early beginning readers, but you should note which ones are causing problems.

• Explain, "I would like for you to write the letters of the alphabet that I call out. If you aren't sure how to make a letter, you can skip it."

• Call out the letters one by one in the same sequence as listed at the top of Form D, or sing the alphabet song *with* the child as she or he writes the letters.

• Record the number of letters produced on Recording Form E.1.

Letter-Sound Production

To assess children's knowledge of letter sounds, they are asked to say the sound, not the name, of the individual capital letters and three digraphs (*sh, th,* and *ch*) at the bottom of Form D.

• Show the uppercase letters to the child, and practice with the letter *M*. Say, "See these letters? I want you to tell me the sound the letter makes. Here's an example: This is the letter *M*. I would say 'mmmm' because that is the sound the letter makes."

• Next, say, "Put your finger on the first letter, and tell me the sound the letter makes. If you don't know it, you can skip it and go on to the next one."

• If a child produces the long vowel sound (i.e., *ay* for *A*), say, "That is one sound it makes, but what is another?" The short sound is the correct response. Do the same if children give the soft sound for *G* (as in *gym*) or *C* (as in *cent*). The correct sound is the hard sound of *C* and *G* as in *cat* and *gum*. A pronunciation guide is provided on Form E.1.

• Circle any incorrect responses on Form E.1. If children take more than 3 seconds to produce the letter sound, count it as an error. You might record what they say to inform your instructional planning.

• Count the number of letter sounds the child pronounced correctly, and record it.

Initial Phoneme Awareness

In this task children are shown four pictures and asked to identify which two begin with the same sounds. Children can mark on a copy of Form E.2 (p. 57) or you can use the book and ask children to simply name or point to the correct answers.

• Display Form E.2 and model how to do the first one. Say, "Here is a *moon*. One of these pictures beside the *moon* starts with the same sound. Listen, *moon, egg, mouse, rock*. Which ones start the same? *moon, egg*; *moon, mouse*; *moon, rock*. *Moon* and *mouse* begin with the same sound. Say those with me: *moon, mouse*. Do you hear the /mmmm/ sound at the beginning of them?" If you have made a copy of the form, circle the two pictures.

• Then say, "We will name the next pictures together, but I want you to find the two that have the same sound at the beginning: *belt, log, corn, ball*. Which two pictures begin with the same sound?" If necessary, support the child by repeating pairs (*belt, log; belt, corn; belt, ball*), but do not emphasize or elongate any of the sounds.

• Continue to name the pictures with the child to be sure he or she says the right word. Record the number of correct responses. The pictures are as follows:

moon	egg	mouse	rock
1. belt	log	corn	ball
2. pie	pig	rain	cat
3. sock	bed	sun	web
4. dog	desk	roof	towel
5. fish	hat	fork	keys
6. tape	box	ring	toes
7. van	kite	vase	tag
8. leaf	bag	ant	lock

Concept of Word Assessment with Sand Castle

To assess emergent readers' concept of word, you will need Form F (p. 59) and a copy of the story *Sand Castle* made into a little book (Form H.1, pp. 62–63). Watch for accurate one-to-one matching of spoken and printed words as the child recites the words from memory and touches the corresponding words on the page. Be especially watchful of two-syllable words such as *playing* or *brother* where the child might get off track. Follow the steps in the box, and record each child's responses on Form F.

Directions for Concept of Word Task

1. Explain to the child that you are going to read a story together.
2. Read the title of the book, touching each word. Then discuss the first picture. Say something like "This is Alvin. What is he doing?"
3. Then say, "Down here it says, 'Alvin is playing in the sand.'" Touch each word as you say it.
4. Talk about the picture on each page by posing a question (Page 2: "What is Alvin making?" Page 3: "Here comes his little brother. What did he do?" Page 4: "What will Alvin do now?"). Then read the text to the child, touching each word.
5. Read chorally. Ask the child to read the story with you as you point together.
6. Echo read. Return to the beginning and ask the child to point and repeat after you as you read each page, again pointing to the words together. Repeat if you feel it is necessary until the child has memorized the sentences.

7. Ask the child to read the story independently and point to the words without help. Score the pointing for each sentence (2 points for accurate pointing, 0 for a mistake). If a child gets off track but self-corrects without prompting, score the sentence as a 2.

8. Assess word identification. Return to the first sentence. Point to the word *sand* and say, "What is this word?" Then point to the word *playing* and ask, "What is this word?" Repeat this for each of the words underlined on the record sheet (Form F). Record 1 point for each word identified correctly.

9. Total the pointing scores and the word identification scores. If children are able to point accurately and can identify some of the words for a total score of 13 points or more, you should give them a chance to read the story *Sam*, described below.

Text Reading Assessment

In Chapter 2, we described how books are organized for instruction and how readers at different levels need different kinds of books (see pp. 13–15). Table 2.1 (p. 16) provides a concordance to show how several leveling systems match up with grade levels and types of readers, and Appendix D offers a list of books by level. At this step in the assessment process, you want to establish the highest level at which a child can read without frustration but with enough challenge to make progress. Use the word list reading task to determine where to start this part of the assessment.

Which Text to Use First?

If children name fewer than 10 words on the preprimer word list, you will need to do the Concept of Word Assessment described above, but if children know 10–17 words, they probably have a concept of word. You can skip *Sand Castle* and start with *Sam* (preprimer 1–2). If a child reads 18 or more words on the preprimer word list, start with *My Huge Dog Max* (preprimer 3). For both *Sam* and *My Huge Dog Max,* there are specific directions below and on the recording sheets. If a child was able to read at least 15 words on the primer list or higher, we recommend you use your own leveled texts or books from the list in Appendix D. Follow the directions below for how to administer and score the text reading, and use the percentage of words read correctly to decide what to do next. The flow chart in Figure 3.1 (p. 37) and Table 3.1, "Criteria for Selecting Books for Assessment and Instruction," will help you use the scores on word list reading to identify the leveled text to use first, as well as the criteria for moving on to the next level.

Where to Go Next?

If a child cannot read *Sam* with accuracy of at least 85%, try her in an earlier preprimer text (numbered level 3, or lettered level C). Move to the easiest levels (1–2 or A and B) if she continues to read with less than 85% accuracy, and watch for accuracy in pointing to words. A child who performs well enough on the preprimer word list but cannot read preprimer text might have been drilled on words in word lists, in which

TABLE 3.1. Criteria for Selecting Books for Assessment and Instruction

Score on Word List	Text to Use for Assessment	Criterion for Placement	Criterion for Moving to Next Text Level	Text Level Range—Basal; Reading Recovery; Guided Reading
Preprimer list				
0–9	*Sand Castle*	0–12 points	13–16 points	Readiness; 1–3; A, B, C
10–17	*Sam*	85% accuracy (26 words)	90% accuracy (27 words)	PP 1, 2; 3–6; C, D
18–20	*My Huge Dog Max*	85% accuracy (61 words)	90% accuracy (65 words)	PP 3; 7–8; E
Primer list				
15 or more	Primer text	90% accuracy	98% accuracy	Primer (1.1); 9–12; F, G
First-grade list				
15 or more	First-grade text	90% accuracy	98% accuracy	First grade (1.2); 13–17; H, I
Second-grade list				
15 or more	Second-grade text	90% accuracy	98% accuracy	Second grade (2.1–2.2); 18–21; J, K, L, M
Third-grade list				
15 or more	Third-grade text	90% accuracy	98% accuracy	Third grade (3.1–3.2); 22+; N, O, P

case word list reading may not reflect contextual reading ability. See Figure 3.1 (p. 37) as a guide to where to go next.

If a child reads *Sam* with accuracy at 90% or above, go on to *My Huge Dog Max* (preprimer 3). If a child can read *My Huge Dog Max* with accuracy at 90% or above, select an early primer level (numbered levels 9–10, or lettered level F) book and ask her to read it to you. Similarly, if a child knows at least 15 words on the primer word list and reads very accurately (98% or higher) on a late primer text (11–12, or G), but has not read at least 15 words on the first-grade word list, you can try books at levels 13–16, or H and I, to test contextual reading at the first-grade level.

We have not included passages or forms for primer level and above, but you can use the Oral Reading in Context forms in Appendix V to score accuracy for the text you use. The 100 Word Chart (p. 220) can be used to keep a tally of errors to calculate an accuracy percentage (number of errors/number of words in the passage). It is also known as a *running record*. The 100 Word Chart also allows you to keep track of progress in oral reading accuracy (text at the same level) over time.

If the child is reading above the preprimer level, you might also use a more formalized assessment, such as PALS (*www.pals.virginia.edu*; Invernizzi et al., 2007) or an informal reading inventory (IRI).

Recording and Scoring Text Reading

For text reading, you will need a copy of Forms G.1 and G.2 (pp. 60–61), as well as the illustrated versions (Forms H.2 and H.3) on pages 64 and 65 for the child to read. You can just use the illustrated versions of the preprimer texts, or you can copy them, cut the pages apart, and staple them to make a little book. (Do *not* give the little book to the child to keep or use it for instruction because you will invalidate any future assessment using that text.)

If the child is reading beyond the preprimer level, you will need the 100 Word Chart in Appendix V (p. 220) for recording oral reading. If the text is at the late primer level or beyond, use a stopwatch and time the child's reading as soon as she begins. Do not time *Sam* or *My Huge Dog Max* because these texts are below the primer level, and we do not measure reading rate below late primer level.

- For the preprimer passages, you will start by placing the text in front of the child and reading the title as you point to the words: "The name of this story is . . . " Specific directions for introducing the preprimer texts are included on the forms. For text leveled at primer and above, you will review the title of the book with the child and ask the child to make a prediction from the title. Then say, "I would like to listen to you read."
- Start timing the child if you are using late primer level text and above. If children get stuck on a word for more than 5 seconds or appeal to you for help, you can supply the word, but it will count as an error.
- *Preprimer passages.* For the preprimer passages, you will mark directly on Forms G.1 and G.2 to record children's errors. Place parentheses around any words you supply. Cross out any words children misname on the record sheet, and write above the word what your child said. Circle any words that are omitted, and write in any added words. Indicate self-corrections by putting a check over the word, and do not count it as an error. Figure 3.2 (top) illustrates some examples of reading errors children might make and how to mark them.
- *Primer and above.* If you are using the 100 Word Chart, each box on the chart represents one word. Put a check in the box if the child read the word correctly. Otherwise, mark errors by leaving the box blank or noting the type of error in the box (e.g., put a circle if the word was omitted, and write in added words). An example of how to use the 100 Word Chart can be seen in Figure 3.2 (bottom). If the text the child is reading is primer or beyond, stop timing the child after 100 words. Record the time beside "Total Time" on the 100 Word Chart. If the selection is not completed, you may want to finish reading it to the child or ask a question about the part the child read in order to simulate a regular reading experience. Count the number of errors and subtract from 100 to calculate the accuracy percentage. If the child did not read a full 100 words, follow the directions on the 100 Word Chart for calculating the accuracy percentage and words per minute if the reading was timed.

Whether you use the text copies of *Sam, My Huge Dog Max,* or some other text and the 100 Word Chart, refer to the chart in Table 3.1 for the criteria for moving to the next text level. Sometimes, you will find that a child just cannot read a text. If you have to supply every word or two, just stop the testing there. Say "Let's read this together," and proceed to read the rest of it in a choral fashion. Then try text at an easier level.

Phonics/Spelling Assessment

For this assessment you will call out 10 words for the child to spell as best he can. Have a copy of the alphabet available (p. 188) for reference in case a child is unsure how to

FIGURE 3.2. Samples of Reading Errors and How to Mark Them

Error Sample Using *Sam*

Sam ~~has~~ *had* a dog.	("had" was substituted for "has")
Sam has a (big) dog.	("big" was omitted)
The dog is so big he can get the cup.	
Look out ^*now* Sam!	("now" was added)
Up (goes) the dog.	("goes" was supplied by the tester)
~~Down~~ *Dog* ✓ goes the cup.	("dog" was corrected to "down")

Sample 100 Word Chart Using *Sam*

▶ Oral Reading in Context:

Student: *Dajonna* Date: *9/27*

Passage Title: *Sam* ☐ expository ☐ narrative Passage Level: *PPA/PPB*

✓	had / ~~has~~	✓	✓	✓	✓	✓	O	✓	✓
✓	✓	✓	✓	✓	✓	✓	✓	✓	✓
✓	now ^	✓	✓	(goes)	✓	✓	Dog ✓ / ~~Down~~	✓	✓
✓									

write a letter. Some children may be comfortable about attempting to spell words they have never written before, but others will not, so encouragement might be needed.

Directions for the Spelling Assessment

- Make a copy of Form E.3, Spelling Assessment (p. 58). Fold under all but the row of empty boxes on the left side. The child is expected to write each word as it is called in these blank numbered boxes.
- Before you begin, model a sound-it-out strategy by slowly saying the sounds of the sample word *map* and writing it for the child as suggested below:
- "We are going to write the word *map*. Listen to me say the sounds in *map*: m-m-

m-a-a-a-a-p. What letter should I write down first? This word starts with *m* [*point to the* m *in an alphabet strip*]. What letter should I write down next? Now I need the letter *a*. What do you hear at the end? Listen again, m-m-m-a-a-a-p [*emphasize the sound of the letter* p]. I'll end this word with the letter *p* [*point to it on an alphabet chart*].

• "Now I am going to call out some words for you to spell. Spell them the best way you can. Think about the sounds you hear in the word and the letters you need to write the sound."

• Pronounce the words clearly and naturally. Repeat them as needed and use in a sentence. Call out all 10 words unless your child is clearly uncomfortable or is unable to spell even a single letter of the first five words.

1. van	2. pet	3. rug	4. sad	5. plum
6. chip	7. shine	8. skate	9. float	10. treat

• If the child does not spell the entire word and is lingering over it, you might ask, "What else do you hear?" But limit your prompts to just that. *Do not* elongate the sounds of the words as you did in the modeling part. If the child asks you whether a word is correct, respond by saying, "You are doing a good job listening for the sounds!"

• Listen as the child works out the spelling of each word. If you are unsure of any letter he has written, ask what letter he intended as soon as he is finished spelling the word. *Letter reversals on this task* (such as *b* for *d* in *sad*) *will not count as spelling errors* (letter formation reversals are considered handwriting errors).

Scoring the Spelling Assessment

Score the spelling at a later time by checking the appropriate boxes on Form E.3 according to the sounds the child was able to represent correctly. You are also encouraged to write in logical substitutions, although they are not scored. For example, the word *chip* might have been spelled *jep*. (Say *chip* and *jep* to yourself, and you might feel how similar those sounds are.) When beginning readers try to spell short vowels, they often confuse them (as in *jep* for *chip*), but it is worth noting that they are attempting them even when they choose the wrong one. A sample test by Jenny has been scored in Figure 3.3 for you. Note that she does not get credit for the long vowels in *float* and *treat* because she fails to represent the silent letter (*a* in both words) that makes the vowels long.

Sum the number of points for each word, adding a bonus point if the word is spelled correctly. Add the number of points at the bottom of the spelling form, and write that total on the Assessment Summary Sheet (Form A, p. 50). Look across the feature scores at the bottom to find areas where the child misses more than one item. These would be considered features that need instruction, beginning with the first one from the left. In the case of Jenny, she knows initial and final consonants but needs work on short vowels and blends and digraphs, the first features on which she missed more than one. With scores of only two out of six on each of these features, it is not surprising that Jenny shows a 0 score at the bottom of the long vowel column. Long vowel instruction is not yet appropriate for her.

FIGURE 3.3. Sample Spelling Test That Has Been Scored

Name Jenny Date 8/20

Student writes words below. Fold paper back so only blanks show.	Initial Cons	Final Cons	Short Vowel	Blends and Digraphs	Long Vowel	Correct	Total
1. van	v ✓	n ✓	a ✓			van ✓	4
2. pat	p ✓	t ✓	e a			pet	2
3. rog	r ✓	g ✓	u o			rug	2
4. sad	s ✓	d ✓	a ✓			sad ✓	4
5. pom	p ✓	m ✓	u o	pl		plum	2
6. jep		p ✓	i e	ch j		chip	1
7. shin		n ✓		sh ✓	i-e i	shine	2
8. scat		t ✓		sk sc	a-e	skate	1
9. flot	f ✓			fl ✓	oa o	float	2
10. jret				tr jr	ea e	treat	0
Add down and across to total	6 /6	8 /8	2 /6	2 /6	0 /4	2 /10	20 /40

The Assessment Summary Sheet

Transfer scores from all the recording sheets to the Assessment Summary Sheet (Form A, p. 50), and staple or clip all the other testing materials together. Keep the results of the initial assessment in a secure place. You will be referring to these test results to decide on the best lesson plan to use, to help you select appropriate reading materials, and to plan specific instructional activities as described in Chapters 4, 5, and 6. You will find that the numerical scores on the summary sheet offer a useful comparison to assess progress when you are ready to determine the effectiveness of the tutoring program and your work with a particular child.

Interpreting the Results of the Assessment

Using the Results to Determine Which Lesson Plan to Use

This book describes lesson plans for readers who are at the emergent stage (Chapter 4), the beginning stage (Chapter 5), and the transitional stage (Chapter 6). The results of the initial assessment will help you decide which plan to use, although it is certainly possible that some children will fall in between, and you will need to draw on ideas from two plans. Begin by comparing the assessment results with the types of readers described below:

- *Emergent readers* still lack complete alphabet knowledge, do not have full awareness of sounds in words, and cannot point accurately to the words in *Sand Castle* (concept of word in text). In terms of word reading, the emergent reader will recognize few if any words on the preprimer list.
- *Beginning readers* know most or all of the alphabet letters and most letter sounds. Beginning readers can spell many of the consonant sounds on the spelling assessment, although they may be spelled incorrectly with phonetically appropriate substitutions (e.g., substituting a *k* for a *c*). Beginning readers can also read at least 10 words on the preprimer word list, and they should be able to read *Sam* or *My Huge Dog Max* with 85% accuracy.
- *Transitional readers* have mastered most of the basic phonics features if they spell consonants, consonant digraphs, two-letter consonant blends, and short vowels in single-syllable words. They can also read all of the words on the preprimer and primer word lists and most of the words on the first-grade word list. Depending on their reading level, they may be able to read words on the second- or third-grade word lists as well. Transitional readers typically read text with at least 90% accuracy on a late first-grade level to a late second- or early third-grade level.

Determining the Child's Reading Level and Selecting Appropriate Books

Table 3.1 (p. 41) can serve as a starting point for deciding which level book to use for instruction. Exact placements will depend on how well children actually read at that level and can only be determined by checking their accuracy with running records on several books. The 100 Word Chart can be used for this.

Emergent Readers in Book Levels: Readiness and Preprimer 1

If children cannot point accurately to the words in *Sand Castle,* they will not be matching their speech to print and will consequently have difficulty learning and remembering words. The simple books from the readiness levels (numbered levels 1–3 and lettered levels A–C) are written with only a few words per page, which supports these children in matching the words they say with the words on the page as they synchronize the beginning sound of each word (as it is spoken) with the beginning letter that matches that sound. The words in these books repeat patterns, may rhyme, and are reinforced by the pictures. For example, the sentence pattern "I see a tiger" changes to "I see a zebra" on the next page, and the pictures support the respective animal names. The picture of the zebra prompts the /z/ sound, and the child then knows to point to the *z* word as he says "zebra."

Even if children can point accurately to the words in *Sand Castle,* they may not have been able to read *Sam* with 85% accuracy. In this case, it is unlikely that they know many words, and they still need to be in the easiest levels. Observations during tutoring will help you determine whether to start with numbered book levels 1, 2, or

3, or lettered levels A, B, or C. If children can name and point to the words accurately after several readings, they are probably at the right level. They should also be able to use the beginning sounds of words to help them stay on track and name words. If not, they may need to be moved back to an easier level.

Beginning Readers in Book Levels: Preprimer 1 and 2

If children can read *Sam* with 85% accuracy and know at least 10 words on the preprimer word list, they are probably ready to begin reading the preprimer materials in numbered levels 3–6, or lettered levels C and D. These texts have a limited range of words in repeated sentence patterns, with two or three sentences on a page. The pictures will continue to help children identify unknown words. As stated earlier, *Sam* spans the preprimer 1–2 levels for initial assessment purposes, and you'll want to get a more precise idea of the reading level for each child. If a child's accuracy on *Sam* was closer to 85%, try placing her in preprimer 1 text (numbered levels 3–4, or lettered level C). If it was on the higher end, try placing her in preprimer 2 text (levels 5–6, or D). Running records, as in the 100 Word Chart, and observations during tutoring will determine which books within these ranges make a comfortable fit.

Beginning Readers in Book Levels: Preprimer 3

If children can read *My Huge Dog Max* with 85% accuracy and know most of the words on the preprimer list, they are ready to try books in numbered levels 7–8, or lettered level E. Although these books will still have only two or three sentences per page, the sentence patterns will vary, and there will be a wider range of words in a story.

Beginning Readers in Book Levels: Primer

Children who can read at least 15 of the words on the primer word list and read text at the primer level with 90% accuracy or better are ready for books at numbered levels 9–12, or lettered levels F and G. These books may still have some repetition of sentence patterns and many illustrations, but the sentences are longer, and there will be many different words in the text. Children will be doing less rereading of these books and should be able to read them the first time through with at least 90% accuracy, or no more than one error in 10 words. A good goal to work on for beginning readers at the primer level is to increase the accuracy of oral reading with practice and to increase the number of words read correctly per minute. You might occasionally start timing their oral reading when children can read with 90% accuracy in level 11, or G. For late beginners reading at a primer level, a reasonable instructional goal for reading speed is at or above 45 words per minute.

Transitional Readers

If children can read most of the words on the first-grade word list and some of the words on the second-grade list, they are probably transitional readers. Transitional readers should be able to read a late first-grade text (numbered levels 13–17, or lettered levels H and I) with at least 90% accuracy. Be sure they can maintain at least 90% accuracy in the text you choose with a smooth and steady pace. If they can read just about every word correctly and quickly, try a book at a higher level (see Table 3.1). If they read with more than one error in 10 words and read slowly and hesitantly, try texts at an easier level. A reasonable goal for reading speed at the late first-grade level is 60 words per minute.

Using the Assessment Results to Plan Word Study

The word study portion of the lesson plan depends on the assessed level of the child's literacy development (emergent, beginner, or transitional) and provides differentiated instruction in alphabet, phonemic awareness, phonics, and spelling.

Alphabet and Letter-Sound Assessments

If a child can name most of the lowercase letters (24 out of 26) and knows most of the letter sounds (20 out of 26), then work on the alphabet and letter sounds can be targeted specifically to those that were missed. In addition, those letters and letter sounds can be isolated during reading and writing activities. For example, the child might be asked to find words that contain a targeted letter or point to a word that starts with a certain letter sound in context. On the other hand, if a child knows fewer than half his letters and letter sounds, he will benefit from more intensive, systematic, and comprehensive work on the alphabet both while reading and writing and during the word study portion of the emergent lesson plan.

Phoneme Awareness and Spelling Assessments

Children's ability to identify initial phonemes can be assessed with the phoneme awareness task in Form E.2. The spelling assessment gives us an insight into the children's ability to separate all the sounds in a word and match those sounds to letters. Table 3.2 will assist you in interpreting spelling as a key to the phonics instruction children will need.

Phonics and spelling development progress hierarchically through a series of stages that are based on the representations children most commonly make as they spell words that are not stored correctly in their memory. These stages are described in depth by Bear et al. (2020) and summarized in Table 3.2.

The Developmental Steps to Literacy

Children's development in alphabet knowledge, phonemic awareness, phonics, and spelling provides the foundational skills that fuel their reading and writing. As shown in Figure 3.4, there are developmental steps to literacy. Understanding these developmental steps, particularly the synchronization of reading stages with spelling stages, will help you plan a comprehensive lesson that addresses your child's literacy needs. For example, beginning readers are typically *letter name–alphabetic spellers* who need instruction in consonants (single, digraphs, blends) and short vowels. Although all learners of alphabetic written languages must ascend the same steps to literacy, some may start in Book Buddies on a higher step than others. Your job is to use assessment information such as that from the Book Buddies assessment to determine the step on which to start climbing.

TABLE 3.2. **Using Spelling to Determine Phonics Instruction**

Spelling Samples	Spelling Stage	What the Child Knows	What to Work On
van=RT pet=ML	Emergent	• Words are made of letters but not matched to sounds	• Alphabet if needed • Picture sorts of beginning sounds
van=F pet=PD rug=G	Early letter name–alphabetic	• Some consonant sounds are represented but incomplete	• Alphabet if needed • Picture sorts of beginning sounds
van=VN pet=PAT rug=RG chip=JP float=FOT	Middle letter name–alphabetic	• Single consonants often correct at beginning and end • Some middle vowels but not always correct	• Picture sorts of digraphs and blends • Compare same-vowel word families
van=VAN pet=PAT rug=ROG chip=CHEP float=FLOT shine=CHIN	Late letter name–alphabetic	• Single consonants correct at beginning and end • Some blends and digraphs • Short vowels used but confused • Long vowel sounds are correct but missing silent vowels	• Compare mixed-vowel word families • Compare short vowels outside word families and include blends and digraphs
van=VAN pet=PET rug=RUG chip=CHIP float=FLOTE shine=SHIN treat=TREET	Early within word pattern	• Short vowels, blends, and digraphs are mostly correct • Long vowel patterns are used inconsistently and are often confused	• Compare long and short vowel sounds • Compare long and short vowel patterns

FIGURE 3.4. **The Developmental Steps to Literacy**

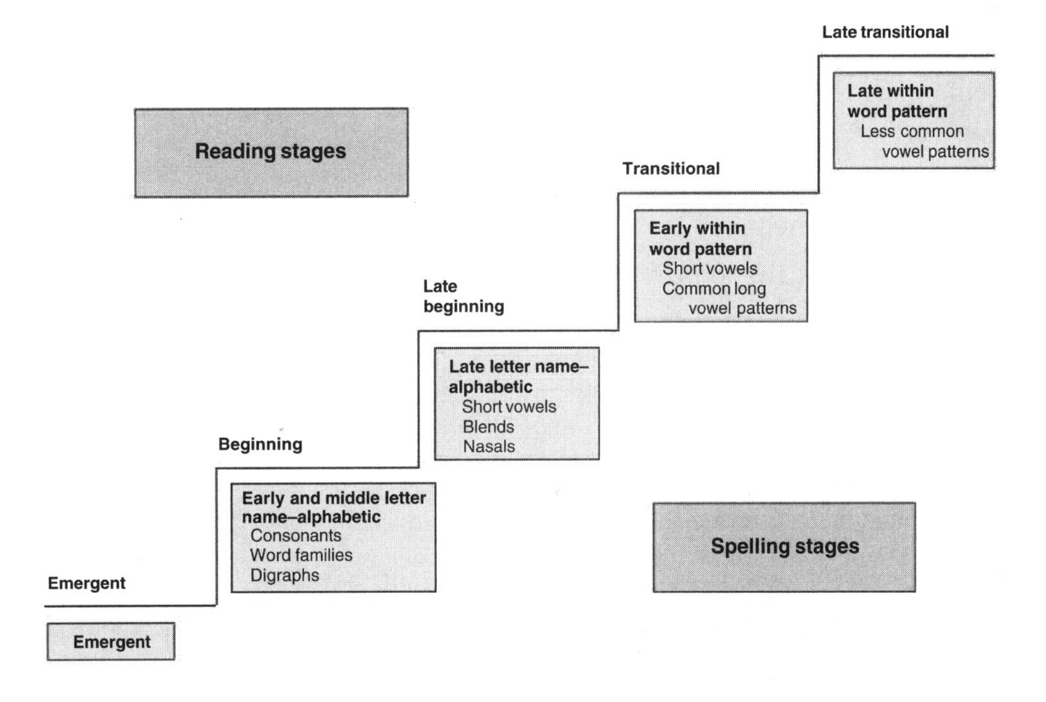

FORM A. Assessment Summary Sheet

Child ______________________ Age ______ Testing Dates ______________________

Examiner ______________________ Teacher/Grade ______________________

		Test Date 1 ___/___/___	Test Date 2 ___/___/___	Test Date 3 ___/___/___
Word List Reading: Form C		% Accuracy	% Accuracy	% Accuracy
Preprimer	(20)	______	______	______
Primer	(20)	______	______	______
First Grade	(20)	______	______	______
Second Grade	(20)	______	______	______
Third Grade	(20)	______	______	______
Letters and Sounds: Forms E.1, E.2, and E.3				
Letter Identification	(26)	______	______	______
Letter Production	(26)	______	______	______
Letter-Sound Production	(26)	______	______	______
Initial Phoneme Awareness	(8)	______	______	______
Phonics/Spelling	(40)	______	______	______
Concept of Word: Form F				
Pointing	(8)	______	______	______
Word Identification	(8)	______	______	______
Total Score	(16)	______	______	______
Text Reading: Forms G.1 and G.2				
PP 1-2 *Sam*	(criterion 85%)	______	______	______
PP 3 *My Huge Dog Max*	(criterion 85%)	______	______	______
Primer	(criterion 90%)	______	______	______
First Grade	(criterion 90%)	______	______	______
Second Grade	(criterion 90%)	______	______	______
Third Grade	(criterion 90%)	______	______	______

Observation/Type of Reader
(Emergent, Beginner, or Transitional)

FORM B. Word Lists (Child's Copy) *(p. 1 of 2)*

the	girl	road
at	yellow	boy
can	mother	move
with	swim	horse
my	sheep	king
go	old	once
did	put	sometimes
run	very	family
red	green	never
bus	eat	paper
get	happy	try
see	play	visit
like	what	grandfather
to	every	ago
she	work	eggs
box	farm	cloud
and	bear	barn
dog	rabbit	table
is	toy	afternoon
up	new	dear

light	danger	towel
cover	scarf	patient
mountain	ruler	carnival
people	husband	instrument
country	travel	furnace
third	blind	parachute
wrong	nibble	pottery
quick	impossible	vegetable
kind	hammer	garbage
together	half	wrinkle
important	worse	citizen
city	kingdom	voyage
neighbor	promise	champion
slowly	understood	article
remember	squeeze	doubt
thought	needle	stampede
busy	huge	wound
herself	thirty	diagram
story	sidewalk	pasture
painting	earn	medicine

FORM C. Word List Reading *(p. 1 of 2)*

Child ______________________________ Date ____________________

Check correct responses, write in substitutions, and check immediate self-corrections.

	Preprimer	Primer	First Grade
1.	the	girl	road
2.	at	yellow	boy
3.	can	mother	move
4.	with	swim	horse
5.	my	sheep	king
6.	go	old	once
7.	did	put	sometimes
8.	run	very	family
9.	red	green	never
10.	bus	eat	paper
11.	get	happy	try
12.	see	play	visit
13.	like	what	grandfather
14.	to	every	ago
15.	she	work	eggs
16.	box	farm	cloud
17.	and	bear	barn
18.	dog	rabbit	table
19.	is	toy	afternoon
20.	up	new	dear

Total ______________ Total ______________ Total ______________

Go on to the next list if the child can name 15 or more of the words in a list.

FORM C. Word List Reading *(p. 2 of 2)*

Child ______________________________ Date ____________________

Check correct responses, write in substitutions, and check immediate self-corrections.

	Second Grade	Third Grade	Fourth Grade
1.	light	danger	towel
2.	cover	scarf	patient
3.	mountain	ruler	carnival
4.	people	husband	instrument
5.	country	travel	furnace
6.	third	blind	parachute
7.	wrong	nibble	pottery
8.	quick	impossible	vegetable
9.	kind	hammer	garbage
10.	together	half	wrinkle
11.	important	worse	citizen
12.	city	kingdom	voyage
13.	neighbor	promise	champion
14.	slowly	understood	article
15.	remember	squeeze	doubt
16.	thought	needle	stampede
17.	busy	huge	wound
18.	herself	thirty	diagram
19.	story	sidewalk	pasture
20.	painting	earn	medicine

Total ______________ Total ______________ Total ______________

Go on to the next list if the child can name 15 or more of the words in a list.

FORM D. Letter Identification and Letter Sounds (Child's Copy)

Letter Identification *(Record responses on Form E.1. Fold this form in half.)*

d	i	n	s	x	
e	j	o	t	y	
c	h	m	r	w	
b	g	l	q	v	
a	f	k	p	u	z

Letter Sounds **Practice** M

B	S	R	F	W	
T	O	J	A	H	
K	Sh	V	I	P	
Z	L	C	Th	U	
E	D	Y	G	N	Ch

FORM E.1. Letters and Sounds

Child ______________________________ Date ____________________

1. Letter Identification (26 possible)

Directions: Ask the students to touch and name each of the lowercase letters on page 55. Circle any incorrect response. Reversals, such as *b* for *d,* are incorrect. Self-corrections are counted correct if they are immediate.

d	i	n	s	x	
e	j	o	t	y	
c	h	m	r	w	
b	g	l	q	v	
a	f	k	p	u	z

Total Correct ____

2. Letter Production (26 possible)

Directions: Call out the sequence of letters presented above. Ask the student to write the letters. Accept either upper- or lowercase letters. Reversals are scored correct but should be noted.

Total Correct ___________

Reversals ___________

3. Letter-Sound Production (26 possible)

Directions: Ask students to touch each of the uppercase letters on the bottom of page 55 and tell you the *sound* it makes. Begin with the example *m.* For the vowels, you are looking for the short vowel sound (see pronunciation guide below for short vowel sounds). If students give the long vowel sound for a vowel, say "That is one sound the vowel (name the letter) makes, but what is the other sound?" Do the same if students give the soft *c* (as in *cent*) or *g* (as in *gym*) sounds. You are looking for the hard sound (*c* as in *cat* and g as in *gum*). Circle any incorrect responses, but check self-corrections (counted correct if they are immediate).

B	S	R	F	W	
T	O	J	A	H	
K	Sh	V	I	P	
Z	L	C	Th	U	
E	D	Y	G	N	Ch

Total Correct ____

Pronunciation Guide
A as in *apple*
E as in *Ed*
I as in *igloo*
O as in *octopus*
U as in *umbrella*
C as in *cat*
G as in *gum*

FORM E.2. Initial Phoneme Awareness (Child's Copy)

Name ______________________________________ Date ________________________

Directions: Ask the child to find the picture to the right that begins with the same sound as the picture in the first column. Model the first one. Name the pictures in each row together. See page 38 for further directions. Record the number correct on Form A.

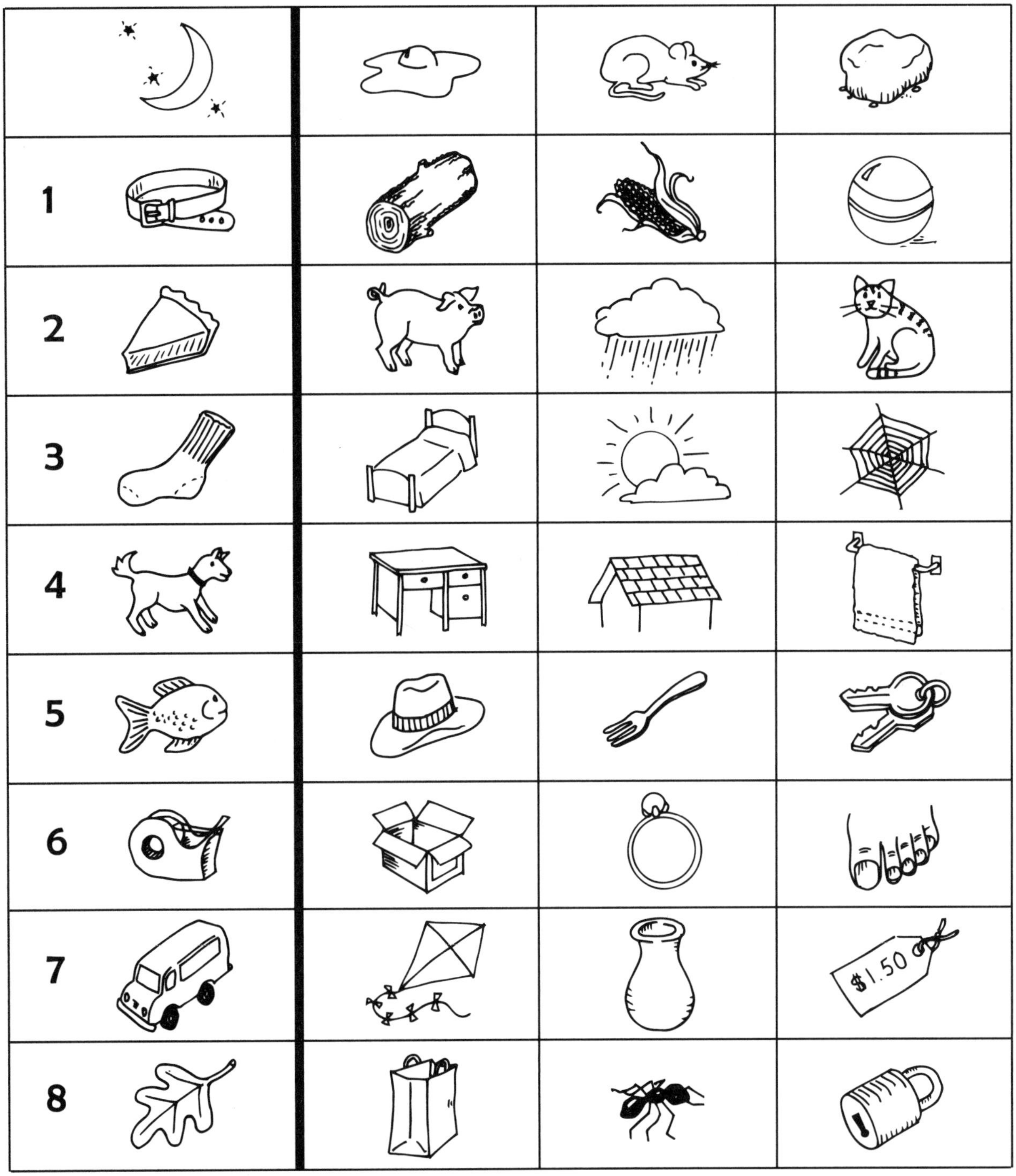

1			
2			
3			
4			
5			
6			
7			$1.50
8			

FORM E.3. Spelling Assessment (Child's Copy)

Name ______________________ Date ______________

Fold paper back so only blanks show. Child writes words below.	Initial Cons	Final Cons	Short Vowel	Blends and Digraphs	Long Vowel	Correct	Total
1.	v	n	a			van	
2.	p	t	e			pet	
3.	r	g	u			rug	
4.	s	d	a			sad	
5.	p	m	u	pl		plum	
6.		p	i	ch		chip	
7.		n		sh	i-e	shine	
8.		t		sk	a-e	skate	
9.	f			fl	oa	float	
10.				tr	ea	treat	
Add down and across to total	/6	/8	/6	/6	/4	/10	/40

FORM F. Concept of Word with *Sand Castle*

Use this with children who know fewer than 10 words on the preprimer list.

See complete directions on page 39.

1. Introduce the story *Sand Castle* by reading the title and then discussing the picture on the first page. Say "This is Alvin. What is Alvin doing?"
2. "Down here it says 'Alvin is playing in the sand.'" Read the first sentence, pointing to each word.
3. Talk about the picture on each page and then read the sentence below, pointing to each word.
4. Now ask the child to read the story *with you* as you point together.
5. Return to the beginning and ask the child to *point and repeat after you* after you read each page, pointing to the words.
6. Once the child has memorized the passage, ask him to read and point by himself. Score the pointing for each sentence on the record form below.
7. Return to the first sentence. Point to each of the two words underlined in the first sentence below, in the order specified, and say "What is this word?" (Point first to *sand* and then to *playing* in the first sentence.) Record a point for each word identified correctly.
8. Repeat for each sentence.

Scoring Pointing: Give 2 points for each sentence pointed to correctly. Also give 2 points if the child corrects himself without prompting. Give zero points for each sentence *not* pointed to correctly.

Scoring Word Identification: Give 1 point for each word correctly identified (there are two in each sentence).

Sentence	Pointing	Word Identification
1. Alvin is playing (2) in the sand (1).	______ (2)	________ , ________ (1 each)
2. He (1) makes a big (2) castle.	______ (2)	________ , ________ (1 each)
3. His little brother (2) knocks it (1) down.	______ (2)	________ , ________ (1 each)
4. Alvin starts (1) all over (2).	______ (2)	________ , ________ (1 each)

Total Pointing (8 possible points) ________

Total Word Identification (8 possible) ________

Total Score for Concept of Word (16) ________

FORM G.1. Text-Reading Assessment for *Sam*

Child ______________________________ Date ____________________

If the child could read at least 10 of the preprimer words, begin with *Sam*. Introduce each book as suggested below. Do not preread, choral read, or echo read.

1. Read and point to the title of the story. "The name of this story is *Sam*."
2. Look at the pictures on the first page and say, "This must be Sam. What kind of a pet does he have? It looks like he has a big dog."
3. Look at the pictures on the second page and say, "The dog is looking at the cup. Can he get it? He is so big he can get the cup on the counter."
4. Look at the pictures on the last page. "Oh no, up he went and down went the cup. What a mess! Let's see if you can read this story about Sam."

Directions for Scoring: If children pause for more than 5 seconds or appeal to you for help, give them the word but place parentheses around it and count it as an error. Cross out words that are misnamed and write above what the child says, circle omissions, and write in additions. If children correct themselves, put a check over the word and do not count it as an error. See Figure 3.2 on page 43 (top) for an example.

Sam has a dog.

Sam has a big dog.

The dog is so big he can get the cup.

Look out Sam!

Up goes the dog.

Down goes the cup.

Words identified correctly in the story (30 words possible) ______ Percentage correct ______

Number correct	30	29	28	27	26	25	24	23	22	21
Percent	100%	97%	93%	90%	87%	83%	80%	77%	73%	70%

Continue with *My Huge Dog Max* if the child reads at least 27 words correctly.

FORM G.2. Text-Reading Assessment for *My Huge Dog Max*

Child ______________________________ Date ____________________

Introduce the story with the following statements and questions. Do not read the story to the child.

1. Read and point to the words in the title of the story. Emphasize the word *huge* as you point to it.
2. Look at the picture on the first page and say "This must be Max. He sure does look huge. He is covered in black spots." Point to the word *spots.*
3. Look at the picture on the second page and ask "What do you think he likes to do with Max? It looks like Max is excited about going out to play ball." Point to the word *ball.* "He is wagging his tail." Point to *tail.*
4. Look at the picture on the third page. Say "Max makes Sam happy when he's sad."
5. Look at the picture on the last page. Say "Where is Max now? Do you think Mom would like to see him there? Where would Mom want Max to be? Now you read this story about that huge dog Max."

Follow the scoring directions for "Sam" on Form G.1.

I have a dog. His name is Max.

Max is a huge dog with black spots.

I like to play ball with Max.

When Max sees the ball he wags his tail.

He knows we will go out and play.

I love Max and he loves me.

Max can make me happy when I am sad.

I take good care of Max.

He sleeps under my bed.

That's what my Mom thinks.

Words identified correctly in the story (72 words possible) ______ Percentage correct ______

To calculate percentage, divide number of words correct by number of possible words.

If the child read at least 65 words correctly or 90%, try a text at the primer level.

Sand Castle

Alvin is playing in the sand.

He makes a big castle.

His little brother knocks it down.
Alvin starts all over.

Sam

Sam has a dog.
Sam has a big dog.

The dog is so big
he can get the cup.

Look out, Sam!
Up goes the dog.
Down goes the cup.

FORM H.3. *My Huge Dog Max* **(Child's Copy)**

My Huge Dog Max

I have a dog.
His name is Max.
Max is a huge dog with black spots.

I like to play ball with Max.
When Max sees the ball, he wags his tail.
He knows we will go out and play.

I love Max and he loves me.
Max can make me happy when I am sad.

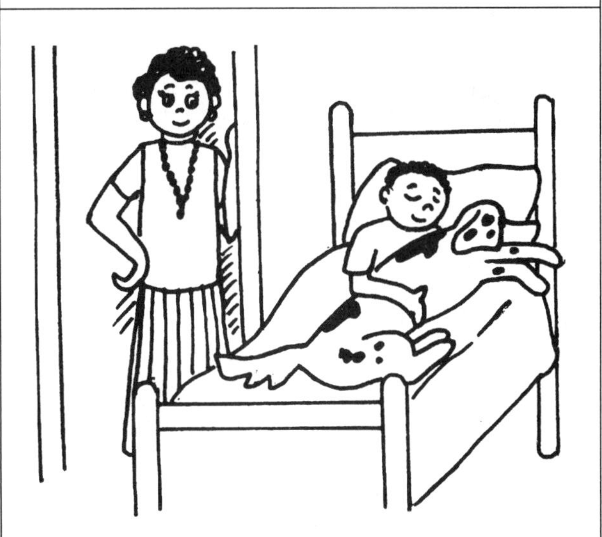

I take good care of Max.
He sleeps under my bed.
That's what my Mom thinks.

Chapter 4

General Tutoring Plan for the Emergent Reader

This chapter presents the lesson plan for the *emergent reader.* Be sure you have assessment information and have considered the criteria in Chapter 3 to determine whether a child is an emergent, a beginning, or a transitional reader.

Characteristics of the Emergent Reader

The emergent stage begins around age 1 and usually ends in kindergarten or early first grade. Emergent readers know few alphabet letters, lack phonemic awareness, and cannot point accurately to the words in *Sand Castle* (concept of word in text). The emergent reader will recognize few if any words on the preprimer word list.

Emergent readers engage in pretend reading as they "read" from a familiar book, using the pictures as a guide. They also read from memory and may recite a text accurately, but their pointing to words doesn't match their spoken words because they have not yet achieved a concept of word in text. To *track* the print and understand where words begin and end, they need to have alphabet knowledge and the ability to attend to the sounds in words.

Emergent learners pretend-write too. Their early written communication usually develops from random marks to pictures to "labeling" pictures. These writers progress from using symbols imitating the shapes of letters to using a combination of letters and numbers to using letters representing the salient, or most noticeable, sounds, including some beginning sounds. By now the writers have developed linearity and directionality—they know to write in a horizontal line from left to right. They may not leave spaces between words yet, but this will come when they develop a full concept of word.

Children who are on the path to developing a concept of word begin by pointing to words from left to right in a text they have memorized. However, they get off track easily, especially on two-syllable words, and usually cannot get back on track without starting over. We say that these children have a rudimentary concept of word. A child with a full concept of word finger-points, or tracks, print accurately as it is spoken. If she gets off track, she will correct herself without starting over, and she can quickly identify individual words within familiar text. We suggest you keep a student in the emergent plan until she develops a full concept of word.

Below is a brief description of the four components of the emergent lesson plan. The rest of the chapter describes each part in detail.

Overview of the Emergent Reader Plan

The lesson plan for the emergent reader consists of four parts:

1. *Rereading familiar materials and concept of word practice* (10–15 minutes). During this warm-up and practice, children reread books, rhymes, poems, and songs they have read in previous sessions. They may also engage in hands-on activities designed to explicitly reinforce the concept of a written word in text as a printed unit with a beginning and an end, bounded by white space.
2. *Alphabet, word study, and writing* (15–20 minutes). In this part, tutors and children work on alphabet knowledge and letter–sound correspondence, or phonics. They also extract known words from stories, and tutors write the words on cards to form a *word bank,* or collection of words they can identify.
3. *Language play* (5–7 minutes). In this part, tutors and children work with *phonological awareness,* or the sounds of speech, including rhyme and beginning sounds.
4. *Reading new materials* (8–10 minutes). In the last part of the plan, tutors introduce a new text.

In each part of the lesson plan children engage in multisensory learning. They say words as they finger-point read. They say sounds and words as they write. They point to letters as they say the letter names and sounds. They manipulate picture cards and letter cards as they say letter sounds and words. Such multisensory practice is a powerful tool for facilitating the learner's connection of letters and sounds and reinforcing those connections.

A sample lesson plan is reproduced in Figure 4.1, and a blank form for the emergent lesson plan can be found in Appendix A.1. As the tutor works through each part of the plan, he or she writes in comments to describe how well the child accomplished the various tasks. These comments will serve as guides for future planning and provide important documentation of the child's progress.

Emergent Reader Lesson Plan, Part 1: Rereading Familiar Material

Every tutoring session opens with reading and finger-pointing to three or more familiar books, poems, and rhymes, including the new text introduced in the previous lesson. This part of the lesson should last 10 to 15 minutes. Rereading gives students practice in developing a concept of word. All reading is done aloud.

FIGURE 4.1. Sample Emergent Reader Lesson Plan

Student: Brandon	Tutor: Jenny	Date: 10/10 Lesson #: 8
Lesson Plan	***Description of Planned Activities***	**Comments**
Rereading and Concept of Word (10–15 minutes)	• "One, Two, Three, Four, Five" rhyme • Can You Find It? • The Color Book — text copy 1) Read 2) B. highlights (w/ highlighter marker) "like" in each line while saying it aloud. Discuss beginning "L" & its sound.	– Needed a lot of support – Fair tracking – Had to match "orange" to book – Highlighted whole 1st line, then OK
Alphabet and Word Study ***Word Bank** ***Letter Recognition** ***Picture Sort/Writing Sort** ***Glue and Label** **Writing** (15–20 minutes)	• Add words from The Color Book. • Review Sidewalk ABC. Match stick-on note lowercase letters to uppercase J-P in book. When you get to L, revisit highlighted text copy. What word did he highlight? What letter & sound did it start with? • Use chalk & chalkboard in book to practice writing uppercase & lowercase J-P.	– Added "like" and "red" – Matched all correctly. Needed some prompting on connecting the "l" in "like" – Backwards "j/J" and "p"
Language Play ***Rhyme** ***Syllable Awareness** ***Beginning Sounds** ***Phoneme Awareness** (5–7 minutes)	• Reread or sing Down by the Bay. • Play rhyming Concentration with pictures of animals/objects from book (envelope in box). Note the sound "llama" begins with. What letter makes that sound?	– Perfect! – Got it! Yes!
New Reading (8–10 minutes)	**Book:** Let's Move **1. Read title to student and look at cover.** **2. Student makes a prediction.** **3. Discuss pictures, words, and patterns in the story.** **4. Read to the student.** **5. Choral, echo, independent reading.**	– Used picture clues – Best 1st independent reading yet!
Take-Home Book	**Book:** Can You Find It?	

Getting Started with Rereading

In the very first tutoring session, you won't have any familiar books to reread, so you will begin with one or two book introductions (see Part 4 of the lesson plan described later in this chapter). Gradually, you will build up a collection of books and poems that have been read before, and you will use these for the rereading. When the child has read a text four to six times, it is retired from the collection. You may also retire a text if it is too hard or too easy, or if the child simply doesn't like it.

Tutor Support

As the emergent reader does not have a concept of word in text, the tutor must strongly support the child in the rereading of familiar, even memorized, text. Reading together, or *choral reading*, is one way to support the reader. Another is *echo reading,* when the tutor points to words, or *tracks,* as she reads a page or line of text, and then has the child do the same.

The emergent reader can be expected to veer off track, especially when pointing to words with more than one syllable. When the child tracks incorrectly, the tutor should first *wait* to give the child time to self-correct. If the child doesn't correct himself, the tutor should prompt the child to reread the line, supporting his finger-pointing if necessary. If that prompt doesn't work, the tutor will want to point to words identified incorrectly and ask the child what letter the word starts with and what sound the letter makes. The child may then be able to identify the word if he has read the text numerous times. If not, the tutor can give it to him. Do not expect an emergent reader to sound out an unknown word letter by letter, because he doesn't yet have the alphabet and phonics knowledge to do so. See Appendix W for a handy reference for tutors, "What to Do When a Reader Needs Help with Words," as they read with their Book Buddies.

After reading, the tutor should revisit any problem words, going back to the sentence where a word occurs and asking the child to reread the entire sentence. If the child reads correctly, the tutor should praise her, point to the word that was previously unknown, and say, "What was this word? How did you know it? What does it start with?" If the child cannot read the word, the tutor should supply possibilities: "Could this word be 'funny'? Why or why not?" However, the tutor shouldn't belabor this. We do not expect emergent readers to remember every word they encounter. This review is designed to draw their attention to the letters and sounds in the word.

The tutor pair continues rereading until all of the texts listed in this section of the lesson plan have been read.

Text Copies

After a book has been read over three or four lessons, a text-only copy of the book can be provided. This is a one-page typed copy of the story in a large font. Without benefit of pictures, the text copy forces the reader to attend to the print, reinforcing concept of word. If the child can't get a word or identifies it incorrectly, the tutor finds the corresponding page in the book and has the child find the word on the page. As the child has read the book many times, he can usually identify the word from memory.

Typing up the texts doesn't take long, and the coordinator can build a file of text copies that can be used in many ways. Text copies can be stapled together or put into personal readers and taken home. They can be cut apart into sentence strips, and the student can rebuild the text. They can also be used to highlight targeted words as described below.

Keeping a Record of Text Readings

Keep a list of all the texts your student reads. (A book list form for this purpose is included in Appendix J.) Each time a story or poem is read, the tutor or student places a tally mark or check beside the title. It is a reasonable goal to expect students to read each text at least four times. Sometimes students are more willing to reread when they have a set goal and can see their progress in the tally marks.

Concept of Word Activities

Next, introduce a concept of word activity:

1. *Cut-up sentences.* Matching individual words to the same words on a sentence strip provides great practice in understanding the boundaries of words. The sentence can be taken from one of the familiar books or poems, or it can be one the child has dictated. Create two sentence strips with the sentence. Leave one intact, and cut up the other into individual words. The tutor pair should read and track the sentence several times on the intact sentence strip. Then the tutor, while reading each word aloud, pushes up the individual words (cut from the duplicate strip) beneath the same words on the sentence strip. Finally, the tutor mixes up the individual words and hands them to the child to repeat the process. Once finished, the child should read the sentence aloud, pointing to each word. Do this both with and without the sentence strip as a model. (See Figure 4.2.)

2. *Highlighting words.* After reading and tracking a text-only copy, the tutor can have the child underline or use a light-colored marker to highlight a given word each time it repeats in the text while he says the word aloud. The pair can then discuss the word's beginning and ending letters and the sounds they make. Other words can also be called out and highlighted by the child as he repeats each one.

3. *Reading and matching word cards.* Pull out a few of the word cards from the pocket in the back of a book that has been reread and ask the child to identify them. If the child can't identify the word on the card, the tutor reads it. The child can then be challenged to find the word on a page (the tutor finds the page first) and say it aloud.

FIGURE 4.2. Cut-Up Sentence Example

Again, the beginning and ending letters/letter sounds can be discussed. This activity should occur immediately after the reading of the book.

Emergent Reader Lesson Plan, Part 2: Alphabet, Word Study, and Writing

A major goal of the emergent lesson plan is for children to attain the *alphabetic principle*: the fusion and application of alphabet recognition, *phonemic awareness,* and letter sounds in reading words and writing them. All these elements are addressed in this second part of the lesson plan.

Alphabet instruction includes learning how to recognize and form the letter shapes, how to name the alphabet letters, and how to associate each letter with an individual speech sound. Word study continues the instruction of letter–sound correspondences, helps children learn new words, improves children's skills in figuring out unfamiliar words when they read, and helps them learn to spell words. Writing may take place during word study and/or separately. Altogether, this part of the lesson should take about 15 to 20 minutes.

- *Alphabet.* Most emergent readers are learning to identify uppercase and lowercase letters of the alphabet. Refer to assessment data to see what letters a particular child needs to study.
- *Word study.* In the emergent lesson plan, word study consists of word-bank work and systematic phonics/spelling instruction.
- *Writing.* This can take the form of writing alphabet letters, completing a simple writing sort, labeling sorted pictures that have been glued into a notebook, writing dictated or original sentences, or pattern writing.

Alphabet

Emergent readers need direct, systematic work with letters and sounds. Here we emphasize letter recognition, letter production, and how to pair those shapes with letter names and sounds. Many letter names contain the associated sound *in* their names, such as the letter name *b* that contains the /b/ phoneme at the beginning of the name, and this is helpful to emergent readers just learning the alphabet (Huang & Invernizzi, 2014; Huang, Tortorelli, & Invernizzi, 2014). You'll know from the assessments in Chapter 3 which letters the child knows and which ones she needs to learn. An alphabet strip or chart for identification and for proper letter formation should always be available for reference. An alphabet chart can be found in Appendix K. It can be attached to the tutoring box or planning folder.

Note that letter sounds can and should be added to the alphabet activities described below.

Alphabet Activities

- *Start with the child's name.* A good starting place for children who do not know many letters is to work on the letters in their names. Names are particularly meaningful to a child. (If your child already knows the letters in his first name, work on those in his last name or a friend's name.) Write each letter of the child's name on a separate card. Lay the cards out in order and name them. Then have the child name them. Scramble the letters and have the child reassemble them, naming them as he does so. Have the child name the letters again, backward and forward, as he touches them.

You might use capitals in one row and ask the child to match lowercase letters in another row below (as shown in Figure 4.3).

- *Recite the alphabet.* Have the child sing the ABC song or recite the letters while touching each letter on an alphabet strip or chart.

- *Arrange the letters in order.* When the student knows 15 letters or more, she can work on putting a set of letters in alphabetical order from A to Z (see Figure 4.4). Use a set of letter cards (see Appendix X), letter cutouts, or magnetic letters. Use both uppercase and lowercase letters. You might put the uppercase letters in order while the child works to match the lowercase letters. The child who struggles with a number of letters should be allowed to refer to an alphabet strip. If this activity seems overwhelming or time consuming, divide the alphabet into halves or thirds.

- *Memory or Concentration.* Use the letters in the child's name, or any other letters you are working on, to play Memory or Concentration. Make two sets of letters so you can match lowercase to lowercase, uppercase to uppercase, or lowercase to uppercase. To keep the game fast and satisfying, don't use more than 10 pairs, or 20 letters. This is a good game, because the child has an excellent chance of winning. Turn all the letters face down to start. Players turn over any two cards at a time. If a player turns up a matching set, she must name them correctly in order to keep them.

- *Use alphabet books.* Look up the letter(s) you are studying in an alphabet book or picture dictionary to find things that begin with that letter. Have the child point to the letter on the page and say its name. The child should also point to the picture and say the name of the picture and its beginning sound: "*A* (the letter name), *apple,* /a/."

- *Make an alphabet book.* You can create an alphabet book by stapling together blank sheets of paper and assigning a letter to each page (or two facing pages). The top of each page is headed by the letter (in both uppercase and lowercase). A personal alphabet book can be used in a number of ways for the child who needs to learn letters:

  - Encourage the child to practice writing uppercase and lowercase forms of the letter on each page while saying the letter name.

FIGURE 4.3. Name Cards for Alphabet Work

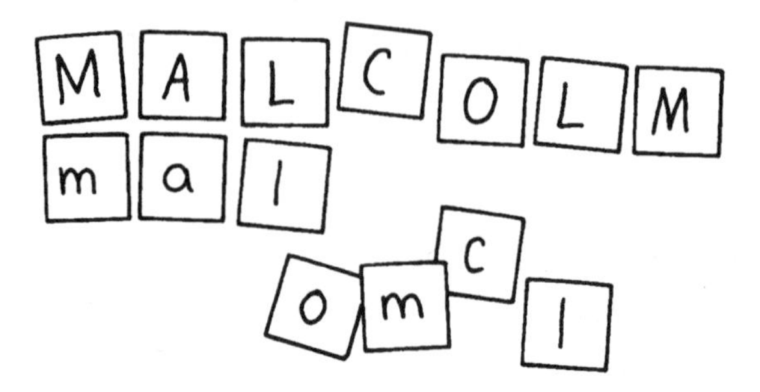

FIGURE 4.4. Letters in ABC Order

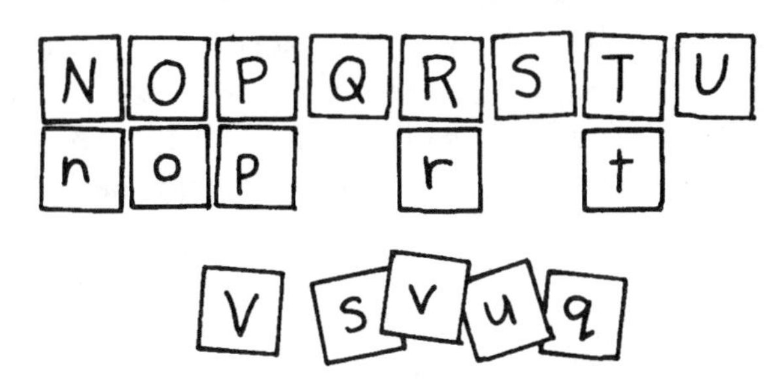

- Glue onto each page a key picture that begins with that sound. The tutor or the child can draw it, cut it from a magazine, or generate it from computer clip art.
- Draw other things that begin with the letter. (Look up things in an ABC book or picture dictionary. Asking the child to think of words that begin with a particular letter is difficult if he has not learned the sound and letter matches.)
- Add word-bank words to the alphabet book to create a dictionary of known words. You can also add the names of friends, family, or pets.
- Use the consonant sound chart (in Appendix K) or another alphabet book as a point of reference to remind children of the letter–sound matches.

• *Font sorts.* Emergent readers need exposure to many different print styles in their progress toward automatic letter identification. Cut out letters in different fonts—both uppercase and lowercase—from print sources, or print them off a computer. These cutouts can be sorted in columns by letter. Avoid cursive styles for now. Font sorts can be found in *Words Their Way: Letter and Picture Sorts for Emergent Spellers* (Bear, Invernizzi, Johnston, & Templeton, 2019).

• *Alphabet eggs.* Draw several pictures of an egg or a seasonal item like a pumpkin or heart on card stock. On each shape write a different lowercase letter on one half and the corresponding uppercase letter on the other. Cut down the middle in a jagged line to create two pieces of a puzzle. Mix up the puzzle pieces for the child to match up as she says the name of each letter.

• *Name That Letter theme games.* Print and cut out pictures of basketballs and laminate them. Laminate a larger picture of a basket. Use a dry-erase marker to write letters on the basketball pictures. Have the child pick up and name each letter. If the letter is named correctly, the child can place the basketball "in" the basket. After playing, wipe off the letters, and the pictures are ready to be reused. You can use the same idea with different themes: footballs and a picture of an end zone, soccer balls and a goal, leaves and a tree, teddy bears and a toy box, and so forth.

Record Progress

Record the letters your child knows by having the child color in the letters on the alphabet sheet in Appendix O or mark them in some other way. Make sure the child says the name of each letter while marking it. This will give you and the child a record of what has been learned and what still needs to be accomplished. Part of the daily routine can be reviewing all the known letters.

Word Study: Word Bank

Word-bank activities and picture sorting for letter sounds and phonics are the ingredients of word study at this stage. A word bank is a collection of words written on small, individual cards or slips of paper (about 1½″ × 3″). These are words a child knows well enough to recognize in isolation. They primarily come from text the child has read. The word bank serves three important purposes:

- In the process of collecting word-bank words, children match the words they say with the printed words in the text. This is particularly helpful for emergent readers, who lack a concept of word and are unsure of where words begin and end on the page.
- As children review their word-bank cards, reading the words aloud, they must pay close attention to the print. By repeated connection of their meaning, pronunciation (sound), and spelling, the words become *sight words,* or words that can be read instantly—"at first sight" (Ehri, 2014; Metsala & Ehri, 2013).
- Word-bank words provide a collection of familiar words for phonics instruction.

Emergent readers know very few words by sight. The ones they know are usually meaningful words such as their names, family names, and words like *mom* and *cat*. In the first lesson, these known words can be written on cards to begin the word bank.

Subsequently, word-bank words will primarily come from the books, rhymes, poems, and songs that are read. The little books used for reading should have book pockets in the back with word cards.

Selecting Word-Bank Words

What should you watch for in choosing word-bank words?

- Concrete nouns, adjectives, and verbs, such as *dog, red,* and *jump,* that evoke strong imagery. These are the easiest words to learn because they convey more meaning than abstract words like *love* and *think* (Rawlins & Invernizzi, 2019; Warley, Invernizzi, & Drake, 2015).
- High-frequency words (*see, am, get, with, for, from*) that children see in many stories.
- Words with a particular phonics feature (e.g., *bee, buzz,* and *bus* all start with the /b/ sound associated with the letter *b*).

Don't be afraid to add plural nouns and present tense verbs ending in *s* if they appear in text. Children will be seeing many such words, and collecting them opens a conversation about singular versus plural nouns as well as verb tense—an introduction to morphology and syntax.

Adding Words to the Word Bank

After reading a book over three or four sessions, take the word cards from the pocket in the back of the book, spread them out on the table, and ask the student to pick up and read the words she knows. Or you can hand the words to the child one at a time and ask her to name each one. Any new words that the child can identify are put aside to be added to the child's word bank.

If you are using a text-only copy or an individual copy of a poem, the child can be asked to underline or highlight words he knows; then ask him to identify those words as you randomly point to them. New words that are read correctly will be added to the word bank.

After the lesson, copy any new, known words onto the Alphabetized Word-Bank List (in Appendix F) and then onto cards for deposit into the child's word bank.

Managing the Word Bank

Store the words in a small box, in a plastic baggie, or on a ring. Once the word bank grows to 50 or more words, you might begin to organize the words alphabetically. Children love to see their word banks grow, and periodically coloring a record form, such as the rocket ship or mountain path provided in Appendix Q, is a motivating activity. Only immediately known words remain in the official word bank. Words that aren't quickly recognized during the review activities described below can be kept separately for matching back to their counterparts in context. However, if a word continues to be a problem, discard it. Emergent readers will not have many words in their word banks, but beginning readers will. More about word banks appears in the next chapter.

Reviewing the Word Bank

The following activities provide some ways to review the word-bank collection:

- *Simple sort.* Hand the collection of words to the child and ask him to go through and read each one, putting known words in one pile and unknown words in another. These unknown words are good ones to include in the "pick-up" game described next.

- *Pick-up.* Lay out 6 to 10 words on the table face up. Ask the child to find and pick up the word you name. Reverse roles. Let the child name the words and you pick them up. Up the ante for this review by laying out words that begin with the same letter, such as *big* and *boy* and *better.* This requires that the student attend to more than just the first letter. Some variations for pick-up are asking the child to pick up words that all begin with a certain letter or to pick up words that start with a particular sound.

- *Paired association.* Word-bank words can be matched to photos, pictures from magazines, or pictures from the cards used for sorting. One motivating activity involves matching photos of classmates to their names. Ask classroom teachers if they can provide some digital thumbnail prints of the Book Buddies children's classmates.

- *Concept sort.* Semantic aspects of word-bank words can be explored by categorizing them by concepts, ideas, and parts of speech. Word-bank words might be sorted by color words versus noncolor words, people versus animals, things you can touch and feel versus things you can't touch or feel (e.g., *bed* and *dog* versus *love* and *smell*), action words versus nouns, and pets versus wild animals.

• *Singular versus plural noun sort.* Word-bank words that are nouns can be sorted into two groups according to whether they are singular or plural. *Dog* and *cat* would go in one column and *dogs* and *cats* in the other. You may be able to note that most plural nouns end in *s*, but there are some exceptions, such as *deer* and *fish*. Exceptions present the opportunity to discuss how some nouns are the same whether singular or plural.

Word Study: Phonics

In the earliest stage, phonics instruction helps children learn the one-to-one correspondence between speech sounds and letters (such as the fact that the words *bell, bat,* and *bug* all begin with the /b/ sound made by the letter *b*). The target for the emergent reader is the beginning sounds.

Word Study: Picture Sorts for Beginning Letter Sounds

A good way to begin teaching phonics is through simple *picture sorting*. Picture sorting is a concrete, hands-on activity for comparing and categorizing speech sounds and matching them with letters. Children sort the picture cards into groups that all start with the same sound by placing them in columns headed with the letter that represents each targeted sound. A key picture that is used consistently to illustrate a particular letter sound is also useful. Materials that come in handy for phonics instruction are described in Chapter 2. *Words Their Way: Letter and Picture Sorts for Emergent Spellers* (Bear et al., 2019) offers a good source for pictures.

Picture sorting can be followed up in each session by adding to the sort any word-bank words that begin with the same sounds. Next comes a writing sort or a glue-and-label activity, which involves gluing a sort into a notebook and labeling each picture. Both these activities are described after picture sorting.

Getting Started with Picture Sorting

Picture sorts always contrast at least two sounds at the same time. After starting with two sounds, we suggest moving to three sounds and adding a fourth if the student is doing well.

A good starting point is sorting pictures of objects that start with *m* and *s*. These sounds are very different from each other and can be said slowly, without distortion. Each sort follows these steps:

1. *Set up.* Prepare a collection of pictures to use for sorting. Use letter cards to head each category (see Figure 4.5). Select a key picture for each sound (such as *mouse* and *sun*) and put it under the corresponding letter to start a sorting column.

2. *Introduce the sort.* Shuffle the rest of the picture cards and say to the child something like "We are going to listen for the sound at the beginning of these words and decide if they begin like *mouse* or like *sun*. I'll do a few first. Here is a sock. Sssock begins like sssun, so I'll put it under the letter *s* and the picture of the sun. It starts with /s-s-s-s/. Here is a man. Mmmman begins like mmmmouse, so I'll put it under the *m*. Now it's your turn. You pick a card and decide where to put it."

FIGURE 4.5. Picture Sort of *S* and *M*, with Several Words at Bottom

When modeling, elongate the beginning sound by stretching it out when possible, as in /s-s-s-s/. However, some sounds cannot be elongated, and you will want to be careful not to add an *uh* after those letter sounds. For example, for the letters *b* and *t*, avoid saying *buh-uh-uh* or *tuh-uh-uh*.

3. *Sort.* After modeling several pictures—saying the name, emphasizing the beginning sound, then relating it to the letter at the top of the column—begin taking turns or turn the task over to the child. Make sure she says the name of each picture, the beginning sound, and the letter that makes that sound, before or while sorting the picture. If the child does not know what to call a picture, simply tell her what it is. If she continues to have trouble naming it, just eliminate it from the deck. Don't make naming the pictures into a guessing game. You can include words from the child's word bank in these sorts as well.

For all children, and especially for English language learners, picture sorts present a way to broaden vocabulary. If an English learner knows just a few pictures for each column, use those and try adding a couple more. Repeat the English word for each picture and ask what the word is in the child's primary language.

4. *Re-sort and check.* After doing a sort together, scramble up the pictures and ask the student to sort again as quickly as she can, naming each picture as it is placed. Leave the letter and key picture in place. Don't correct the student as she sorts by herself, but when she is through, have her check herself by first identifying the header (both the sound and the letter) and then naming the pictures in each column and stating what the pictures have in common. If she fails to find misplaced cards, tell her how many she missed and ask her to try to find them herself.

Further Studies of Beginning Sounds with Picture Sorts

If your child can easily sort *m* and *s,* you can add *b* words and then *r* words over the next two sessions until you have four categories of initial sounds. Repeat this kind of sequence with all the letters, working with up to four categories at a time. If your child knew many letter sounds in the assessment in Chapter 3, a quick review that compares four sounds at a time over 4 or 5 weeks is all that may be needed. *Words Their Way: Word Sorts for Letter Name–Alphabetic Spellers* (Johnston, Bear, Invernizzi, & Templeton, 2018) offers ready-made picture sorts for this purpose. Later, in the beginning reader lesson plan, you will target consonant sounds as needed. You will also study consonant sounds as you work with same-vowel word families.

In your beginning sounds instruction, include pictures of words beginning with short vowels (see the suggested sequence below). Short vowel sounds are harder to learn than consonant sounds, and consonants will be mastered first. Medial short vowels will be studied in word families later, in the beginning reader plan. Words such as *apple* and *ax* are good to use for the beginning short *a*. *Octopus* and *ox* are good for short *o*. Avoid words such as *elephant* or *Indian* because children are likely to confuse the beginning sound with *l* (elephant) and *n* (Indian), respectively. Pictures for sorting beginning short vowel sounds may be found online or in the appendices of *Words Their Way* (7th ed.; Bear, Invernizzi, Templeton, & Johnston, 2020). *Digraphs,* or units of two letters that make one sound, like *sh,* can be introduced here and will be studied in the beginning reader plan as well.

Suggested Sequence for Beginning Sound Study

There is no set order for the study of beginning sounds, but you'll want to start with those that occur most frequently, and you'll want to make sure to compare sounds and letters that are distinct both phonologically, or sound-wise, and visually. A suggested sequence is shown below and in the Suggested Word Study Sequence in Appendix P.

Suggested Sequence for Initial Sound Sorting

(1) M/S, M/S/B, M/S/B/R

(2) T/G, T/G/N, T/G/N/P

(3) C/H, C/H/F, C/H/F/D

(4) L/K, L/K/J, L/K/J/W

(5) Y/Z, Y/Z/V, Y/Z/V

(6) TH/SH, TH/CH, TH/CH/SH

(7) A/O, I/U, E/I/O/U

Before moving to a sort with all new letter sounds, make sure the child has a solid understanding of the sounds that have been taught. Observation, writing sorts (described below), and contextual writing provide assessment opportunities during each lesson. If a child is still struggling with one or two sounds, continue practicing those and add a new letter sound, and then another.

Assessment

Cumulative *spell checks* provide an opportunity to assess learning over a longer period of time. For a cumulative spell check, simply call out several words beginning with the sounds that have been taught over the previous 2 or 3 weeks and have the child write the words in a column. Encourage children to spell as much of the words as they can, but assess them for correct representation of the initial sound. Review any beginning sounds that are represented incorrectly.

For more ideas and materials for teaching beginning phonics to emergent learners, see *Words Their Way: Letter and Picture Sorts for Emergent Spellers* (Bear et al., 2019).

Word Sorts for Beginning Sounds

It is important to add word-bank words to each of the picture sorts described earlier to help children see the connection with reading. After sorting the picture cards into categories headed by the corresponding letters, pull out the child's word bank and give him those words that start with the same letter sounds. This is easy if you have arranged the word bank alphabetically. Let the child sort the word cards into the correct categories, naming each word as he does so.

Writing Sorts for Beginning Sounds

In writing sorts, children are asked to write a few words after sorting them as part of the phonics portion of the lesson plan. Writing sorts strengthen the multisensory connections between sounds and letters and can also be used for assessment. The following steps outline the procedure:

1. *Set up.* Before the lesson, the coordinator prepares the notebook or a piece of paper by writing the beginning sounds to be studied at the top of the page. These serve as headers for the lists of written words. The coordinator might also glue a picture beginning with the appropriate letter beside each letter header. Select several pictures from the sort you have just completed. Generally, two or three pictures for each sound will be enough. Scramble the pictures and turn them face down.

2. *Writing.* First, have the child identify the header letters and their beginning sounds. Next, invite the child to turn over a card, say the name of the picture, and then write as much of the word as she can beneath the proper header. She should sound out the word while writing, listening for the beginning and other sounds. Since you have been working on the initial consonant sound, that is all that you can really expect the child to write correctly, but children can be encouraged to listen for and write more sounds in the word. Just don't expect these additional sounds to be correct. Proceed with the rest of the pictures.

3. *Check the sort.* After she finishes writing all the words, have the child identify the first header, read the words in the column, and state the beginning sound they have in common. Have her follow this procedure with the other headers and columns.

Glue and Label

This activity is an alternative to the writing sort described above. The child sorts pictures under picture/letter headers glued onto the top of a page or pages of his notebook following picture sorting. Then the child glues the pictures down, leaving enough room beneath each one to label it. The child says the name of the picture and then sounds out the word while writing, listening for the beginning and other sounds.

As they have been studied, the beginning sounds should be represented correctly when labeled. After labeling, the child reads down each column's words and tells the tutor what the words have in common.

For the glue-and-label activity, you can make reduced-size copies of the pictures from *Words Their Way* (Bear et al., 2020) or pictures you've purchased. It's a good idea to keep many copies of little pictures representing beginning sounds so you can easily pull the ones you need as you write lessons. A large storage box with small, separate compartments, like ones used for beads or nails, is a perfect receptacle for keeping the pictures in alphabetical order.

Word Hunts for Beginning Sounds

A word hunt is a quick and valuable add-on activity after children have completed picture/word sorting and a writing sort or glue-and-label task. Look up targeted letters in an alphabet book to find pictures of more things that begin with a sound. Also ask children to look for words that start with targeted sounds in the books they have already read. This will go faster if you can open the book to a particular page where you know one or more words appear. Say something like "Let's look for words that start with the same sound as *mouse*. What letter would you look for at the beginning of that word? Can you find a word on this page that starts with the same sound as *mouse*? Point to the word. What is that word? What sound does it start with?"

Other Beginning Sounds Activities

While sorting, writing sorts, and gluing and labeling provide the foundation for teaching letter sounds, games afford fun opportunities for instruction and review. One of the games described below can substitute for sorting in the lesson plan after a set of letter sounds has been sorted once or twice, or it can serve as a culminating activity after repeated instruction in a set of letter sounds. A game also serves as a good cumulative review of previous lessons. Make sure the child says the letter sounds and names as he is playing!

- *Memory or Concentration.* This is the same game as the one described for alphabet practice, but the child matches a letter card (use both uppercase and lowercase forms on the card) to a picture beginning with the letter sound.

- *Letter-Sound Eggs.* Again, this requires the same procedure as Alphabet Eggs puzzles, but one half of the shape is the letter, and one half is a picture beginning with the letter sound.

- *Board games.* Two sides of a manila folder become the board. You can create a path of squares, each square labeled with a letter. Players take turns choosing from a pile of picture cards with beginning sounds corresponding to the letters on the board. Each player identifies the picture chosen (e.g., a sun) and emphasizes the beginning sound (*s-s-s-un*) or isolates the beginning sound (/s-s-s-s/) before moving her game piece forward to the closest square sporting *Ss*. The first person to finish wins. You can make a permanent game, or you can laminate a folder with a blank game path and simply add the operative letters to the squares with a dry-erase marker, wiping off the board after use.

Another variation on this game is to fill the game path with pictures and use a pile of letter cards from which the players choose.

Writing

Emergent writers practice what they know about letters: how to form them, the sounds they make, and how to put them together to create a representation of speech. Their growing understandings of reading and writing inform each other. By the time they develop a solid concept of word, emergent learners also understand word boundaries in their writing. Writing is an important part of literacy instruction for children at this stage, as it is for readers in the later stages of development. Just remember to hold emergent writers accountable only for the features they know. At this stage few, if any, words will be spelled correctly, but the writer knows what he just wrote. Don't forget to have him read it back to you. In the Book Buddies emergent reader lesson plan, writing can take several forms:

- *Alphabet letters.* An emergent reader just learning the alphabet can practice writing the uppercase and lowercase letters she's working on with her tutor, or she can draw and label pictures of words she's discovered that begin with the letter.

- *Lists of names.* Children can apply their knowledge of letter sounds to create lists of names: friends, family members, and pets. *Katy* may be written as *KT*; *Ellen* may be spelled *LN*.

- *Writing sorts; glue and label.* As outlined above, the child represents what she knows about letter sounds by writing words the tutor calls out or by labeling pictures. Although the focus has been on the beginning sound, the tutor can verbally draw out the word to see if the child can represent any more sounds. If you have done this after sorting it can comprise the writing task for the lesson when time is short.

- *Writing after games.* After playing a game, children can be instructed to write the names of pictures.

- *Picture drawing and labeling.* The child might draw a picture of her choice and label it with a title or a description of what's happening and then read it to her tutor. Because emergent readers don't possess a concept of word, there may not be spaces between the "words." Early on, letters may be mixed with other symbols. Don't let the drawing take more than 5 minutes, and remember: hold the writer accountable only for what she's been taught.

- *Dictated sentences.* A sentence incorporating the beginning sounds being studied provides an opportunity for the child to apply what she's learned. These sentences can offer a "fill-in-the-blank" for the child to complete as she wishes: "Bob bit into the big ____________." When dictating sentences, read them once completely and then dictate one word at a time while the child writes each one.

- *Patterned sentences.* These are sentences based on the pattern of a familiar text. For greatest support, they can take the form of a cloze sentence. After reading *Can You Find It?* by Amy Casey (1997), you can repeat the pattern in the book by writing a sentence in the child's notebook with a blank for her to fill in however she wishes: "Can you find the ____________?" After reading *Let's Move!* by Kate McGovern (2000), where different animals "love to" move in different ways, you might write the following in the child's notebook: "__________ love to __________." Or, a child can write a whole, original sentence based on a pattern.

• *Original sentences.* An original sentence can be in response to reading, or about something that's important to the child, such as an upcoming birthday. After the child writes the sentence, it can be written by the coordinator on a sentence strip, with corrected spelling and spacing between words, and can be placed in the rereading collection for future lessons. It can also be used with a matching, cut-up sentence strip for concept of word practice.

It's important to point out here that the purpose of rewriting the sentence is *not* to correct the child's writing. Rather, it is to create authentic practice for reading and concept of word development.

• *Notes and cards.* Birthday and holiday cards and notes to friends and family members provide engaging opportunities for writing practice. They also reinforce the concept of writing for communication purposes. The desire to communicate and be understood offers powerful motivation to work hard at applying those sound–symbol correspondences!

Questions Tutors Often Ask about Writing

Over the years, we have found that tutors tend to ask many of the same questions regarding student performance. We have included some of these, along with their answers, in this chapter and in the next two chapters.

"What If My Child Is Having Trouble with Handwriting?" You should certainly assist your child in forming letters. If a child is struggling with writing a letter properly, model writing the letter, following the directions showing which part of the letter to make first and where to start and finish the part (a handwriting guide is provided in Appendix M). Verbalize as you write. For example, as you make an uppercase *B,* say something like "Start at the top and make a line down; start at the top and curl around to the middle; start at the middle, and curl around to the bottom." Then have the child trace and verbalize after you.

Be sure to tell your coordinator about any letters your child is having trouble writing. For the next lesson, the coordinator can use dashes to fashion two or three examples for a letter in the child's notebook; the child can trace over them and then make the letter on his own several times.

"How Can My Child Be Able to Read a Word but Then Be Unable to Spell It?" Late emergent readers and beginning readers are reading with partial clues. In the early phases of word recognition, readers store only partial representations of words: They know words in bits and pieces. They might see the word *for* and read it correctly because they know *for* begins with *f* and ends with *r,* and it makes sense in the sentence. So they might read a word correctly in context or even sometimes in isolation, but they haven't retained the knowledge to summon a correct spelling when they try to write the word.

This kind of word recognition also explains why a child may know a word one day and not the next, or know it on one page and not another, or know it *without* an *s* on the end but not *with* an *s* on the end (Ehri & McCormick, 1998).

Emergent Reader Lesson Plan, Part 3: Language Play

This part of the lesson plan targets phonological awareness, or awareness of the sounds in spoken words, including rhyme, syllables, and phonemes—the smallest units of speech. The ability to recognize and manipulate phonemes in a word, such as segmenting a word into phonemes (*bag* is /b/-/a/-/g/) or blending phonemes to make a word (/p/-/o/-/t/ is *pot*) is called phonemic awareness and is the most difficult skill to attain under the phonological awareness umbrella. This section of the lesson plan should last about 5 to 7 minutes.

A conscious awareness of the sounds of the language represents the first step in the developmental progression to literacy in an alphabetic language like English. Emergent readers identified as at risk for reading difficulties need extra, direct instruction in phonological awareness. Phonological awareness instruction is about speech sounds, but research shows that phonemic awareness instruction becomes more effective when letter sounds are matched to print, and so we also introduce letters into the phoneme awareness portion here (Bryant, Bradley, MacLean, & Crossland, 1990). Once sounds are matched to print, the lesson becomes phonics instruction.

Where to Start

This section of the lesson plan is called "language play" because it does involve playing with oral language. The instructional areas appearing on the lesson plan—rhyme, syllable awareness, beginning sounds, and phoneme awareness—are listed in descending order according to the developmental progression of phonological awareness as shown in Figure 4.6 (Invernizzi & Tortorelli, 2013). Use the assessment results from Chapter 3 to determine where to start a child here. If the child performed very poorly on the alphabet, letter sounds, initial phoneme awareness, and spelling tasks, you might begin with rhyme. On the other hand, if the child did moderately well on the letter sounds and represented some beginning sounds in the spelling, you might start with beginning sounds or phoneme awareness practice.

Not all emergent readers will need to spend much time in this part of the lesson plan. Children who knew many letter sounds and spelled a fair number of initial consonants on the assessments but still don't have a solid concept of word might engage

FIGURE 4.6. Developmental Progression of Phonological Awareness

Rhyme
⇩
Syllable Awareness
⇩
Beginning Sounds
⇩
Phoneme Awareness

in a quick phoneme awareness activity, but they should spend more of their Book Buddies time working in the other areas of the lesson plan.

Rhyme

Several activities support the development of rhyme. Note that while most children develop an awareness of rhyme easily, some do not. If a child is receiving instruction in rhyme awareness in both the classroom and Book Buddies and is not getting it, try moving on to syllable awareness tasks.

- *Sorting by rhyme.* Picture cards can be sorted by rhyme.
- *Odd One Out.* Here, sets of three cards are presented. Two cards rhyme, and one—the "odd one out"—does not (for example, *cat, man, bat*). The child says aloud the names of the pictures and determines which one is the "odd one out" (*man*) and then repeats the two rhyming words to reinforce the rhyme awareness (*cat, bat*).
- *Rhyming Concentration.* Rhyming sets of pictures are used in this game. The pictures can be generic, or they can refer to a reading or a read-aloud. For example, after reading aloud Raffi's *Down by the Bay* (1988), the tutor and child can play rhyming Concentration with pictures of objects and animals from the book. These can be drawn or found in computer clip art.
- *Rhyming Bingo.* Prepare sets of rhyming pictures. Glue one set to the board and use the other as the deck for the game. The deck cards themselves or other markers are used to mark the squares. *Words Their Way* (Bear et al., 2020) offers a list of rhyming groups from its pictures in the back of the book.

Syllable Awareness

Syllables are probably the easiest segment of speech to separate because each syllable corresponds to a physical release of air. Integrating syllable awareness into concept of word practice, particularly when using poetry or nursery rhymes, is very important (Mesmer & Williams, 2015). Multisyllabic words will throw emergent readers off track as they point and recite, so awareness that a word can have more than one syllable is an essential part of developing word awareness and a concept of word in print. For example, after reciting and tracking the printed rhyme "Sam, Sam, the baker man / washed his face in a frying pan," the tutor pair can clap the syllables. The tutor can then point to each word as the child is reciting and clapping syllables. This is the perfect opportunity for the tutor to point out that *baker* and *frying* are "two-clap" words, while all the other words are "one-clap" words.

Some activities to support development of syllable awareness are presented below.

- *Clapping syllables–words in isolation.* You can clap the child's and tutor's names, along with the child's family names. Say the whole name aloud and then one syllable at a time while clapping once: "*Landon. Lan* (clap), *don* (clap)." Ask, "How many syllables are in *Landon*?"
- Lay out pictures of objects or the child's classmates and clap syllables too. Pictures from sorts and books you've read also offer opportunities for syllable play.

• *Clapping syllables–words in sentences.* Move on to use a sentence from a reading, a sentence from a story dictated by the child, or another sentence meaningful to the child (e.g., "Today we go to art class"). The tutor repeats the sentence aloud and announces, "We're going to clap for the syllables we hear in each word of the sentence. We'll clap once for each syllable. The first word is *today*: *to* (clap), *day* (clap). Now try it with me: *to* (clap), *day* (clap). How many syllables are in the word *today*?" The tutor pair proceeds through the sentence this way and then recites the whole sentence together while clapping.

• *Sliding syllables.* Gather picture cards depicting one-, two-, and three-syllable words. Start with the one- and two-syllable words and work your way up to three syllables. Cut the two-syllable pictures into two pieces and the three-syllable pictures into three pieces. Pictures representing single syllable words remain uncut. Have the child say the whole word, and then slide each piece of the picture while saying the syllable: "*Window*: *win* (slide the first piece on the left), *dow* (slide the second piece). Don't forget to reinforce the total number of syllables: "So how many syllables are in the word *window*?"

Beginning Sounds

Identifying the beginning sound in spoken words is a rudimentary phonemic awareness skill and absolutely necessary to move an emergent child into beginning reading. Some activities to support beginning sound awareness are offered below.

• *Matching sounds to names.* Start with a child's name. Say the child's name and repeat the initial sound: "*Janae* starts with /j/." Lay out a group of pictures, some of which begin with the same sound as the child's name. Identify the pictures. Then say the child's name, again isolating the initial sound. Have the child say the name of each picture, and then her name, and state whether those pictures belong in her "name pile." After creating the "name pile," have the child repeat the name of each picture and tell you why they all belong together in the pile ("They all start with /j/, like "*Janae*.")

• *Using readings.* You can connect beginning sound instruction to a text that has been read or read aloud. For example, after reading aloud *Animals Should Definitely* Not *Wear Clothing,* by Judi Barrett (1970), lay out picture cards of animals from the book. Say, "I'm thinking of an animal that should not wear clothing. It begins with the sound /p/-/p/-/p/." The child can make a pile of pictures he gets right, saying the name and beginning sound of each picture he collects.

• *Sorting by sounds.* Under picture headers, the child can sort pictures representing two or three beginning sounds.

• *Odd one out.* Proceed as you would with the rhyming version, but the criterion is beginning sounds.

Phoneme Awareness

Phoneme awareness is the most difficult of the phonological awareness skills. For this reason we suggest starting phoneme awareness instruction with segmenting and blending words by their *onset,* or the part of the word before the vowel, and *rime,* or the part of the word including the vowel and the letters that follow: /c/-/at/. (Note that the rime is the part of the word that rhymes: *cat, bat, sat*!) Once the child gets the hang of that, try introducing the more difficult process of segmenting and blending words by individual phonemes (/c/-/a/-/t/). The following activities support the development of phoneme awareness.

• *It's in the Bag.* In this game you'll be asking the child to identify a word by blending together the onset and rime of the word. Lay out several objects or pictures with one-syllable names and identify them. The words can have short or long vowels. Explain that you'll be placing them in a bag, and you—or a puppet—will be saying each object in a funny or slow way. It is the child's job to figure out which object you're about to pull out of the bag. When saying each word, you'll separate the onset and rime: /c/-/at/.

Once the child becomes adept at blending the onset and rime to identify words, try individual phonemes. When you say each word, drag out the word, phoneme by phoneme: /c/-/a/-/t/. The greater the number of phonemes, the more difficult the task is. You'll want to work your way up. Note that initial or ending consonant *blends* (i.e., the *st* in *step* or *mast*) represent two phonemes and are more difficult to blend than single consonants or digraphs such as *sh* or *ch*.

You can match this activity to a reading too. After reading aloud *Animals Should Definitely* Not *Wear Clothing,* lay out pictures of animals from the book. Only use the animals with one-syllable names. Have the child identify each one. Then pick up the cards and hold them so the child can't see. Say the name of the first animal, separating the onset and rime or dragging out the name phoneme by phoneme, if the child is ready for that. If the child blends the sounds to make the correct word, he gets the picture to hold. It's a good idea to warn the tutor that each letter in a word doesn't always represent a phoneme, or sound. For example, the *sh* in *sheep* is one phoneme. The *oa* in *goat* is one phoneme.

• *Sound boxes.* For this onset-rime activity, create a sound box by drawing two contiguous boxes on a sheet of card stock and laminating it. The child pushes up a marker (e.g., a penny or small disk) inside the first box for each word's single phoneme onset (the *m* in *mat*) and another marker inside the second box for the rime (the *at* in *mat*). The child says each sound while pushing up the marker and then blends the sounds together to say the word.

You can add to this activity by then having the child push letter cards (these can be found in Appendix I) corresponding to the spelling of the onset and rime. For this phonics exercise, you would use simple CVC words. CVC is the basic short vowel syllable structure in the English language and the first syllable type we study in our phonics instruction. The procedure for pushing markers followed by pushing letter cards is as follows:

1. *Pushing markers*: Gather pictures of one-syllable words that begin with a single consonant or digraph (e.g., *sun, gate, ship*). Say the name of the first picture and explain you are going to "split off" the first sound. Then model how you push up a marker for the beginning sound, saying the sound aloud (e.g., the /s/ sound in *sun*). Do the same with the rime (e.g., the /un/ sound in *sun*). Then blend aloud the onset and rime to make the word as you sweep your finger from left to right: *S-un, sun*). Have the child try. Continue with the other pictures.

2. *Pushing letters:* Remove the markers, and for those pictures representing CVC words, introduce one letter card with the initial letter written on it (*s*) and one card with the rime (*un*). Repeat the process with the sound box, this time using the letter cards instead of the markers.

With late emergent readers you can try pushing markers for the beginning, middle, and ending sounds for three-phoneme words and follow up with pushing the letters for CVC words. Just make a three-box mat.

• *Cut-up pictures.* Another way to practice segmenting a word into onset and rime and blending it again is with pictures cut into two pieces.

1. As with the sound box activity, gather pictures of one-syllable words that begin with a single consonant or digraph. Cut each picture into two pieces, making the piece on the left slimmer than the other. With the pieces together, say the name of the picture and explain you are going to "split off" the first sound. Then model how to push up the first, slimmer piece and say the initial sound. Do the same with the second piece, representing the rime. Next blend aloud the onset and rime to make the word, sweeping your finger from left to right. Give the picture to the child to try.

Variation: Instead of pushing up the pictures on a surface, you can hold up the picture pieces in the air, keeping them together, and say the whole word. Then actively "split off" or "peel off" the beginning sound: Move the first piece away to the left, saying the initial sound. Then move the second piece to the right while pronouncing the rime. Finally, bring the pieces back together and say the whole word. This manipulative activity can be particularly powerful for the struggling learner.

2. As with the sound box activity, repeat with letter cards representing the onset and rime of those pictures representing CVC words.

• *Initial phoneme manipulation.* In this activity the student segments and substitutes the beginning sound/letter of a three-phoneme CVC word and blends each new initial sound/letter with the rime. For example:

1. Place a picture of a cat before the child. Have the child say the name of the picture and isolate and repeat the beginning sound /c/. Then place three letter tiles or plastic alphabet letters together beneath the picture to spell the word *cat*: *c, a, t*. Say that these letters spell *cat,* and again establish the initial sound and point to the *c*. Slide your finger under the *at* chunk and say it; then blend the onset and rime to make *cat,* sliding your finger beneath the word.

2. Now remove the *c,* and establish what is left: *-at*. What word would we get if we added the sound /p/ to /at/? Repeat "/p/-/at/." Establish that the new word would be *pat*. Introduce a *p* letter tile. Point to the *p* and repeat the sound: "/p-p-p/." Repeat the rime. Then, again sliding your finger beneath the tiles, blend the new initial sound with the rime to make the word *pat*. Repeat with *m,* allowing the child to try herself. If she has trouble, support as necessary.

For more phonological awareness activities, refer to *Words Their Way for PreK–K* (Johnston, Invernizzi, Helman, Bear, & Templeton, 2014), *Phonemic Awareness in Young Chil-*

dren (Adams, Foorman, Lundberg, & Beeler, 1998), and *Phonics from A to Z* (Blevins, 2017).

Emergent Reader Lesson Plan, Part 4: Introducing New Reading Materials

New reading material is introduced at the end of every tutoring session and should never be skipped. If the tutor is running short on time, she should speak to the coordinator about cutting short another part of the lesson plan. Generally, about 8 to 10 minutes should be saved for new reading.

The emergent reader will be reading nursery rhymes; jingles; easy poetry; and the easiest, predictable little books leveled at lettered reading levels A, B, and C, or numbered levels 1–3. These books offer heavy support through pictures on each page and patterned, repetitive language.

Introducing a New Book

Because emergent readers do not have a full concept of word, knowledge of many sight words, or the ability to sound out words, the tutor must lend a great deal of support. There are five steps to consider when reading a new book with an emergent reader:

1. *Before Reading.* Preview the text with the child. Read aloud the title as you point to the words and talk about the pictures on the cover. Ask the child what the book might be about based on the title and cover illustration. You may need to model how to make a prediction by thinking aloud. For example, a tutor might think aloud, "This book seems to be about colors. I wonder if it will include my favorite color?" Then walk through the book page by page, talk about the pictures, and point to and name any unfamiliar vocabulary. You might stimulate the child's interest by asking questions that relate the pictures to the child's life.

2. *Read To.* Read the text to the child while pointing to each word. If there is a two- or three-syllable word, model how you must point to it more than once. Also point out features of print such as bold print, punctuation marks, and capital letters. React to what you are reading! Is there something surprising, funny, or sad? Don't hesitate to model how reading evokes feelings.

3. *Read With.* Return to the first page or line and read the page or line together (choral read) while finger-pointing together. Proceed through the whole text in this manner if needed. If more support is necessary, use echo reading: Read a line while finger-pointing; then have the child do the same.

4. *Read Independently.* Go back to the beginning and have the child try reading herself. If the child is struggling, try choral reading or echo reading. Then, once again, ask the child to try reading on her own. It is important to provide *only* as much support as is needed.

5. *Discuss.* Engage the student in a conversation about the book–not an inquisition to test comprehension. Invite the child to react to the book. For example, after

reading a book about colors, ask the child if she has changed her mind about her favorite color. What objects of her favorite color would she have added to the book?

Using Songs, Rhymes, and Poetry

Easy songs, rhymes, and poems that children first memorize make very appropriate reading materials for emergent readers who are developing a concept of word. A collection of easy poems and rhymes, such as *Hey Diddle Diddle* and *Jack and Jill,* ready to photocopy, can be found in *Words Their Way: Letter and Picture Sorts for Emergent Spellers* (Bear et al., 2019). Copies of nursery rhymes in large-font format can also be found at many websites such as Webbing into Literacy (*https://webbingintoliteracy.com*). Familiar songs like *There was a Little Turtle Who Lived in a Box, The Itsy Bitsy Spider* and *Happy Birthday* are good choices. In general, limit the text to four to eight lines.

1. Prepare a copy of the text in a large font on a sheet of paper leaving an extra space between the words if possible.
2. Songs should be sung and poems or rhymes should be read aloud by the tutor and enjoyed and discussed before displaying the printed form. This is the time to react to what has been read or sung: "Could a cow really jump over the moon?" "I wonder why Jack fell down the hill?"
3. Next the printed text is displayed and the tutor reads it aloud several times while pointing to the words. If there is a two- or three-syllable word, model how to point in the same spot for each syllable. As the text is read, point out features of print such as the title, punctuation, capital letters, and so forth. Help the child identify rhyming words by pausing so the child can supply the second one of a pair (Jack and Jill went up the ____________). Also point to, and talk about, new vocabulary when appropriate. What does *fetch* or *crown* mean in *Jack and Jill*?
4. The child is then invited to choral read as she points to the words, while the tutor is ready to fade out if she senses the child can take the lead. Fall back on echo reading if there is a part that seems to be especially difficult. Finally, the child tries reading alone. If the child still cannot read a poem after choral reading several times, it may be too hard.

Supporting Independent Readings

Emergent readers will veer off track when reading independently, even when they've memorized a text. When that occurs, let them get to the end of the line. As they develop a rudimentary concept of word, they'll realize they've finished reciting the line too early or that they've run out of print before finishing, and they'll correct themselves. They'll probably start over from the beginning of the line. Later, they'll be able to correct themselves without starting from the beginning. Such behavior signals their growth! If they don't correct themselves, prompt them to try again. If that doesn't work, return to a word and draw attention to the beginning letter. Because the child is quite familiar with the text by this time, he may know the word, which will help him to track more correctly.

Once the child gets the word, point out the ending letter so you are highlighting the other boundary of the word. "What to Do When a Reader Needs Help with Words," in Appendix W, provides a valuable reference for tutors as they work with emergent readers.

As a child progresses toward a concept of word, he will track more correctly even on a first reading. At this time, it's important for the tutor to reduce the amount of support in new reading, and especially in rereading.

A Note about Support through "Cueing"

A debate about the value of any kind of cueing in reading instruction—using pictures, beginning letters/sounds, meaning, or the predictability of sentence structure as support for reading words—has gone on for decades. Those educators who find any kind of cueing ineffective, even harmful, for reading development point to phonics as the only viable method of identifying words. They warn that cueing only leads to guessing words as opposed to identification through decoding. Research has proven that phonics instruction *is* key to reading development. By mapping speech sounds onto letters and spelling patterns in meaningful words, children learn to recognize words (Metsala & Ehri, 2013).

We view the foundational role of phonics in reading as fact. However, when we look at how children develop as readers, we see the value of cueing as a means of support for the emergent and very beginning reader. The reason is that emergent and very beginning readers do not yet have the alphabet or phonics knowledge to identify many words or sound out unknown words without using other cues. It's impossible to only use phonics and decoding when you don't yet know all your letters or beginning sounds and when you aren't sure where a word begins and ends on the page.

We often say to children, "Reading is *not* guessing!" When we draw attention to a picture and a beginning sound to prompt accurate identification of an unknown word, we are asking emergent and very beginning readers to coordinate and apply their alphabet knowledge with their phonological awareness and phonics in a way that results in a word that makes sense. Learning to read is about coordinating pronunciations and meaning with the letters and spelling patterns on the page, but only to the extent possible. It's such hard work that sometimes a picture cue can remind the readers of the word they are trying coordinate. It's like saying, "What word starts with this letter sound (and makes sense here)?" Ultimately, once emergent learners have enough alphabet, phonological, and phonics knowledge to support independent reading, they will rarely need additional cues beyond those provided by the word's spelling.

Post-Reading Activities

After reading you can add some extension activities for vocabulary and comprehension development.

- *Reviewing new vocabulary.* Vocabulary included in emergent texts is simple, but there could be words that are unfamiliar to some children. After reading, return to any unfamiliar words in the text. For each word, point and ask the child if she knows what it means. Say the word and have the child point to it and repeat it. Then write the word on a sheet of paper or a card. Study the letters and sound out the word with the child.

Here the child is connecting meaning, sound, and spelling to gain a deeper understanding of the word. This *anchored word instruction* helps words "stick" (Juel & Deffes, 2004). As stated earlier in our discussion of word-bank instruction, linking the dimensions of meaning, sound, and spelling also supports the development of sight words (Metsala & Ehri, 2013; Rawlins & Invernizzi, 2019). In fact, the new words can be added to the word bank for further review.

- *Concept sorts.* Emergent text also offers simple concepts, but these, too, can be explored through concept sorts to extend comprehension. For example, the little book *A Pond,* by Brenda Parkes (1998), about animals and plants that can be found in ponds, offers an opportunity to contrast and discuss things that live in or on water and those that live on land.

A picture sort can be created with two picture headers labeled "Land" and "Pond" along with various pictures of animals and plants that the child sorts beneath the headers. The process of distinguishing between the concepts and the ensuing discussion kick up the level of thinking *and* engagement. And for children who are unfamiliar with what a pond is, such an activity reinforces both the word and its concept.

Further Reading of the New Text

When the new text has been read, the tutor should update the book list with the title and the date it is first read. Place the new text in the collection for rereading in the next lesson. It can go home with the child in her Book Buddies baggie after rereading it in the following lesson.

Text copies of poems, songs, and rhymes that have been read over several lessons and taken home for rereading can be kept together in a special folder in the tutoring box. At the end of the year they can be stapled together into a book, with a cover illustrated by the child, and added to the child's home library.

Note the importance of having children say letter names, sounds, and words as they engage in all learning activities. The multisensory practice of simultaneous seeing, saying, writing, and manipulating goes a long way to helping learners make that connection between sounds and symbols and jump into reading!

English Language Learners

English language learners in the emergent stage of reading need additional and intensive practice with the sounds and rhythm of the English language, its vocabulary, its letters, and the letters' corresponding sounds. The Book Buddies emergent lesson plan, incorporating these areas of instruction, delivers an excellent intervention for English learners at this stage of reading development. And the one-on-one, personalized instruction offers the ideal situation for learning, discussion, and inspiring confidence.

English learners may not have grown up with the English ABC song, and they are unfamiliar with print in English, so they need extra work with English letters (Helman et al., 2012). Also, English learners may substitute letters and sounds from their primary language that are closest to certain letters and sounds in English. For instance, the English sound for the letter *j* doesn't exist in Spanish; a Spanish speaker may pronounce the letter *j* as /h/, or even a vowel.

English learners at the emergent stage of literacy need systematic and explicit word study instruction in English. Be aware that more time will need to be spent on explaining pictures used for sorting, and you may need to use fewer pictures in sorts. A word study resource for Spanish-speaking English learners at the emergent stage is *Words Their Way: Emergent Sorts for Spanish-Speaking English Learners* (Helman, Bear, Invernizzi, Templeton, & Johnston, 2009a).

Note that rhyme may pose a problem for English learners whose home language does not contain many final consonant sounds. Do not put off the study of syllable awareness and initial sounds when English learners struggle with rhyme, as both skills are critical for moving into literacy. Rhyme will be addressed again in the study of word families where students have the chance to see and manipulate the visual patterns of rhyme as well as hear the sounds.

The predictable and patterned language in the books read at this stage provide support to children learning English, but some pictures and words will need explanation. Also, English learners might need more support with choral or echo reading, as some words might be unfamiliar and the pictures may not offer much help.

Activities like concept sorts after reading are powerful tools for concept and vocabulary development. Discussion surrounding the activity also offers a great opportunity for the English learner to practice speaking the language.

Just as we would with any children with whom we work, those of us working with English learners should get to know them. We should ask them about their lives and what their parents read in their home language. We must be mindful of cultural differences, such as holidays the children do not observe. We should celebrate the children's heritage and faith, even if different from our own. While we are teaching them, English learners have much to teach us!

Learners with Challenges, Including Dyslexia

Much of what was said above about English language learners in the emergent stage goes for any learners exhibiting challenges with reading development. Along with dyslexia, challenges include language-based issues that may show up as speech difficulties. Children experiencing challenges with language, particularly in the area of *phonology* (sounds of speech), run the risk of prolonging their time in the emergent stage. Language-based difficulties can make it harder to learn early literacy skills like the alphabet, letter sounds, and segmenting initial sounds of words.

For these children, early intervention is vital to building foundational literacy skills and facilitating progress beyond the emergent stage. They will need additional and intensive practice with each area of the Book Buddies emergent lesson plan. The multisensory nature of the instruction offers essential practice for such learners. Skill development may take longer, but it is vital that the skills built in the emergent stage be mastered before moving on, as they constitute the foundation of reading development. A note about rhyme: If a struggling learner is just not getting rhyme, do not delay the study of syllable awareness and initial sounds. Rhyme will be addressed again later in the study of word families, which is covered in the next chapter about beginning readers.

Positive Reinforcement

Praise, praise, praise is important at every turn in all the Book Buddies lesson plans, but it should be specific. Tutors should be instructed to be generous with comments such as "I like the way you fixed that mistake" and "Great job remembering to say the name of each of those pictures and the sound at the beginning when you were sorting!" We are building confident readers and writers, and there's no such thing as too much praise.

Looking Ahead

This lesson plan is appropriate for the emergent reader. While a reader with a rudimentary concept of word is considered an early beginning reader, we suggest you keep Book Buddies children in the emergent plan until they possess a full concept of word. This way, they'll have practice with the concept of word and language play sections offered in this plan.

In the next chapter we discuss the beginning reader lesson plan.

Chapter 5

General Tutoring Plan for the Beginning Reader

This chapter presents the plan for the beginning reader. Be sure you have assessment information and have considered the criteria in Chapter 3 to determine whether a child is an emergent, a beginning, or a transitional reader.

Characteristics of the Beginning Reader

Beginning readers read text at the preprimer and primer levels between lettered levels C and G, or numbered levels 3 to 12 (see Table 3.1 on p. 41). Early beginning readers know most or all of their alphabet letters and many letter sounds. In spelling they are in the letter name–alphabetic stage, where sound is the strategy they use to spell words. They represent the salient, or most prominent, sound(s) in a word, usually the beginning consonant. They know at least 10 words on the preprimer list presented in Chapter 3.

Late emergent/early beginning readers may still have a *rudimentary* concept of word in text: They can point to the words in memorized text accurately but may get off track with two-syllable words, and they cannot quickly and consistently find particular words in the text when asked. For Book Buddies lessons, we suggest that only beginning readers who have attained a *full* concept of word be placed in the beginning reader lesson plan. These students track print accurately. If they veer off track, they correct themselves without starting over and they can quickly find individual words in familiar text when prompted.

Beginning readers learn a lot about reading by the end of this stage. They significantly increase their store of automatically recognized words, or sight words, and they learn how to correctly spell short vowel words with blends and digraphs. They continue to read slowly, aloud, and word by word, but they move through many gradations of reading levels and pick up some speed. Their writing is slow, with most words written as they're sounded out, but more sounds are represented and more words are spelled correctly by the end of the stage.

Below is a brief description of the beginning reader lesson plan. In each part of the lesson plan, children engage in multisensory learning. They say words as they finger-point read. They say sounds and words as they write. They point to letters as they say the letter names and sounds. They manipulate picture cards and letter cards as they say letter sounds and words. Such multisensory practice is a powerful tool for facilitating the learner's connection of letters and sounds and reinforcing those connections. The remainder of the chapter describes each part of the lesson plan in detail.

Overview of the Beginning Reader Plan

The lesson plan for the beginning reader consists of four parts:

1. *Rereading familiar material* (10–12 minutes). Children reread texts they've read in previous lessons, including poetry, for practice with fluency and to develop a store of words they know automatically.
2. *Word study* (15–20 minutes). In this section children work with the word bank and phonics features.
3. *Writing* (8–10 minutes). Here children write dictated sentences or original responses to text or questions.
4. *Reading new material* (8–10 minutes). In the last part of the plan, tutors introduce a new text.

A sample lesson plan for a beginning reader is reproduced in Figure 5.1, and one for a late beginning reader is reproduced in Figure 5.2. These plans correspond to the lessons in the online videos accompanying this book (for more information on where to find the online videos, see the box at the end of the table of contents). The same plans, without tutor comments, are offered in Appendix T along with a guide to using the online videos for tutor training. A blank form for the beginning reader lesson plan can be found in Appendix A.2.

Beginning Reader Lesson Plan, Part 1: Rereading Familiar Material

Beginning readers are acquiring new words to support fluency, and rereading affords excellent practice to this end. It gives students the chance to develop smooth, accurate reading in easy, familiar materials. Children see the same words over and over again, and increase the number of words they recognize automatically. This rereading also serves as a warm-up and confidence builder. As children read with confidence, they are more likely to read with understanding and enjoyment.

Rereading Books

The tutoring session begins with the reading of three or more familiar books, including the new book introduced in the previous lesson. This part of the lesson should last

FIGURE 5.1. Sample Beginning Reader Lesson Plan

Student: *Minuette* **Tutor:** *Ms. Flory* **Date:** *12/3* **Lesson #:** *14*

Lesson Plan	*Description of Planned Activities*	*Comments*
Rereading (10–12 minutes)	• *Little Green Frog — text copy* 1) *read* 2) *highlight -og words* 3) *underline -op words* } *(Highlight while saying words aloud)* • *Who Can Be a Friend?* → • *My Clock Is Sick* → • *"Chili in a Pot" poem 1) Model 2) Choral read 3) M. reads* →	 *(depend ~~on~~, send)* *tock/tick* *Easy*
Word Bank and Word Study (15–20 minutes)	**Word Bank:** *Add words from Little Green Frog* **Push It Say It:** *#32 Make these words: d-og, d-ock, l-ock, l-og, cl-og, cl-ock* **Picture/Word Sort:** *-ot, -og, -ock* **Writing Sort:** *Call out 2-3 words for each header: -ot, -og, -ock* **FastRead:** *Word Families #5 1) Model 2) Time for 1:00*	*frog, went, said, hop* *trouble with cl (clog)* *trouble with "og"—still wants to say "ock"* **Score:** *26/30* **(# read correctly in 1:00)**
Writing (8–10 minutes)	*Dictate this sentence:* *Minuette and the frog can hop on the hot rock.*	*nice job—no trouble*
New Reading (8–10 minutes)	**Book:** *Polly's Shop* **1. Read title to student and look at cover.** **2. Student makes a prediction.** **3. Discuss pictures, words, and patterns in the story.** **4. Student reads the book to you.** *Read 2x if time*	*were/with* *trucks/toys* *Here/There* *I'll—needed help*
Take-Home Book	**Book:** *My Clock Is Sick*	

FIGURE 5.2. Sample Late Beginning Reader Lesson Plan

Student: Ashley **Tutor:** Donna **Date:** 12/16 **Lesson #:** 16

Lesson Plan	Description of Planned Activities	Comments
Rereading (10–12 minutes)	• Dragon's Lunch—text copy 1) Read 2) Highlight dr- words while saying words aloud • "See You Later, Alligator" poem 1) Model 2) Choral read 3) A. reads • Choice—A. reads her favorite part	– "sandwich" for "sandwiches" — otherwise perfect – super, liked the poem – Brave Norman — no problems
Word Bank and Word Study (15–20 minutes)	~~**Word Bank:**~~ **Push It Say It:** tr-, ch- **Picture/Word Sort:** tr-, ch- blind sort **Writing Sort:** Call out 3-4 words for each header: tr-, ch- **FastRead:** r-blends #2 1) Model 2) Time for 1:00	great job perfect All spelled correctly, but read back "chop" as "trop" DRIP/grip BRAN/brand **Score:** 22/24 (# read correctly in ~~1:00~~ :51)
Writing (8–10 minutes)	After new book, answer questions on sheet about armor for people.	– Wrote thoughtfully — hard words! – I helped her hear some sounds after she wrote — she added. Good job! – PES/pads
New Reading (8–10 minutes)	**Book:** Animal Armor **1. Read title to student and look at cover.** —Discuss "armor." **2. Student makes a prediction.** **3. Discuss pictures, words, and patterns in the story.** —Animal names **4. Student reads the book to you.**	protect, enemies, spines Did well w/this! Worked hard!
Take-Home Book	**Book:** A Hole in Harry's Pocket	

10 to 12 minutes. The child reads aloud and should point to each word. These processes give the child time to attend to each word and help him keep his place. Books are retired from the warm-up routine after at least four rereadings. Children continue to reread other books that they have not yet learned to read smoothly and accurately.

Other Text for Rereading

Poetry, jingles, songs, and jump-rope rhymes are used along with books for developing phrasal, expressive reading. Just be careful that the items chosen are ones that aren't too difficult. Text-only copies of books that have been previously read at least three times are especially helpful for rereading. These copies, without the support of illustrations, serve to "glue children to print"—the readers must attend to the words. At the end of the year the text copies can be stapled together into a book and sent home to add to the child's personal library.

Phonics-featured books targeting the current word-study focus can be used at this point in the plan for a first reading *if* they are easier than what the child is currently learning to read. These books and text-only copies can be used for word hunts, which are described in the word study section of this chapter.

Tutor Support

The beginner may need support with rereading materials, particularly text that was just introduced in the previous lesson, although not as much as the emergent reader. The child placed in this lesson plan has a full concept of word and points accurately. If the child is really struggling with a familiar text, the tutor can support him with choral or echo reading, but if this is still happening after two lessons, the text is probably too difficult, and the higher level of support should appear in the comments section of the lesson plan.

During every lesson the tutor updates the book list (you'll find a book list in Appendix J) by tallying the number of times each text—book, poem, and so forth—is read.

Questions Tutors Often Ask about Student Performance

As in the last chapter, we include some questions tutors often ask regarding student performance, along with the answers the coordinator can offer the tutor.

"What Do I Do When My Child Has Trouble Reading?" During rereading time, your student should be zipping through one text after another with very few errors or hesitations. However, he will forget words he knew the session before and confuse words with one another. If he hesitates or makes an error, the first thing you do is *nothing*! Resist the impulse to correct it immediately. Give him the chance to work it out or discover the error for himself. That may not happen until he gets to the end of the sentence and realizes that something didn't make sense.

Beginners often remember words not as entire letter strings but in bits and pieces. What they remember about *car* may be only that it starts with *c*. In that case, they may well confuse it with *cat* and read "I saw a *cat*," instead of "I saw a *car*." Listen to the words your student substitutes and consider what parts, if any, of that word fit what is on the page. Help the child to see the source of the problem when appropriate.

"What Do I Do When My Child Asks for Help?" Often, your child will come to a word she doesn't know and simply stop or appeal to you for help. Tutors are often tempted to say "Sound it out" as a strategy, but early beginning readers cannot yet sound their way through an entire word because they know very little about vowel sounds. However, they may be able to use the first sound, which is often a consonant, as a clue. You might use the following prompt: "Try that sentence again, and when you come to this word [*point to the problem word*], say the first sound." As readers learn more about vowel sounds, "Sound it out" works better as a strategy if the vowel has been taught.

If your child is still stuck on a word after you've offered a few prompts, you can give her the word, perhaps modeling how it can be sounded out. You might want to keep handy a copy of "What to Do When a Reader Needs Help with Words," from Appendix W, as you work with your beginning reader.

If your child is having too much trouble with texts at a certain level, she needs to read at an easier level. Missing more than two or three words in books after several rereadings is usually a sign that the books are too hard. Your comments will guide your coordinator to take a step back and try books at an easier level.

"What If My Child Just Seems to Be Memorizing the Book?" The beginning reader *does* rely on memory and illustrations a great deal, and this is a good thing. Without these sources of support, earlier beginners would not be able to read much at all. However, we want children to be paying attention to the words in the text as they point to each word while reading it aloud. If you suspect a child is just relying on memory and pictures as he rereads a book, go back after reading and point to some words in the text. Ask the child to point to the word and tell you what it is. Then ask him *how* he knows. Prompt him to talk about the beginning letter/sound and ending letter/sound. You might model how to sound out the word. Text-only copies of books that have been reread multiple times also offer a way to assess if a child is attending to words.

Beginning Reader Lesson Plan, Part 2: Word Study

The second part of the lesson plan is word study and consists of two parts: (1) word-bank work and (2) systematic phonics instruction. This part of the lesson should take about 15 to 20 minutes.

1. *Word bank.* The word bank was introduced in the previous chapter. The beginning reader should be adding many new words in this stage.

2. *Phonics instruction.* Early beginning readers may still need to study initial letter sounds. *Picture sorts* will also focus on beginning *blends* (e.g., *st, bl, gr*) and *digraphs* (*sh, th, ch,* and *wh*). Later the readers will learn about short vowels along with ending consonants through the study of *word families* and sorts featuring CVC words (consonant–short vowel–consonant).

Instructional activities consist of manipulation of letter tiles to spell and decode words, sorting tasks with picture and word cards, a *writing sort,* and an activity called *FastRead* that builds automatic recognition of word families and short vowel words. Each of these components is described in more detail next.

Word Bank

A word bank is a child's personal collection of known words written on small cards (it is better if the tutor writes the words neatly rather than having the child write them). The word bank is kept in a plastic baggie or on a ring to be reviewed, sorted, and played with regularly, as described below. Word-bank words are intended to be *known* words, that is, words that the child recognizes immediately.

As children review their word-bank cards, reading the words aloud, they must pay close attention to the print. By repeated connection of their meaning, pronunciation (sound), and spelling, the words become *sight words,* or words that can be read instantly—"at first sight" (Ehri, 2014; Invernizzi, 2014; Metsala & Ehri, 2013). Sight words comprise the foundation of children's reading vocabulary, and their familiarity with the words' spellings, together with explicit phonics instruction, help beginning readers decode new words that follow similar spelling patterns. Sight words are added to phonics instruction in the word study part of the lesson plan to increase beginners' ability to transfer their growing spelling knowledge to decoding new words.

Creating the Word Bank

From the very first tutoring session, you should begin to create a word bank, even if the child hasn't read anything yet. The first words might include the child's name, the tutor's name, family members' names, or a friend's name. You might add words the student identified on the word list task of the assessment, or you might simply ask whether there are any words that she knows. Common words such as *I, the,* and *a* may be known. After a few sessions, you can begin to collect words from the materials you are rereading during the first part of the lesson plan.

With books that have been read over three or four sessions, the tutor presents word cards from pockets at the back of the books for the child to read. Words known automatically can be added to the word bank. For text-only copies and copies of poems, words can be underlined for the child to read as the tutor points randomly to each word. Again, only words known automatically will be deposited in the word bank.

Selecting Word-Bank Words

What should you watch for in choosing word-bank words from books?

1. Concrete nouns, adjectives, and verbs that evoke strong imagery, such as *dog, red,* and *jump.* These are the easiest words to learn because they convey more meaning than abstract words like *love* and *think* (Rawlins & Invernizzi, 2018; Warley et al., 2015).
2. High-frequency words (*see, am, get, with, for, from*) that children are likely to see in other texts.
3. Words with a particular phonics feature (*log, pot,* and *chop* are all CVC words that contain the short *o* sound in the middle).

Don't be afraid to add plural nouns and present tense verbs ending in *s* if they appear in text. Children will be seeing many such words, and collecting them opens a conversation about singular versus plural nouns as well as verb tense—an introduction to morphology and syntax.

Reviewing the Word Bank

The "simple sort" and "pick-up" activities described in Chapter 4 work well for beginning readers too. As the beginning reader builds up the word bank to include at least 100 words, we offer several more activities for review:

- *Bingo or Lotto.* In advance, prepare a board by lining off a plain sheet of paper into boxes, either a 3 × 3 or a 4 × 4 array. Select enough words from the word bank to write in each box (see Figure 5.3). Place the matching word cards in a pile.

  You will need something to cover the spaces as the words are called out. Pennies, small squares of paper, poker chips or small tiles will do the job. To play the game, shuffle the word cards and turn them face down. The caller draws a card and names the word, and the player covers the word on the board after reading it aloud. Three or four in a row is a winner. Switch roles and play again.

- *Create sentences.* Once the child has a good collection of word-bank word cards, you can create sentences. Begin by making a sentence; then ask the child to read it aloud, pointing to each word. Or call out a sentence for the child to make with the available words. You might want to lay out a limited collection of word cards to choose from. For example, lay out *like, to, I,* and *fish,* and ask your child to make the sentence "I like to fish." Eventually, you want the child to make up his or her own sentences, but continue to make it a joint tutor–child effort if needed. The child should say each word while building the sentence and then read the entire sentence while pointing to each word.

- *Rebuild words.* Select a word from the word bank and have the child spell it with letter cards (see Appendix I for letter cards you can cut apart) or three-dimensional letters made of plastic or wood. Or you can simply write the word on a blank word card and cut it apart to put back in order. You can also call out words (three- and four-letter words such as *red* or *here*) to be spelled on paper or on a dry-erase board.

  The child should repeat the word before building it or writing it and say each sound within the word while writing it. If it is an irregular word like *said* or *from* that can't be fully sounded out, target the beginning and ending sounds and discuss what

FIGURE 5.3. Word-Bank Bingo and Sentences

is irregular. Finally, the child should read the completed word aloud. Let the child check and, if necessary, correct his spelling by looking at the word card. Words that the student misses when reviewing the word bank are good candidates for rebuilding and writing.

• *Concentration or Memory*. Make a duplicate set of cards so you have two copies of each word. Be sure that the words cannot be read through the back of the card. Use 5 to 10 words and their duplicates to play a game of Concentration or Memory. Turn all the words face down and take turns turning two up at a time. Read the words aloud. If you turn up a matched pair, put the set in your played pile. Unmatched pairs are turned face down before the next turn. Limit sets to no more than 10 for a fast game.

• *Sorting*. Look through the child's word bank for words that share some similarity. Prepare a collection for sorting by pulling out two or more related groups, and then have the child sort the word-bank cards into columns (see Figure 5.4). These sorts can take different forms:

- *Concept sort*: Sort words that share a concept, such as people words, food words, color words, or animal names. Animal names can be further sorted into groups, such as pets versus wild animals. Here, in categorizing words by concepts and ideas, we bring in semantic aspects of words.
- *Sound sort*: Sort words that have the same sounds—for example, beginning sounds, vowel sounds, and words that rhyme. Here, in categorizing words by speech sounds, we bring in phonological aspects of words.
- *Pattern sort*: Sort words by spelling pattern—for example, words that begin with two consonants (consonant blends or digraphs) versus words that begin with single consonants. In categorizing words by their spelling patterns, we focus on phonics.
- *Singular versus plural noun sort:* Sort word cards into two groups. You may be able to note that most plural nouns end in *s*, but there are some exceptions, like *children*. You may also have the opportunity to discuss how some nouns are the same whether singular or plural, such as *deer* and *fish*. Here we bring attention to morphology as well as syntax.
- *Parts of speech sort*: Sort verbs and nouns in two columns. Verbs can be further sorted into action words and nonaction words. Nouns can further be sorted

FIGURE 5.4. Word-Bank Sorts

Mom	yellow	fish	boy	you	man
man	red	dog	be	yellow	me
Daddy	blue	cat	bat	yes	most
	green		baby		mud

into people, places, and things. Such attention to syntax informs the study of sentence structure in writing.

- *Multiple meaning words*: Find word-bank words that can be both nouns and verbs (e.g., *top, lap, run, block, play, drum,* and *trick*) and make a second card for each. Discuss and sort by the parts of speech. This exercise brings semantics and syntax into play. It also offers an opportunity to stretch vocabulary and lay the foundation for comprehension!

Remember to have the child read each word while sorting it; then read the words in each column after sorting. She should tell you what the words in each column have in common.

Managing the Growing Word Bank

As the child's collection of known words grows, you may find that she will have too many word cards to be stored in a plastic baggie or on a ring, or to review all at one time. As a general rule, word banks are discontinued when a child has accrued 100 or more known words.

To avoid duplication when adding words to the word bank, it is helpful to use the Alphabetized Word-Bank List provided in Appendix F. We recommend that tutors wait until after the lesson to add new words to the alphabetized list and to copy the words onto new cards for deposit in the bank. As the word bank grows, you might consider organizing the word cards alphabetically too.

Recording the Growing Number of Words

From the child's point of view, the most important thing about the word bank is its size. The number of words a child knows is like money in the bank, and we all like to see that bank account grow. Everyone enjoys measuring success in a concrete way. For children struggling with learning to read, the positive feedback provided from a graphic display of word growth is especially important. Record the number of word-bank words the child automatically knows using a fun form such as the rocket ship or mountain path in Appendix Q. You might plan a special reward for the child when he reaches 100 words, such as a colorful pencil, an eraser, a certificate, or a book. In some schools, children reaching the 100 mark join the "Hundreds Club," and their names are announced on the loudspeaker or added to a special list posted in the hall.

Questions Tutors Often Ask about Word Banks

"What Do I Do When My Child Forgets Words?" Beginning readers will frequently be able to name a word one day and not the next, so don't be surprised when this happens. As previously explained, it occurs because these learners read with partial clues. They store words by the parts they know: They might store the words *what* as *wh-t* and *this* as *th-s*. So they might read a word correctly in context or even sometimes in isolation, as in word-bank review, but they might not get it every time (Ehri & McCormick, 1998).

If your child cannot identify a word when you are adding cards to the word bank from a particular book, open the book to the page where the word appears and ask your child to find the word. Usually, the child can use the familiar context and the beginning sound to find the word. The word card is then compared to the word in the text to make sure they match. This activity encourages the child to look closely at all the letters in the word, increasing the likelihood that she will remember the word.

If your child doesn't recognize words out of context during review, place the card in a separate pile to be revisited after going through all the words to be reviewed. "Pick-up," described in the previous chapter, is a good way to review unknown words because you say the word for the child to find. If the child still doesn't recognize the word, tell him what it is and place a sticky note or paper clip on the word card to try next time (or place it in a baggie marked "practice words"). Be prepared to discard a word if it continues to be a problem. Remember that the word bank should consist of *known* words. If the child is frequently missing words during review, consider the possibility that you might be adding too many words at one time, or that they have not been reviewed regularly.

The word bank is important, but it shouldn't take more than 5 minutes of the lesson. It is best to alternate between gathering new words one day and reviewing the word bank on another day.

Phonics Instruction

The phonics portion of word study immediately follows the word-bank work and takes another 10 to 15 minutes. The phonics activities focus on speech sounds, letters, and spelling patterns. Word bank words that fit these speech sounds, letters, and spelling patterns are incorporated. Although the focus of the phonics lessons varies, the instructional activities follow a set routine. First, children are given letter cards to do a Push It Say It activity (Blachman, Ball, Black, & Tangle, 1994). With this activity they learn in a concrete way how to blend parts of words together as they manipulate the letter cards while simultaneously saying the sounds.

After Push It Say It, children sort picture cards, word cards, or both into categories of sound with corresponding letters or letter patterns. This is called a *picture sort* or a *word sort.* After that, children engage in a *writing sort,* in which they are asked to write some of the words or names of pictures they just sorted. Finally, children read quickly through a set of word families or short vowel words in the FastRead activity.

Where to Start and Where to Go

What you will be teaching each child depends on what the child already knows, as demonstrated in the initial assessments. Not all children begin in the same place or progress at the same rate. You will be tailoring the phonics instruction to each child's individual needs. Only one-on-one instruction can really do this. As mentioned earlier, the beginning reader is in the letter name–alphabetic stage of spelling development. In general, the sequence for phonics instruction for the beginning reader begins with the study of unknown beginning consonant sounds and moves through the study of short vowel sounds in the middle of words, along with consonant digraphs (e.g., *sh, th, ch,* and *wh*) and blends (e.g., *s* blends such as *smell, skip,* and *spoon*; *l* blends such as *sled, black,* and *plum*; *r* blends such as *crab, frog,* and *grass*). See the phonics ladder in Chapter 1 and the suggested word study sequence in Appendix P.

Continuing Assessment

Remember that where you begin and how fast you move through this sequence depends on what the child already knows and how easily he learns the features you work on. Observation of children's performance on writing sorts and writing in context, as well as regular cumulative *spell checks,* will inform you of their progress and therefore guide you in planning continuing instruction.

Push It Say It

Throughout the letter name spelling stage, children need practice manipulating the sounds in words, exchanging one sound for another to make a new word. This skill will eventually help them sound out unfamiliar words as they read by blending sounds and word parts together. The activity involves manipulating letter tiles or cards, as displayed in Figure 5.5. Push It Say It comes before the sorting and the writing sort, introducing the child to the features he'll be blending and segmenting in those sorts. The activity can also be used to review features previously studied. It is meant to move very quickly.

At first, the words are divided into two parts: the beginning sound(s) before the vowel, or *onset* (such as the *c* in *cat* or the *ch* in *chat*), and the *rime* or word family that follows (such as the *-at* in *cat* or *chat*). Words containing the same rime spelling also *rhyme* (e.g., *cat, mat,* and *rat*). With children we refer to these units as *word families* and talk about how they rhyme. Beginning sounds or onsets are exchanged with other beginning sounds and added to rimes to illustrate concretely how to make new words.

There are three levels of focus for Push It Say It:

1. The first level focuses on final consonants in *same-vowel* word families. The critical place to look to differentiate words like *mat, sat,* and *cat* from words like *can, man,* and *tan* is the final consonant. This level also includes manipulation of the onset, thereby reviewing both beginning and ending consonants.

2. The second level focuses on the medial vowel within *mixed-vowel* word families, where the vowels are different but the following consonant or consonants are the same (e.g., *at* versus *it*). Here the focus is squarely on the medial vowel sound. The critical difference between the words *hat, mat,* and *sat* and the words *hit, kit,* and *sit* lies in the vowel sound in the middle.

FIGURE 5.5. Push It Say It with the Onset S and the Rime AT

3. The third level also targets the medial short vowel, but without the support of word families. Instead children push together three letter cards representing the onset, the vowel, and the consonant or consonants following the vowel. Each of these levels is described in turn.

Although Push It Say It comes before sorting in the lesson plan, we describe each level after we present the procedure for each type of short vowel sort. In the context of the sort, the Push It Say It activity becomes clearer.

Beginning Sounds

Use the results from the letter-sounds and spelling assessments in Chapter 3 to determine which, if any, initial letter sounds a beginning reader needs to learn. In the spelling assessment you'll be looking for the representation of beginning consonants. The beginning reader will probably miss only a few beginning consonant sounds at most. Target for instruction only the letter sounds identified incorrectly. You may find that a child will miss only vowel sounds in the letter-sounds assessment. Remember that short vowel sounds in the medial position will be studied extensively in this stage, so brief instruction of short vowels as initial sounds is fine.

Beginning sound picture sorts described in Chapter 4, including glue-and-label activities, provide excellent instruction for initial sounds. For example, if a child has confused *v* and *f* on the spelling of *van* as FN, an appropriate sort would be to compare pictures of words that start with /v/ and words that start with /f/. While comparing these two consonants would be inappropriate in first teaching because of their phonological similarity, it is perfectly appropriate if these confusions linger and most consonant sounds are known. After sorting with pictures, include words from the student's word bank. If, in writing sorts or labeling pictures in a glue-and-label activity, a child is not attending to ending sounds, prompt her to do so by elongating the sounds in the word.

Digraphs and Blends

If your assessments show the child knows his single-consonant beginning letter sounds, start instruction by introducing beginning digraphs and blends in sorts comprising pictures and word-bank words. Pictures and word-bank words will be sorted beneath printed header cards (e.g., *sh, st, bl, cr*). Follow sorting with a writing sort or glue-and-label activity. As in instruction with beginning sounds, if a child is not attending to ending sounds when writing, prompt him to do so by elongating the sounds in the word. This instruction is meant as a brief introduction and does not aim toward mastery. Later, you'll explicitly teach digraphs and blends in short vowel word sorts and Push It Say It activities (see the phonics ladder in Chapter 1 and the suggested word study sequence in Appendix P).

Beginning Digraphs. Digraphs are units of two letters that make one sound. The consonant digraphs to be studied at this stage are *sh, ch, th,* and *wh.* A good way to begin teaching beginning digraphs is to compare, with picture sorting, a whole digraph to the consonants that constitute it, focusing on the difference in sound. For this brief introduction, we suggest sorting *c, h,* and *ch* to start off, followed by sorts including whole digraphs:

1. c/ch/h
2. sh/th
3. sh/th/ch

Each category should be headed by the corresponding letters. For this pictorial introduction we do not recommend sorting *wh,* because it usually doesn't sound different from *w*. Rather, *wh* will be presented in the context of question words (*who, what, when, why,* and *where*) and studied with word sorting (as opposed to picture sorting) later on. After sorting the pictures, it is important to add any word-bank words that fit the features.

Beginning Blends. Consonant blends are two consonants that are blended together, such as the *c* and *l* in the word *clock*. We can still distinguish each separate sound, but the two letters work together as a tightly meshed sound unit. Most consonant blends occur at the beginning of words, and it is on this position that we focus our attention here. Blends are studied at this time through picture sorts (see Figure 5.6). Once again, this sorting is not meant to be exhaustive but rather as a brief introduction. *S* blends (e.g., *st, sn, sm*) are probably the easiest of the blends and make a good starting point. *L* blends (e.g., *bl, cl, fl, gl, sl*) and *r* blends (e.g., *br, cr, dr, fr, gr, tr*) are more difficult. Like all picture sorts, each column should be headed by a card with the letters being taught (e.g., *s* versus *st*). Also make sure to add word-bank words that start with the targeted sounds. We suggest the following sequence to expose children to blends:

1. S/ST/T
2. SN/SM/SK
3. B/BL/L
4. B/BR/R

FIGURE 5.6. Picture Sort with Blends

5. BL/BR
6. Additional *s*-blends, *l*-blends, *r*-blends as needed

Some children need extensive work with digraphs and blends, particularly English language learners. For example, native Spanish speakers will want to add a vowel before an *s*-blend in words like *Spain* because there are no *s*-blends in Spanish (e.g., *Spain* in Spanish is *España*).

Introducing Short Vowels in CVC Words

If the spelling assessment shows a student is already consistently representing beginning and final sounds but not consistently including a vowel in the middle of words, you will start your phonics instruction with same-vowel word families. Work with word families encourages children to think of the vowel and the letter(s) that follow in the rime (such as the *at* in *cat* or the *ack* in *back*) as a *chunk* that always "says the same thing." Most of the words you will use at first will be simple CVC words that serve as a review of consonants. But word family study will also be used to reinforce consonant digraphs and consonant blends.

See the suggested word study sequence in Appendix P. Comparing the *at* and *an* families is often a good place to start, since they commonly occur, in words such as *cat, man,* and *can,* in beginning books.

Sorting Procedure for Same-Vowel Word Families. The following sorting activity can be used to introduce word families that share the same vowel. Both word cards and picture cards are used. The sort should be preceded by a Push It Say It exercise and followed by a writing sort. You can find lists of words to use for these sorts in Appendix H. Ready-made sorts can be found in *Words Their Way: Word Sorts for Letter Name–Alphabetic Spellers* (Johnston et al., 2018). The procedure described here will guide you through the steps of a word family sort and need to be followed carefully (see Figure 5.7).

FIGURE 5.7. CVC Word Family Sort with AT and AN

1. Prepare word cards for sorting (e.g., *cat, hat, mat, sat, pat,* and *rat* to compare with *can, man, fan, ran,* and *van*), along with a few picture cards. Be sure that your child can read one or two of the words in each family (typically those would be *cat* and *man*). Start with three-letter words, but add at least a few words with digraphs and blends later on (e.g., *that, chat, flat*). Use any word-bank words that fit the patterns, but be careful not to overwhelm the child with the total number of cards to sort. Four to six cards for each column, depending on the total number of columns, is fine.

2. Lay down a known word to start each category (e.g., *cat* and *man*) or a card with the word family written on it (*at* and *an*) and read each header aloud. Have the child repeat each header after you. Shuffle the rest of the words and pictures.

3. Place a word card under the header word that rhymes. Read the header word first and then the new word (e.g., "cat, rat"), and model how you use the header to figure out the new word by substituting a different beginning sound as the child did in Push It Say It. Sort another word and then a picture for each category. When sorting a picture, name the picture while placing it under the header.

4. Now invite the child to do the next word. The child can sort it visually, under the corresponding header pattern, and then read the header and the new word. When sorting a picture, he should name the picture before sorting it so he can hear the sounds in the word. Have the child sort the rest of the cards.

5. After all the words and pictures have been sorted, ask the child to read down each column, starting with the header, and ask him how the words are alike. You want the child to pay attention to the sounds, letters, and the position of those letters. Probe for answers such as "They rhyme," or "They all have an *a* and a *t* in them." Explain that the words in each column are called a *family* because they all end with *a* and *t*; they all end in *at*.

6. If the child makes an error in sorting, wait to see whether she catches the error upon reading down the column. If she catches the error and moves the card, ask her to explain why she did that. If she doesn't catch the error after reading down a column, ask, "Do all those words belong there?" and have her read the header, then the first card, then the header, then the second card, and so on. If she still doesn't see the problem, point out the error and ask where the card should go.

When a child is sorting for the very first time, he'll require some extra modeling for the first couple of lessons. If he's familiar with sorting but working on new features (like the first time he sorts short *i* word families or short *o* word families), the process should begin with some brief modeling. After that, the child will become an expert sorter and can proceed on his own after he and the tutor identify the headers. The tutor might say, "Now you be the teacher. Tell me what you're sorting and why you're doing it that way."

Further Studies of Word Families. The first word families that are compared should share the same short vowel, as in the *at* and *an* sort described earlier. Start by just comparing two and then try three or four different families at a time, adding new ones to the ones you have already studied so that they are reviewed. A suggested sequence for sorting is listed on the next page.

Learning the first few word families may go slowly, but most children will need much less reinforcement with later families as they transfer their learning to new vowels within the rime. There is no reason to study every word family. Even the suggested list below has more sorts than many children will need. To really solidify children's understanding of short vowels, you will need to compare words containing families with different vowels (e.g., *chat* and *spot*) and words that do not share the same vowel *or* consonant following the vowel (e.g., *flat* and *ship*). These sorts provide the basis for the next steps in short vowel instruction and are described ahead.

Possible Sequence for the Study of CVC Word Families with the Same Vowel

Short *a* families:	1. AT and AN	(Start with two families.)
	2. AP and AT	(Add another and review one.)
	3. AT, AG, AP	(Try three, but include a familiar one for review.)
	4. AN, AD, AP, ACK	(Try four, but include some familiar ones.)
Short *i* families:	5. IG, IT, IP	(Start with two or maybe three on the second short vowel you tackle.)
	6. IN, ILL, ICK	(Be ready to pick up the pace whenever you can.)

(*Note:* At this point, you could continue with sorts that have the same short vowel, or you could begin contrasting vowels by comparing word families such as AT and IT, or IP and AP.)

Short *o* families:	7. OT, OG, OP, OCK	(You might be able to start off with four, but drop back to two or three if needed.)
Short *u* families:	8. UT, UG, UN, UM	(It should be getting easy by now to do three or four at a time.)
Short *e* families:	9. ET, EN, EG, ELL	

Writing Sort for Same-Vowel Word Families. The writing sort for word families is similar to that for beginning sounds, except that now you can expect your child to spell the entire word correctly. The writing sort comes immediately after the word sort and ensures that children are not simply sorting by the spelling they *see* but that they can also *hear* and *feel* each sound as they voice it and write the associated letter.

1. Set up the headers for the categories you will need by writing a keyword at the top of each column. These might be *cat, man,* and *sad* (see Figure 5.8). Or you can write the word family as a header. Some coordinators also like to paste or draw a picture next to the word or word family. Have the child read aloud each header.

2. Call out two to four words for each category, depending on the number of cat-

FIGURE 5.8. Writing Sort for CVC Word Families AT, AN, and AD

egories, in a scrambled order for the child to spell. If you call out *mad,* he should write it under the word header *sad* or *ad.*

3. Assist the child when needed by saying the word slowly, drawing out the sounds, and stressing each one: "mmmm-aaaa-t." Ask the child to say each word too.

4. After finishing the writing sort, have the child read down each column, beginning with the header, and then state what the words have in common. With this he may catch any errors. If he fails to note an error, have him read the header, then the first word in the column, then the header and the second word, and so on. If he still fails to catch the error, point it out and ask him how he can fix it. Then have him correct the error, and show him the word card. There is no reason to erase an error. Just have the child draw a line through it and write it again in the correct column.

Push It Say It for Same-Vowel Word Families. Push It Say It routines for same-vowel word families represent the first level of the activity. They teach children to pay attention to the vowel and the letters that follow, and to treat these letters as a chunk that can be peeled off and combined with other beginning sounds to make new words. The procedure moves quickly and goes as follows:

1. Choose the word family cards in Appendix I that match the word sort you are about to do or features from a previous lesson that need reviewing.

2. If you are working with the *at* and *an* families, cut out these rimes as well as an assortment of beginning sounds such as *m, r,* and *f.* Two or three word families are enough for one sitting.

3. Spread out the cards. First, establish the word families and the beginning sounds. Have the child repeat them after you. Then push the *m* card up on the table while saying "m-m-m." Next, push the *at* card next to it while saying "at." Say the word *mat* while sweeping your finger beneath the cards from left to right.

4. Tell the child that you can take the *at* away and change the word into *man.* Push the *m* card up a little farther, saying "mmmm-m"; then push the *an* card next to it saying "an." Then say "man," again sweeping your finger from left to right.

5. After modeling this procedure, ask your child to push and say "mat." Then ask her how she can make *man*. The child should sweep her finger beneath the cards from left to right while blending the sounds to make a word.

6. Repeat with one or two other beginning sounds to make *man* into *fan, fan* into *fat, fat* into *rat,* and *rat* into *ran.*

Children will usually need a lot of support when first trying Push It Say It, but they will soon become experts. If they are really struggling with the process, try modeling the manipulation of a few beginning sounds with just one word family card. For example, try blending the *m, r,* and *f* cards with the *at* card only. Then try moving on to two word family cards in the next session with just one beginning sound. Progress from there. Push It Say It will usually not have to be modeled once the child becomes very familiar with it.

Comparing Mixed-Vowel Word Families

If children used short vowels to spell words on the initial assessment but used the wrong short vowels, they may have created efforts that look like this: PAT for *pet,* ROG for *rug,* and PLOM for *plum*. You can start your phonics instruction with mixed-vowel families that compare different short vowels followed in the rime by the same consonant or consonants (e.g., *ig* versus *og* versus *ug*). Because young spellers often get the short *a* correct but confuse the other vowels, it makes sense to start by comparing something known (short *a* families) with something unknown or often confused (such as short *o* word families). A sample mixed-vowel sort is shown in Figure 5.9.

Sorting Procedure for Mixed-Vowel Word Families

1. Set up headers such as *cat* or *at* for the *at* words and pictures and *hot* or *ot* for the *ot* words and pictures.

2. For the first time a child sorts mixed-vowel word families, model the sorting of some words and pictures after establishing the headers. Read each word card, and then the header, before placing the word cards in the proper column. With pictures, name the picture before sorting it.

FIGURE 5.9. Mixed-Vowel Word Sort

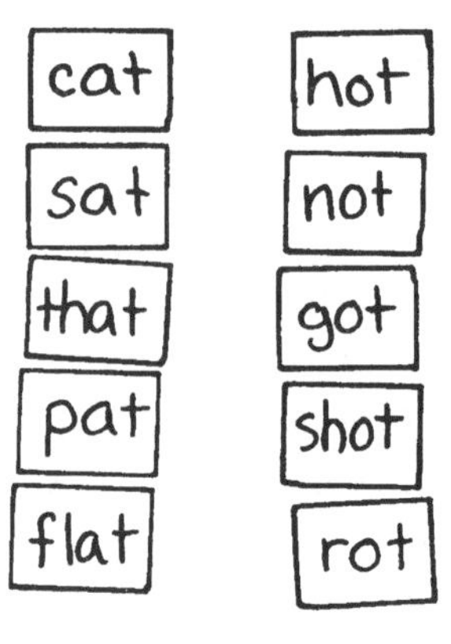

3. Invite the child to sort the rest of the words and pictures, reading each word or naming each picture before sorting.

4. After the words and pictures are sorted, have the child read down each column, starting with the header, and then say how the words in the category are alike. Remove the pictures and ask the child to read the words without the picture support.

5. As with the previous type of sort, if the child makes an error in sorting, wait to see whether he catches the error after reading down the column. If he catches the error and moves the card, ask him to explain why he did that. If he doesn't catch the error, ask, "Do all those words belong there?" and have him read the header, then the first card, then the header, then the second card, and so on. If he is still puzzled, point out the error and ask where the word should go.

In subsequent mixed-vowel word family sorts, the tutor does not have to model. Rather, as mentioned earlier, the tutor can establish the headers with the child and hand him the cards to be sorted, saying, "Now you be the teacher. Tell me what you're sorting and why."

Possible Sequence for the Study of CVC Mixed-Vowel Word Families

1. AT and OT (Start with two families.)
2. IT, AT, and OT (Add another family with a different vowel.)
3. IT, OT, UT, and ET (Try four, but include some for review. Be ready to go back to two or three if this is difficult.)
4. AN, IN, AP, and IP (Mix up different vowels and ending consonants.)
5. AD, AG, ID, and IG
6. IG, OG, UG, and EG
7. OP, UP, OCK, and UCK
8. ACK, OCK, ICK, and UCK (Remember to include words with blends and digraphs such as "*snack*" and "*shock*.")

(Try other combinations depending on the words you encounter in the materials you read. The list of common word families in Appendix H will give you other ideas as well.)

Writing Sort for Mixed-Vowel Word Families. The procedure is exactly like the procedure for same-vowel families.

1. Set up the headers for the categories you will need by writing a keyword at the top of each column. These might be *cat, not,* and *sit.* Or write the word families as headers. Again, some coordinators like to paste or draw pictures as part of the headers. The child should read each header.

2. Call out two to four words for each category, depending on the number of categories, in a scrambled order for the child to spell. If you call out "hot," she should write it under the header *not* or *ot*.

3. Assist the child, when needed, by saying the word slowly, drawing out the sounds and stressing each one. Ask the child to say the word.

4. After finishing the writing sort, have the child read down each column, beginning with the header, and state what the words have in common. With this he may catch any errors. If he fails to note an error, have him read the header, then the first word in the column, then the header and the second word, and so on. If he still fails to catch the error, point it out and ask him how he can fix it. Then have him correct the error, and show him the word card. Errors should be crossed out and rewritten in the correct category.

Push It Say It for Mixed-Vowel Word Families. Push It Say It routines for mixed-vowel word families teach children to pay attention to the vowel in the middle. This is the second level of the activity. With practice, children will see that medial vowel sounds are crucial to identifying words. The procedure is very similar to the Push It Say It for same-vowel word families. Include any blends or digraphs you have worked on. Blends and digraphs cards are included in the Push It Say It materials in Appendix I. Note that a digraph such as *sh* is on *one* card, not separated into an *s* card and an *h* card, because *sh* makes one sound. We've also included blends on one card, even though the letters represent different sounds (e.g., in the blend *st* we can hear both the /s/ and the /t/). This way the onset is represented as a unit and is easier to manipulate. Later, when the child has progressed to contrasting short vowel words outside the support of word families, we suggest you use individual letter cards for blends. Remember, the activity moves quickly.

1. Choose the rime cards in Appendix I that match the word sort you will be doing later in the lesson. Or you may wish to choose rime cards representing features from a previous lesson that need reviewing. If you are working with the *ap, op,* and *ip* families, cut out these rimes as well as two or three onsets, or beginning sound cards, such as *sh, ch, t.*

2. Spread out the cards and establish the word families with the child. Then push the *sh* card up on the table while saying "shshshsh." Next, push the *op* card next to it while saying "op." Finally, say the word *shop* while sweeping your finger beneath the cards from left to right.

3. Tell the child that you can take the *op* away and change the word to *ship.* Push the *sh* card up a little farther, saying "shshshsh." Then, push the *ip* card next to it, saying "ip." Then, say "ship."

4. After modeling this procedure, ask the child to push and say "shop"; then ask him to make *ship.* Don't forget to have him sweep his finger from left to right while saying the words.

5. Repeat with one or two other beginning sounds to change *ship* to *tip,* then *tip* to *tap* to *top* and perhaps on to *chop* to *chip* to *chap.*

Modeling will be necessary the first time a student does Push It Say It with mixed-vowel word families. After that, he can usually proceed on his own after you've had him establish the word families. Just call out the words you want him to make. If you find he is struggling, model first each time until he can do the activity on his own.

Teaching the Short Vowel Sounds

When children are showing great facility with comparing mixed-vowel word families, progress to sorting words that do not share similar rimes (i.e., words that don't have the same vowel or consonant[s] following the vowel) to focus on medial short vowels in isolation. You should begin by sorting pictures by the short vowel sound. Words from the child's word bank should be added, as well as words you used in the word family sorts described earlier (see Figure 5.10).

Below is a suggested sequence for contrasting the short vowel words and pictures by vowel sound only, without the support of similar word families. Start with short *a,* since it is confused the least. The particular sequence isn't very important, but short *a* and short *e,* and short *e* and short *i,* are the toughest contrasts and should be dealt with last.

Sequence for Short Vowel Contrasts

1. Compare short *a* with short *i* (these sounds are fairly distinct).
2. Compare short o with short *a* (add a new sound to one already studied).
3. Compare short *i,* short o, and short *a* (try three categories to review).
4. Compare short e and short *u* (compare two more).
5. Compare all short vowels in various combinations (*a, e, i, o, u*).

FIGURE 5.10. Picture Sort of Short Vowels with Word-Bank Words

Sorting Procedure for Short Vowel Words

1. For sorting, use picture cards and word cards that your child can already read. Look through your child's word bank for words with the short vowel sounds you are studying. Words from the different word families you have been sorting are good candidates for short vowel sorts, but avoid more than one or two in the same family.

2. Lay down a header to start each category, and have the child read or name each header aloud. The headers can be vowel letters (as in Figure 5.10), keywords, or pictures labeled with the vowel letter or name of the picture. Whichever type of header you use, be sure to stress the vowel and its sound.

3. The first time the child sorts short vowels outside the support of similar word families, the child sorts pictures first. With pictures the child must attend to the *sound* of the medial vowel to sort it into the correct category. The tutor models one picture for each column, naming it and placing it under the header with the same vowel sound. Isolate the vowel sound by segmenting the word (e.g., /s/-/a/-/k/ for *sack*).

4. Invite the child to sort the rest of the cards. The child should name each picture first and then sort it. If the child has difficulty sorting, have her isolate the vowel as described in Step 3.

5. After the child has sorted all the pictures, add the word cards. The child will most likely want to sort word cards visually by simply matching the vowel in the middle of word with the vowel in the header. To ensure that the child is not sorting visually, remove the headers at this point so that she must sound out the word and then place it under the pictures containing the same vowel sound.

6. Have the child read all the picture cards and word cards in each column without the headers, checking to see that all the words and pictures have the same vowel sound. Ask the child how the words and pictures in each column are alike (e.g., "They all have the same short *a* sound, /a/"). Finally, have the child replace the header at the top of each column.

7. In subsequent short vowel sorts, use pictures without labels as headers for the medial vowel sound and have the child sort words. Follow the same procedures as described above, ensuring that the child says each word aloud before sorting it.

Contrasting short vowels in isolation, outside word families, can be challenging, and as we stated earlier, children will often simply sort visually after seeing the vowel in the middle of the word. For this reason, after sorting the same vowel sounds several times as described above, we recommend *blind sorts,* in which the child only hears the word and does not see it until she has already identified the medial vowel sound.

Blind Sort. In a blind word sort, the headers are placed and identified, and the tutor holds the word cards hidden from the student. As the tutor reads the first word aloud, the student listens for the vowel sound and then points to the header under which the word belongs. The tutor gives the child the word card and asks, "Were you right?" The child answers and sorts the word card under the proper header. After sorting, ask the student to check her work by reading all the words in each category and identifying the common vowel sound/letter. If there's time, the child and tutor can trade places and repeat the procedure.

Writing Sort for Short Vowel Words. The procedure for writing sorts for short vowel words is very similar to writing sorts for word families.

1. Set up the headers for the categories you will need by writing a short vowel at the top of each column. These might be *a, o,* and *i.* You might want to add a picture, pasted or drawn, for each. Have the child name each header aloud.

2. Call out two to four words for each category in a scrambled order for the child to spell. If you call out "hot," he should write it under *o.*

3. Assist the child *when needed* by saying the word slowly, drawing out the sounds and stressing each one. Ask the child to say the word too.

4. After finishing the writing sort, have the child read down each column, beginning with the header, and state what the words have in common. With this he may catch any errors. If he fails to note an error, have him read the header, then the first word in the column, then the header and the second word, and so on. If he still fails to catch the error, point it out and ask him how he can fix it. Then have him correct the error, and show him the word card. Errors should be crossed out and rewritten in the correct category.

After sorting the same vowel sounds several times, try using pictures without labels as headers for the writing sort.

Push It Say It for Short Vowel Words. Because of the focus on the medial vowel, you will be pushing cards representing the onset (a single consonant, digraph, or blend); the vowel alone; and the final consonant, digraph, or blend (see Figure 5.11). This represents the third level of the activity. Choose letter cards from Appendix I that, when put together, will make a CVC word (blends and digraphs might produce a CCVC, CVCC, or CCVCC word). You will need a consonant (or digraph or two consonant cards to make a blend), several vowels, and another consonant (e.g., *o, e, u,* and *n* and *t*). At first, two or three words are enough for one sitting, as shown in this example. You will quickly be able to work your way up to more words.

FIGURE 5.11. Push It Say It with Three Letter Cards

1. Choose vowel letters that match the word sort you are going to do (such as *e, u,* and *o*) as well as two consonant sounds (such as *n* and *t*). Or you can choose vowels sorted in a previous lesson but needing review. Spread out the cards and have the child name the vowels and their sounds.

2. Push the *n* card up on the table while saying "n-n-n." Next, push the *o* card next to it while saying "o-o-o" (as in *octopus*). Finally, push the *t* card up while saying /t/; then say the word *not* while sliding your finger beneath the cards from left to right.

3. Tell the child that you can take the *o* away and change the word into *net*. Push the *n* card up a little farther, saying "n-n-n." Then push the *e* card next to it, saying "eh-eh-eh" (as in *Ed*). Then push the *t* card up once again, saying /t/. Then say "net," sliding your finger beneath.

4. Repeat the same procedure, substituting the *u* to make *nut*.

5. After modeling this procedure, call out the same words for the child to make with the cards, having her push and say the letter sounds of each word as she builds it. Next she should sweep her finger beneath the cards while blending the sounds to make a word.

Once the child has tried this type of Push It Say It, she will probably be able to manage it in future sessions without the tutor's modeling it first. She can lay out the cards and make words as the tutor calls them out. You can add more consonants, blends, and digraphs to make a few more words too. In the example above, add a *c* to make *cut* and *cot*.

Some other Push It Say It combinations focusing on the medial short vowel are listed below. To push and say *clock,* you would need four cards to represent each phoneme: *c, l, o,* and *ck*. *Cl* is a blend of two sounds, whereas *ck* is a digraph that has only one sound.

Push It Say It Suggestions for Short Vowels in CVC Words

fan, fin, fun/cat, cot, cut/net, not, nut/jig, jog, jug/tap, tip, top/cap, cop, cup/rat, rot, rut

sack, sick, sock/slap, slip, slop/chap, chip, chop/clap, clip, clop/track, trick, truck/stack, stick, stuck

bag, beg, big, bog, bug/ham, him, hum

pat, pet, pit, pot/hat, hit, hot, hut/bat, bet, bit, but/tack, tick, tock, tuck/lack, lick, lock, luck/clack, click, clock, cluck

Although each of these possible combinations substitutes only the vowel, you can substitute the onset and/or ending sounds of words as well. This procedure affords practice with beginning, medial vowel, and ending sounds within words. For example, in a lesson comparing the medial short vowels *a, e,* and *i,* the Push It Say It sequence might look like this: *beg, bag, big, bin, thin, then, than.*

Consonant Digraphs and Blends. During the instruction of short vowels you will also be explicitly teaching consonant digraphs and blends with words, as outlined in the phonics ladder in Chapter 1 and the suggested word study sequence in Appendix P. Initial blends and digraphs are taught first, and then ending blends and digraphs. Note that after beginning blends, the blends *tr* and *dr* are revisited, along with *ch* and *j*. These represent speech sounds called *affricates,* and because they are articulated in a similar manner, children often confuse them. Common misspellings include CHRUCK for *truck* and JRIP for *drip*. For this reason, we contrast the sounds in sorts: tr/ch, dr/j, and tr/ch/dr/j.

After final consonant digraphs and blends, the word study sequence continues with some *r*-influenced vowels (e.g., the *a* in *car*) and preconsonantal nasals (e.g., *ink, ent, ump*).

Introducing r-Influenced Vowels

r-Influenced, or *r*-controlled, vowels are vowels whose sound is overtaken by the *r* immediately following them, changing the sound so that it is no longer an easily detected short vowel. For example, in a word like *car,* the short-*a* sound cannot even be separated from the /r/. While the short vowel is difficult to detect, *ar* and *or* are introduced at this point in the phonics sequence because beginning readers encounter many words containing these patterns in the text they read. We compare *ar* (*car*) with short *a* (*cat*) and *or* (*for*) with short *o* (*fog*) to draw attention to the influence of the *r* on the short vowel before it. The patterns are studied again later in the phonics sequence for transitional readers, along with other *r*-influenced vowel patterns.

In addition to sorting, Push It Say It provides a great instructional activity here. We use words to which *r* can be added after the short vowel to create new words containing the *r*-influenced vowel pattern:

Push It, Say It Suggestions for *r*-Influenced Vowels—*ar* and *or*

cat, cart/pat, part/chat, chart/ham, harm/ban, barn/mash, marsh/pot, port/shot, short

Preconsonantal Nasals

Here we study rimes in which the vowel is followed by the nasals *m* or *n* (called nasals because the sound passes through the nose) plus another consonant. Preconsonantal nasal patterns are *ng, nk, nd, nt,* and *mp*. In these patterns the *m* and *n* are difficult to detect because the sound of the nasal seems to disappear. Say "pin" and "pink" to yourself and try to feel the sounds in your mouth. What happened to that *n* in *pink*? (It passed through your nose on the way to the /k/ sound.) It is not surprising that children often omit preconsonantal nasals in spelling (e.g., JUP for *jump*).

In addition to sorting, Push It Say It provides a powerful instructional activity to study these difficult words. We contrast words to which *m* or *n* can be added after the short vowel to create new words with preconsonantal nasal patterns.

Push It Say It Suggestions for Preconsonantal Nasals

rag, rang/rug, rung/wig, wing/log, long/pat, pant/set, sent/bet, bent/wet, went/cap, camp/but, bunt/chip, chimp/plum, plump/had, hand/bed, bend/led, lend

FastRead

The FastRead activity was created by Mary Fowler, one of our first Book Buddies coordinators, to help children build automatic word recognition. It was designed as a 1-minute activity. In FastRead, children read, as quickly as they can, a series of randomly ordered words containing phonics features they are currently studying or have previously studied. In the sample CVC words sheet in Figure 5.12, the focus is on short *a* word families. During the study of word families, some FastRead sheets in a collection may display only word families instead of entire words. The sample word families sheet in Figure 5.12 offers practice with short *i* word families and includes a few short *a* word families for cumulative review. FastRead moves phonics and spelling into the realm of decoding and word identification, which are vital aspects of word study.

The FastRead sheets can be numbered to correspond with your word study sequence. For example, CVC Words 1 would feature CVC words incorporating the word families *at* and *an*. CVC Words 2 might add words containing *ap*, and 3 might add words with *ag* to review four word families. Subsequent FastRead CVC word sheets targeting short *i* word families may include a few short *a* words for review. A practice box containing words, both words and pictures, or word families (for sheets displaying only word families) prepares the child for the task ahead.

The first few times the child tries FastRead will probably be slow going. The tutor and child should first identify the words/pictures or word families in the practice box.

FIGURE 5.12. FastRead Sheet Samples

CVC Words Sheet
FastRead
at an ap

Practice Box

bat	fan	cap

pat	ran	tap
can	map	man
hat	pan	rap
fan	sat	nap
mat	lap	cat

Word Families Sheet
FastRead
Word Families

Practice Box

ig	ip	it	in

ig	ip	it
in	ip	ig
it	ig	in
ack	ip	it
ig	ad	in

Next, at a slow pace, the tutor should model pointing to each item and reading it aloud (this kind of modeling is, in fact, beneficial each time the child reads a new sheet). Then the child reads alone, pointing to each item. If she is having trouble focusing on one word or word family at a time, use a word finder or piece of card stock with a cutout window to isolate each item.

Once the child gets the hang of the activity, the tutor should time her for 1 minute, keeping track of the number of items she reads correctly. Although the tutor can correct the child during the timing, it is best simply to write down the items read incorrectly and revisit them after the timing. The tutor should then record the score—the number of words or word families read correctly out of the total number. The same FastRead sheet should be revisited until most or all items are read correctly in 1 minute. The tutor pair can keep track across lessons, watching accuracy and rate increase.

A sampling of FastRead sheets containing words and representing a range of phonics features can be found in Appendix S. Coordinators can create their own FastRead sheets and may wish to increase the number of words or word families if their Book Buddies are speeding through them with good accuracy!

Other Word Study Activities

There are other activities that are engaging and involve the child in further experiences with words. We recommend that you use these as time permits to extend and review the word study activities described above.

- *Word hunts* help children extend their understanding of spelling to reading. By finding new words with the same phonics feature they are learning, children apply their growing knowledge of spelling to decode new words in text.

In this activity children hunt through text they have already read to find additional words with the same sounds they have just sorted. Books targeting relevant phonics features provide a wealth of words. The chosen text can be revisited here after it was reread in the first section of the lesson plan, or it can be saved for rereading in this section, right before conducting the word hunt.

The word hunt can occur after the day's sort and writing sort, and the newly found words added to the writing sort in the word study notebook. The child should read aloud each word upon discovering it. After adding the new words to the writing sort, the child should then read down each column again and state the feature(s) the words have in common. Figure 5.13 displays a writing sort followed by word hunt entries.

Many words may turn up in word hunts that appear to fit a vowel pattern but don't fit the sound, or vice versa. For example, the child may find *was* and *car* in his reading material and be ready to write them under *cat* or *a* simply because they have an *a* in the middle. These words may look like they fit, but they don't have the right vowel sound. Make sure the child is reading the words aloud so he can hear the difference! If he doesn't catch the difference right away, he may catch it upon reading all the words in the column at the end of the word hunt. Words that don't fit should be listed in an "oddball" column of the word study notebook.

- *Word hunts during the rereading section of the lesson plan.* Word hunts can also be conducted in the rereading part of the lesson plan just after reading a phonics-

FIGURE 5.13. Writing Sort with Word Hunt Additions

featured book, or on text-only copies right after reading the text copy. The text copies would be from books read during at least three previous lessons. For a word hunt in this section of the lesson plan, the word features to be hunted should have been previously introduced. They may be the same as those to be practiced once again in that day's word study section, or they may represent those just previously studied. With a text copy, if the child is studying medial vowels *a, i,* and *o,* she can be instructed first to highlight with a marker all the short *a* words (the tutor makes the short *a* sound) while saying each word aloud. When finished, she can underline all the short *i* words while saying each aloud. Finally, she can circle the short *o* words while saying each aloud.

- *Sorting games.* The child and tutor can take turns sorting. The tutor should make some errors on purpose, so the child can correct him. The child must point out the error and verbalize what the tutor did wrong. In another game, when features in a sort are familiar, the tutor can time the student in a "speed sort."

- *Push It Say It on a dry-erase board.* This exercise demands greater attention at the phoneme level. The activity is best used when the child is very familiar with the targeted phonics feature. The tutor will have to model the procedure the first time and support as needed.

Instead of pushing up letter cards to make a word called out by the tutor, the child uses a dry-erase marker to write the word on a dry-erase board. After writing, the child "pushes up" each sound from left to right, saying the sound /l/-/o/-/t/. Then she uses her finger to sweep beneath the word from left to right while saying the whole word aloud.

When the next word is called out by the tutor, the child determines which letter she must change to make the new word. To change *lot* to *log,* the child must erase the *t* and replace it with *g.* To change *skin* to *spin,* she must erase the *k* and replace it with *p.*

- *Word study games.* Games offer practice and fun as a culminating instructional activity. Or, especially if a child is struggling with certain word study features and needs extended practice, games can add an element of fun. Games can substitute for sorting on the day they're played. Writing words from the games after playing and then reading them aloud is an important way to reinforce learning. In some games, the tutor and child write as they play and then reread the words after they finish. For prepared games, templates, and other activities, see *Words Their Way* (Bear et al., 2020).

- *Bingo.* A Bingo board can be made with pictures; words matching the pictures are written on the playing cards. Or the board can be made with words and the cards with corresponding pictures. In another version, both the board and the cards have matching words, giving the players an opportunity to read and say a word twice. Word-bank words representing particular phonics features and high-frequency words can be used in this latter version. Use dry-erase markers on a laminated, blank Bingo board to write word-bank words. Match the word-bank word cards to the board.
- *Tic-Tac-Toe.* Fill a laminated, blank board with the word families being studied. Write onsets on the playing cards. The players take turns making words with the onset cards and the rimes.
- *Path games.* There are many variations of path games. If you're studying blends, fill the squares with pictures; the playing cards are blend combinations (*cl, pr,* etc.). The player reads and says the blend sound, moves to the closest picture representing the blend, and says the name of the picture. The player can then write the word. Or the players can roll a die and move the appropriate number of spaces. They must say the name of the picture on which they land and identify the blend and then write the name of the picture. As for spelling accuracy, hold the child accountable for what she's been taught. For example, the child probably won't get the *oo* in *spoon,* but she should represent the *sp* and *n* correctly.
- *Memory or Concentration.* Concentration is played as described in the previous chapter, but with short vowel words. The matching pairs can be identical words or words with the same short vowel family or simply the same short vowel, depending on the features you're teaching.
- *Dice games.* Various rimes are written on the surfaces of one die and onsets on another die. For example, one die might contain the word families *op, ot,* and *og* (each written on two of the die surfaces). On the other might be the letters *h, t, l, p, c,* and *d* (chosen to help make real words). The child and tutor take turns rolling the dice and then putting them together and blending aloud the onset and rime. If the dice make a real word, the player writes it down. The first player to make three real words wins. After playing, the tutor and child must reread aloud the words on their lists.

When playing word study games, players should not forget to read aloud words or onset/rimes as they are playing and writing! Multisensory practice–seeing, saying, writing, and manipulating–is a powerful tool for reinforcement of learning.

Beginning Reader Lesson Plan, Part 3: Writing

The writing section of the beginning reader lesson plan provides opportunities for instruction and practice with speech sounds, syntax, and semantics. Below we address these components of writing instruction, offer activities appropriate for earlier beginning readers and later beginning readers, and describe what happens after the child writes.

This part of the lesson plan should take about 8 to 10 minutes.

Components of Writing Instruction

Writing for Sounds

Children's understanding of letters and sounds is further enhanced through writing. Writing demands that children segment their speech into sounds and match those segmented sounds to letters. You will often need to model the segmentation process by stretching out the sounds in the words and then encouraging the child to do the same. This kind of writing exercises beginning readers' phonemic awareness and phonics knowledge in a meaningful way.

Note that we hold children accountable for correctly spelling only the phonics features we've taught them. Also, as they grow as readers and writers, we want them to attend to correct spelling of high-frequency words that they often encounter, even if the spelling is irregular. These include words like *of* and *was*.

Writing for Syntax

Children attend to grammar, sentence structure, and punctuation as they write. This is accomplished through both original writing and dictated sentences. Children learn that to communicate effectively through writing, their writing must be readable and follow basic conventions, such as beginning a sentence with a capital letter and ending it with a period.

Writing for Semantics

Children attend to the meanings of the words and phrases they write in their original sentences/compositions. Children are taught to remain aware that their written communication must be readable not only from a syntactical and mechanical perspective (grammar, sentence structure, punctuation, and spelling) but also from a meaning perspective. It must make sense *and* convey the intended meaning.

The writing can take a variety of forms, as described below. With earlier beginners—those reading preprimer text (lettered levels C–E, numbered levels 3–8)—it is usually a single sentence. Later beginners—those reading primer text (lettered levels F and G, numbered levels 9–12)—should be writing two, three, or more sentences. After writing, the child should read aloud her sentence or sentences to her tutor. (We hope each Book Buddies child has the opportunity to write extensively and freely on topics of personal interest in the classroom, where more time can be allotted to this activity.)

Writing for Earlier Beginning Readers

The sentence you use for writing with earlier beginners may grow out of the word study portion of the lesson plan, may repeat words from a text that has been read, or may be an original sentence composed by the child. Whether the sentence is created by the child (and voiced aloud to the tutor) or created by the coordinator, the tutor's job is to say the whole sentence and then repeat the sentence word by word as the child spells as well as he or she can. The child should say each word before writing and sound it out while writing. As beginning readers start to represent vowels in their writing, they should be encouraged to use lowercase letters where appropriate. They may need reminders. Below are some examples for each type of dictated sentence for earlier beginners.

Story-Based Sentences

A story-based sentence comes from, or is suggested by, a book the child has recently read. This can be a complete sentence or one with a blank or blanks the child can complete, which increases motivation. For example, after reading about the things "super fox" and other "super" animals can do in *As Fast as a Fox,* by Gary Pernick (1996), a child might be asked to write, "Super (child's name) can ____________." Or the written sentence can be in response to the question "What can Super (child's name) do?"

Pattern writing involves the creation of one or two new sentences based on the patterned sentence structure of a book. After a reading of *All through the Week with Cat and Dog,* by Rozanne Lanczak Williams (1994), the book's sentence pattern represented by "On Monday morning, Dog made cookies. On Monday afternoon, Cat ate the cookies" can be used as the basis for new sentences. A child can be given his choice of characters, days, and food to compose a new sentence such as "On Friday morning, Isaiah made hot dogs. On Friday afternoon, Charles ate the hot dogs."

Personal Sentences

Personal writing reflects something of interest to the child, like a birthday, new shoes, a snowy day, or a new pet. Take advantage of these occasions, which provide motivating writing material. Decide on a sentence that summarizes the subject and use it for dictation, or ask the student to write about the subject. The child may want to write more than one sentence or wish to write a note or card to someone. Earlier beginners will need support in constructing a sentence, which can then be dictated word by word.

Word Study–Based Sentences

A word study sentence uses word-bank words or phonics features. During the study of digraphs (with words), a dictated sentence might be "She sells shells and thin chips."

Writing for Later Beginning Readers

Later beginning readers, who are reading primer materials, can be expected to write more. Responses to reading, predictions about reading, personal responses to questions or statements written by the coordinator in the child's notebook (e.g., "What did you do on your birthday?" or "Tell me about your field trip!"), and free choice are all options in the writing section. (When the writing involves responses during or after the new reading or predictions during reading, be sure to indicate on the lesson plan that the writing section is incorporated into the new reading section, or follows it.) You might also want to slip in a one- to two-sentence word study–based dictation now and then. When dictating to a later beginning reader, the full sentence would be read first, and then several words can usually be repeated at a time.

The later beginning reader will need less support in constructing sentences than the earlier beginner. In fact, she may simply wish to write on her own and surprise her tutor. A surprise is very motivating. Also motivating for all beginning writers is having their tutors join them in writing. We suggest the tutor have his own writing book, which can be made of several pieces of paper folded in half and stapled. Children and tutors love to share their writing with one another.

After Writing

After the child finishes writing, don't forget to have him read aloud the sentence or sentences he has produced. This allows the child to put it all together: the words that have been analyzed for sounds and their corresponding letters, the syntax, and the semantics. The child may realize on her own that she has overlooked a word or words in the process of reading or writing; if there's a spelling, grammatical, or punctuation error; or if a word doesn't convey the correct meaning. If she doesn't correct herself, the tutor should suggest the child read the sentence again. If she still doesn't catch the error, the tutor can provide such prompts as follows:

Did that make sense?
Is there a word missing?
What is this word? Is there a letter missing in this word *win*: /w/-/i/-/n/?
Do we say, "He *get* a cookie?"
What do we put at the end of a sentence?

Questions Tutors Often Ask about Writing

Tutors often have many questions about writing. Here we respond to the ones we hear most:

"What If My Child Doesn't Leave Spaces between the Words When He or She Writes?" The spaces are important, but where to put them is a common dilemma for young writers. Early beginners can be helped by your drawing a separate line on the paper for each word in the sentence (see Figure 5.14). Say the sentence and ask your child to tell you the first word. Then say, "Let's write that word on the first line." Point to

FIGURE 5.14. Writing with Lines for Words

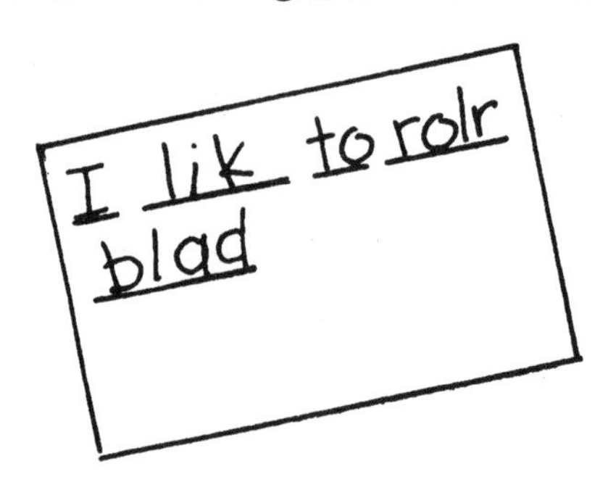

the next line and say the next word. Proceed in this manner word by word, repeating the sentence from time to time. Support your child's effort by saying the words slowly, emphasizing individual sounds. Children can also be encouraged to place a finger space between each word they write.

"What If My Child Can't Remember How to Form Some of the Letters?" Always have an alphabet chart or strip and a handwriting guide available for reference during writing. These are included in Appendices K and M, but your coordinator will find out what handwriting system is used by the school and get other copies if the system is different. If your child is unsure of how to make a letter, direct his attention to the alphabet chart and/or handwriting guide and help him with the correct movements. Familiarize yourself with the letter formation system used by the child's school, and use those forms yourself when you write for the child.

"How Accurate Does the Child's Spelling Need to Be?" In the writing section it is not necessary for the final product to be written in perfectly correct spelling, because these sentences will not be used as reading material. Hold your child accountable for what she has been studying during the word study portion of your lessons, but do not hold her accountable for word features she has not yet been taught. It is important that you accept your child's best effort at a reasonable phonetic spelling, although you can always stretch your child's understanding by saying the word slowly, emphasizing additional sounds as well.

At the beginning stage, it is unreasonable to expect your child to write any silent letters unless they are in words your child has learned to spell from frequent exposure. For example, it is possible that your child might spell the word *like* correctly, including the silent *e* on the end, because it is familiar to her. However, her efforts at spelling *road, light,* and *sheep* might look like ROD, LIT, and SHEP.

"What about High-Frequency Words?" High-frequency words, including prepositions (e.g., *of, from*), pronouns (e.g., *they, you*), and conjunctions (e.g., *although, because*) can be particularly difficult for children to learn to read and spell, because they don't mean much all by themselves and because they are often not phonetically regular. Consider words such as *said, was,* and *of.* Spelling these words by "sound" might result in phonetic efforts such as SED, WUZ, and UV.

Many of these high-frequency words will probably be included in the child's word bank, so keep the Alphabetized Word-Bank List (see Appendix F) handy for reference during writing. Feel free to help your child spell the words correctly when checking over his finished writing—not *during* writing—by pulling out the word cards or pointing to them on the word-bank list. If the words in question are not in the child's word bank, you might write them on blank cards and keep them in a baggie of words to be practiced.

These words are used so frequently that it makes sense to ask your child to memorize the correct spelling, so that when the word is needed for writing or encountered in reading, it can be spelled or read immediately and accurately. However, it also makes sense to treat high-frequency words like any others among your phonics words, and even add them to your phonics sorts—noting consistencies in letter–sound correspondences (e.g., the word *from* is completely regular in the spelling of the onset, or consonant blend, and in the final consonant) and discussing inconsistencies where they exist (e.g., the *o* in *from* is odd because it sounds more like /u/ than /o/). Greater exposure to the words and attention to their spellings will help cement them into the child's memory.

"What If My Child Wants Help with Spelling?" We want children to become confident, independent writers. We want them to take chances by using words they may not know how to spell. When they ask for help with spelling, tell them to say the word and listen for the sounds, and then do their best to represent each sound. For earlier beginners, you can even hold up a finger for each sound you hear as you both say the word. Then have the child write the word herself.

One of our Book Buddies once asked if a word she attempted to write was correct. Our answer: "You represented 95% of the sounds of that word correctly! That's almost 100% completely correct!" The missing 5% was then revealed. If you remain consistent in telling the child to do her best and in answering questions positively and honestly, she will quickly adopt a more independent attitude. It also helps if you are writing busily at the same time.

"What about Punctuation and Capitalization?" By all means, give your child pointers about punctuation and capitalization and encourage their use, but don't expect mastery of them for some time. Don't worry about quotation marks and commas, but do remind your child to start with a capital and end each sentence with a period or question mark if she misses them. Ask, "How do we start a sentence—with a capital (or uppercase) letter or a lowercase letter?" And/or: "What do we put at the end of a sentence (or sentence that is a question)?"

Beginning Reader Lesson Plan, Part 4: Introducing New Reading Materials

New reading material is introduced at the end of every tutoring session. This is a critical part of the lesson plan and should not be omitted. If the tutor feels he is running short on time, he should speak to the coordinator. The writing part might be skipped (you might find you can squeeze it in later), or word study might be cut short, but there should always be adequate time to read a new book. Time spent reading is the most important component of the lesson plan. Generally, save about 8 to 10 minutes to do this.

Selecting Books to Introduce

Book selection is the first critical step when planning a new book introduction. Use the guidelines in Chapter 3 to help pinpoint an approximate reading level and then select from your available leveled books or the list in Appendix D. Also consider what phonics elements the child is working on in the word study part of the plan and look for books that have many examples of that element (see Appendix C for a list of publishers of phonics-featured books). Children's knowledge and use of phonics will be enhanced if you provide reading materials that contain examples of the features being studied.

The books you will be using for readers in the beginning stage start off offering a lot of support for reading through the pictures and the patterned or repetitive language. Early beginning readers need this support. As the books get more difficult, pictures provide less support, and language becomes less patterned and repetitive, offering a blend of oral and written language structures.

New books should offer just the right amount of challenge. There should be a few problems to solve but not so many that the child will feel frustrated. In general, the new books will be at the same level of difficulty for several weeks before moving on to a higher level.

Conduct *running records* every couple of weeks to determine how your child is faring on a certain level, and to check whether he is ready to move up. The 100 Word Chart for running records is provided in Appendix V. (Note that you won't be timing running records for beginning readers until they are reading late primer–lettered level G, or numbered levels 11–12.)

Reading a New Book

There are four steps to consider when introducing a book:

1. Preview the book with your child by looking at the illustrations and talking about the contents. Draw attention to any words you suspect will be difficult for the child to read or are unfamiliar in meaning.
2. The child reads the book on her own, with assistance as needed.
3. The reading is followed by some more informal discussion.
4. The child reads the book a second time to reinforce what she has learned the first time through. It is important to try to read the book twice. Later in the beginning stage, as books become longer, this is usually not possible.

The preview is important and should be planned by the tutor in advance. It serves several purposes: It sparks the child's interest in the story; it stimulates the child's background knowledge of the topic, offering her an opportunity to talk about personal experiences relating to the events or characters in the story; and it prepares the child for a successful reading by highlighting new ideas, new words, and language patterns.

Early beginning readers have a limited sight vocabulary and limited letter-sound knowledge, which makes it unlikely that they can read much of anything without some introduction. As children acquire a store of known words and strategies for using context clues, they will gradually be able to read more and more independently, and new books may require only a brief introduction. Books containing unusual language or unfamiliar topics will still need a more thorough review.

Preparing a Book Preview

The tutor should look through the new book before using it with the child to familiarize herself with it and think about the support the child will need to read it. She should try to anticipate where the child might have a problem and decide whether the child can solve it alone or should be prepared in advance. The preview for a preprimer reader (lettered levels C–E, numbered levels 3–8) will offer more support than one for a primer reader.

For the Preprimer Reader

Here are the steps for previewing a new book for an earlier beginner, or preprimer reader:

1. Read the title of the book aloud to the child as you point to the words. Often the title will include key-words that will reappear in the story (e.g., the book *I Went Walking,* by Sue Williams [1992], repeats the words "I went walking" throughout). Ask the child to repeat the title.

2. Look at the cover of the book and discuss the illustration. You might ask, "What do you see?" Ask for a prediction: "What do you think this story will be about?" You may need to model how to make a prediction by thinking aloud. For example, before reading *I Went Walking,* a tutor might say, "I think the girl on the cover is going to go walking. Maybe the duck will go, too. I wonder what they'll see."

3. Take a picture walk: Look through the pictures in the book and talk about what is happening. Point out character names that the child may not know. Also draw attention to other words that may be unfamiliar. Often these words correspond to illustrations. Point to the picture and the word on the page: "That machine is called a crane, and here is the word *crane.*" Discuss any new vocabulary.

   As you walk through the pictures engage the child in conversation, giving her the opportunity to use some of the words and language of the story. If there is a sentence pattern that repeats throughout the book, work it into this introduction. If there is a change in pattern, bring it to the child's attention.

4. If the book has an unexpected ending, do not look at the final page or pages during your picture walk. Leave the ending as a surprise. Often a child will change her prediction after a picture walk, which is encouraged! Next, ask the child to read.

For the Primer Reader

Later beginning readers, or those reading primer materials (lettered levels F–G, numbered levels 9–12), will not need a complete picture walk, unless it's an informational book with many new vocabulary terms. Nor will they need language patterns brought to their attention. In fact, primer materials are less patterned and repetitive because primer readers don't need that level of support. Rather, the tutor and child should discuss the title and the cover. Then the tutor should ask the child to make a prediction about what the story will be about or, if it's an informational book, what she thinks she might learn from it. Next, they can discuss the pictures on the first few pages and the tutor can ask the child what she knows about the subject. Then the child should be ready to read.

A well-planned book preview includes information and questioning but should come across in practice as informal and conversational. Observing as the child reads and reflecting on the problems he has will help the tutor plan future book previews.

Over time, the tutor will become better at anticipating potential problems and dealing with them in previews.

Support during Reading of a New Book

Offering just the right amount of support as children tackle new materials can be challenging. Over time, tutors will develop a repertoire of responses and become better at intervening during reading. A reference you might want to photocopy for your tutors, "What to Do When a Reader Needs Help with Words," appears in Appendix W. The reference, taking reader type (emergent, beginning, and transitional) into account, offers a specific guide for reading with the beginning reader.

Sometimes a tutor will find that his child needs more than occasional support on the first reading of a book. If the book is difficult, the tutor might say, "Let's read this together" and proceed with a choral reading of the book, or he might ask the child to repeat a sentence after he reads it, using the echo reading technique. These forms of support should be used only until the child can go it alone. With choral reading, the tutor can often fade out or hold back while the child begins to take the lead. Like a parent teaching a child to ride a bike, the tutor must be prepared to provide support when the child is teetering and to let go when the child is steady. But if a child continues to miss more than a few words on the second reading, it may be a book that is just too difficult.

A Note about Support through "Cueing"

In the previous chapter we included a note about cueing in reading instruction—using pictures, beginning letters/sounds, meaning, or the predictability of sentence structure as support for emergent and early beginning readers. Some educators warn that cueing only leads to guessing words as opposed to identification through decoding.

Research has proven that phonics instruction *is* key to reading development. By mapping speech sounds onto letters and spelling patterns in meaningful words, children learn to recognize them (Ehri, 2014; Metsala & Ehri, 2013). As stated earlier, we view the foundational role of phonics in reading as fact. But when we look at how children develop as readers, we see the value of cueing as a temporary means of support for the earliest readers who may not yet have all the tools they need to sound out every letter.

For early beginning readers who are still learning their letter sounds, especially vowels, cueing continues to provide an important means of reading support. Of course we don't want children to simply guess at words based on what makes sense or what the pictures show, so it is important to draw their attention to at least the beginning sounds to assist word identification. As children learn more about letter–sound matches, you can draw their attention to more phonics features in the word. If none of this helps, then model how you sound out the word. Note that although irregular words like *was* cannot be *completely* sounded out, it can be helpful to point out to children that *was* should technically be pronounced *waz,* so we have to remember that the *a* in the middle of *was* sounds like a *u*. It is important to call attention to the sound properties of high-frequency words that do and do not fit consistent letter–sound correspondences.

A Note about Finger-Pointing

Note that most beginning readers need to finger-point as they read to glue their eyes to the print and keep them from losing their place. Finger-pointing should be encouraged for beginning readers who are truly just getting started. As they become more proficient, however, late beginning readers' finger-pointing may taper off naturally because they no longer need the support. They may begin sliding their finger under text, or they may not touch the page at all. Either way, there is no need to be concerned about this development unless the children are repeatedly losing their place in the text while reading.

After the First Reading of a New Book

There are several things the tutor should do after the child completes the new book.

Praise. First of all, she should offer some positive feedback in a sincere and specific way, such as "That book had a couple of difficult spots, but you worked very hard to figure out those new words."

Discuss. Next, the tutor should engage the child in a brief conversation about the text. If the tutor thinks the child might not understand something, she shouldn't hesitate to talk about it with the child or to revisit the illustrations.

Reread. Children will nearly always read better the second time through, making them feel more successful and making the reading more fun. So be sure to allow time. The second reading will also increase the familiarity of the book, so when the child returns to it in the next lesson several days later, he will have a good chance of success.

Post-Reading Activities

After the second reading, explore further with a short vocabulary/concept activity like one of those described next.

Review New Vocabulary

Vocabulary included in preprimer texts is simple, but there could be words that are unfamiliar to some children. For example, in Eric Carle's *From Head to Toe* (1997), the elephant says, "I can stomp my foot," and the buffalo says, "I can raise my shoulders." After reading, it would be worthwhile to return to the words *stomp* and *raise* to discuss along with the illustrations. *Raise* is particularly interesting because of its multiple meanings: One can raise the window, get a raise in salary, or raise children. Primer texts may include vocabulary that is a little more challenging, particularly in nonfiction selections.

For each revisited word, point and ask the child if she remember what it means. Say the word and have the child point to it and repeat it. Then write the word on a sheet of paper or a card. Study the letters and sound out the word with the child.

Here the child is connecting meaning, sound, and spelling to gain a deeper understanding of the word. This *anchored word instruction* helps words "stick" (Juel & Deffes, 2004). As stated earlier in our discussion of word-bank instruction, linking the dimensions of meaning, sound, and spelling also supports the development of sight words (Metsala & Ehri, 2013; Rawlins & Invernizzi, 2018). In fact, the new words can be added to the word bank for further review if the child automatically recognizes them after several rereadings.

Make Word Webs

Even familiar words in the text can be used as springboards to learning new vocabulary and extending comprehension. The tutor and child can create a word web around one of the words. For example, after reading a text containing the word *run,* the tutor can write *run* in the middle of a sheet of paper and draw lines emanating from it to create strands of a "web." The tutoring pair brainstorms synonyms for *run* and writes each new word at the end of a line or on the line. Shades of meaning are discussed for such synonyms as *jog* and *dash*.

Engage in Concept Sorts

Text for beginning readers offers concepts that are generally simple but are critical for developing comprehension skills. These concepts can be explored through concept sorts and then discussed. The process of distinguishing between the concepts and the ensuing discussion kick up the level of thinking *and* engagement. Such sorts also serve to reinforce concepts and vocabulary that may have been unfamiliar to your child.

The new texts read in the videotaped lessons accompanying this book (online) both lend themselves to concept sorts (for more information on where to find the videotaped lessons, see the box at the end of the table of contents). For *Polly's Shop,* by Beth Jenkins Grout (1996), the reader can sort into categories the many different things Polly sells. Category headers might include toys and clothing. For *Animal Armor,* by Cathy Smith (2001), the reader might sort various animals by their protective coverings. Headers could include skin and shells. These sorts would use word cards. Concept sorts at the very early beginning stage may use both pictures and words. Children can be prompted to add other examples for each concept.

Don't forget to have the child read the words after they finish sorting. Words can be discussed according to their relationship with the concepts and also examined for spelling patterns. Meaning, pronunciation, and spelling are thus linked to help anchor new words into memory (Juel & Deffes, 2004).

Further Reading of the New Book

Put the new book in the collection of books for rereading at the next tutoring session. After the next lesson, if possible, send the book home in a personalized baggie or envelope so the child can reread it to himself and family members.

Using Rhymes, Jingles, and Poetry

Poems and jingles also make appropriate reading materials, but they must be introduced in a different way, because they seldom have much support from pictures and may have many unfamiliar words. Poems are meant to be heard in order to enjoy the rhythm, colorful language, and imagery. Children may enjoy poems more if they can hear them read first by an expert reader. The tutor begins with an introduction that stimulates interest and then briefly summarizes what the poem is about. Then she reads the poem or jingle once or twice. The tutor then invites the child on the next reading to choral read along with her as the child points to the words, ready to fade out if she senses the child can take the lead. She can fall back on echo reading if there is a part that seems to be especially difficult. Finally, the child tries reading alone.

Poems and jingles are good reading material and are fun to reread, but they are not leveled. You will need to use your judgment about how appropriate they are in terms of difficulty. If the child still cannot read a poem after choral reading several times, it may be too hard.

Easy poems, songs, and jingles can also be introduced in the rereading for fluency section, rather than the new reading section. *Words Their Way: Letter and Picture Sorts for Emergent Spellers* (Bear et al., 2019) has a collection of easy poems and jingles, such as *Hey Diddle Diddle* or *Jack and Jill,* ready to photocopy. Copies of nursery rhymes in large-font format can also be found at many websites, including the Webbing into Literacy website (*https://webbingintoliteracy.com*).

Copies of poems, songs, and jingles can be sent home for rereading in the child's personalized baggie or envelope. Afterward they can be kept in a special folder in the tutoring box. At the end of the year, they can be stapled together into a book, with a cover illustrated by the child, and added to the child's home library.

English Language Learners

English language learners who have developed a full concept of word need additional, intensive instruction in fluency, phonics, writing, and reading on their current level of achievement. The Book Buddies framework, with its comprehensive beginner lesson plan and its one-on-one, individualized instruction, offers an excellent intervention for the English learner who is a beginning reader.

It's important to keep in mind that English learners substitute sounds and letters from their primary language that are closest to certain sounds and letters in English. Most other languages do not have as many single consonants, consonant blends, or vowel sounds as English has. Beginning and ending English consonants, digraphs, and blends present challenges to English learners in the beginning reader/letter name speller stage. For example, /b/ may be pronounced as /p/ and /l/ as /r/ by Chinese, Hmong, and Vietnamese speakers. The digraph *sh* doesn't exist in Spanish and is often pronounced as *ch*. In their spelling of English words, Spanish speakers who are literate in Spanish will use the letters representing vowel sounds in Spanish that are closest to the English vowel sounds. For example, the long *e* sound in English is spelled with an *i* in Spanish, and the English word *peep* may be spelled as *pip*. English learners may also leave ending consonants and consonant blends off words. Explicit and systematic word study instruction in English addresses these issues.

Explicit English vocabulary instruction comprises an important area of instruction for English language learners too. Book Buddies coordinators and tutors must realize that these students need explanations for many words they encounter in word study and reading, and these new words open up new areas for concept exploration. The one-on-one tutorial provides a situation ripe with opportunity to further vocabulary growth, generate conversation, and build confidence.

We must remember that English language learners have much to teach us—about their lives, what their parents read in their native language, and traditions they may have for reading and writing. We must be aware of cultural differences and celebrate the children's heritage and faith, even if different from our own.

For more information on word study for English learners, see *Words Their Way with English Learners: Word Study for Phonics, Vocabulary, and Spelling Instruction* (Helman et al., 2012) and *Words Their Way: Letter Name–Alphabetic Sorts for Spanish-Speaking English Learners* (Helman, Bear, Invernizzi, Templeton, & Johnston, 2009b).

Learners with Challenges, Including Dyslexia

As with English language learners, native English speakers who exhibit reading challenges in this stage need *more*. They need additional, intensive instruction in fluency, phonics, writing, and reading on their level. The Book Buddies framework, with its comprehensive beginning reader lesson plan and its one-on-one, individualized instruction, offers an excellent intervention for learners in this stage who display challenges with reading development. Along with dyslexia, challenges include language-based issues that may show up as speech difficulties.

The pace of skill development may be slower, but struggling readers must exhibit a solid understanding of the skills studied in the beginning reader stage before moving on. Explicit instruction together with systematic and cumulative instruction provide the building blocks for reading development.

Positive Reinforcement

Praise, praise, praise is important at every turn in all the Book Buddies lesson plans. Tutors should be instructed to be generous and specific with comments like "I like the way you figured out that word" and "You are really listening for all the sounds in that word!"

Looking Ahead

This lesson plan is appropriate for the beginning reader, as described in Chapter 3. If the child you are working with can read beyond the primer level (lettered levels H and above, numbered levels 13 and above), either initially or after you have worked with her for a while, and is ready to study long vowel patterns, use the transitional reader plan described in Chapter 6.

Chapter 6

General Tutoring Plan for the Transitional Reader

This chapter presents the plan for the transitional reader. Be sure you have assessment information and have considered the criteria in Chapter 3 to determine whether a child is an emergent, beginning, or transitional reader.

Characteristics of the Transitional Reader

Transitional readers are ones who are transitioning between two stages: the beginning stage, where readers are just developing their literacy skills, and the intermediate stage, where readers are reading and writing fluently. As their finger-pointing drops off, transitional readers begin to read in phrases and with more expression. They build speed and begin to read silently. The texts they encounter increase in complexity, and comprehension becomes more of a focus in instruction. In their writing they are expressing themselves more substantively and with greater sophistication.

Transitional readers are in the *within word pattern stage* of spelling. When they enter the stage, they spell short vowels in single-syllable words, consonants, blends, digraphs, most preconsonantal nasals, and some *r*-influenced vowels correctly. They may use but confuse the spelling of long vowel words (e.g., FLOTE for *float*). They spell many high-frequency words and a growing store of sight words correctly. They are ready to study long vowel patterns in single-syllable words, beginning with the silent *e,* or CVCe, pattern in words like *ride* and *came.* Transitional readers no longer process unfamiliar words sound by sound, but in chunks and syllable patterns, and they can acquire new words more quickly with fewer encounters.

Transitional readers read between lettered levels H and N or between numbered levels 13 and 22. Typically, these reading levels span the middle of first grade to the end of second/beginning of third grade, but struggling readers do not travel a typical path. Transitional readers who are candidates for Book Buddies will usually be second or third graders.

Using the Transitional Reader Lesson Plan

It is best to begin using the transitional lesson plan if a child is a transitional reader *and* ready to study long vowel patterns. When a child is solidly representing consonants, short vowels, digraphs, blends, most preconsonantal nasals, and some easier *r*-influenced vowels, he is ready to study long vowel patterns. Sometimes a child at the end of the letter-name stage will still occasionally slip up on short vowels, but these will be reviewed in comparison to long vowels in the within word pattern stage. Likewise, if the student is not perfect with digraphs and blends, you'll be revisiting these features in the study of long vowel words.

This plan schedules more time for comprehension and does not include the word bank described for the emergent and beginning readers. Transitional readers still need to study words and increase the number and kinds of words they can recognize automatically, but they acquire new words more readily and have become more adept at applying their understanding of the spelling patterns of known words to decode unknown words.

Overview of the Transitional Reader Plan

The lesson plan for the transitional reader consists of three main parts:

1. *Reading for fluency* (5–10 minutes). During this warm-up and practice, children read aloud familiar texts or excerpts as well as easy materials to enhance their speed, expression, and accuracy.
2. *Word study* (10–15 minutes). During this time, children work with phonics features, examining and comparing the spelling of words to help them develop understandings and generalizations about how letters represent speech sounds and meaning and form patterns.
3. *Reading and writing* (20–30 minutes). In this part of the plan, children read new materials at their level and engage in comprehension activities.

A sample lesson plan can be seen in Figure 6.1, and a blank form that may be copied for your use can be found in Appendix A.3. You will see that there is a space for the tutor to write in comments to describe how well the child accomplished the various tasks. These comments will serve as guides for future planning and provide important documentation of the child's progress.

Transitional Reader Lesson Plan, Part 1: Reading for Fluency

Every transitional reader tutoring session begins with the oral reading of easy material or the rereading of familiar material to develop children's reading fluency. Until children can read smoothly with good speed and a high degree of accuracy, reading will feel like hard work. When children read easy materials, they feel successful and enjoy the experience of reading for fun. Reading easy and familiar materials serves as

FIGURE 6.1. Sample Transitional Reader Lesson Plan

Student: *Nikita*	**Tutor:** *Richard*	**Date:** *4/16* **Lesson #:** *42*
Lesson Plan	*Description of Planned Activities*	*Comments*
Reading for Fluency (5–10 minutes)	*Sparky's Bone* 1) Read 2) Long & short o word hunt in notebook	NO PROBLEM PUT "MOTHER" IN AN ODDBALL COLUMN
Word Study (10–15 minutes)	**Picture/Word Sort:** *short o vs. long o blind sort* **Writing Sort:** *Call out 4 words to write under each header* **Word Hunt:**	NO ERRORS. KNEW THE SOUNDS IMMEDIATELY. WROTE "ROP" FOR "ROPE" UNDER LONG O, BUT CAUGHT HER MISTAKE AS SHE READ DOWN COLUMN –
Reading and Writing (20–30 minutes)	**Book:** *Finish Bony-Legs* **Before Reading:** *Revisit prediction she wrote last time. Review events thus far.* **During Reading:** *Stop @ stick-on note questions. Discuss as necessary. What connections can she continue to make to the Russian folktales she knows? N. writes a new prediction in response to stick-on note near end.* **After Reading:** *N. pretends she's writing a sequel – what will happen to Sasha or Bony-Legs or both? Write a paragraph – @ least 4 sentences.*	WANTED TO CHANGE HER PREDICTION – SO SHE WROTE A NEW ONE! LOVED THE BOOK! CHOSE TO WRITE ABOUT B-L – WATCH OUT! I WROTE TOO – WE BOTH ENJOYED THIS!
Take-Home Book	**Book:** *BONY-LEGS*	

a warm-up, helps children grow as they gain more familiarity with words, and builds confidence.

Reading for fluency includes one or more of the following: (1) reading easy books, (2) poetry reading, (3) Readers' Theater, (4) rereading text read during previous sessions, and (5) timed repeated readings. This part of the plan should last about 5 to 10 minutes.

Reading Materials to Develop Fluency

Easy material for transitional readers includes poetry, simple books, and other text that they can read with about 95% accuracy or better, or no more than one error in every 15 to 20 words. More challenging materials at or slightly above the child's reading level should be introduced during the reading and writing portion of the plan.

There are a number of different things you might invite children to read during this time, and transitional readers benefit from practicing their reading in a variety of formats. Have a collection of materials at hand so you can offer a choice.

- *Books at easier levels.* The materials used for easy reading might include some of the same books used for the beginning reader. Whereas the beginning reader could read these books only with support, the transitional reader can read these books independently. You'll also want to include easy books targeting phonics features the child is studying. Books that the child particularly enjoys might be read over several sessions. Others may be read only once. Adjust the reading levels as you observe the child's success. If books at a particular level seem too easy or fail to interest the child, try higher-level books. Go back to easier levels if the child cannot read nearly every word on his or her own.

- *Poetry.* Reading poetry provides an excellent opportunity to practice expressive, fluent reading. Because poetry is meant to be read aloud, it is a particularly appropriate medium for oral reading practice. Eloise Greenfield, Gwendolyn Brooks, Karla Kuskin, Nikki Grimes, Jack Prelutsky, Maya Angelou, Shel Silverstein, Kalli Dakos, and many others write or have written delightful poetry for children. Children especially enjoy humorous poems, but avoid poems with lots of tongue twisters. Songs and jump rope rhymes also provide fun fluency practice.

First, the tutor reads a selected poem, song, or jump rope rhyme to her child in her best oral reading style. After this first reading the tutor should engage the child in a brief discussion about the poem. Then she invites the child to read chorally along with her a second time before the child tackles the reading independently. Troublesome lines can be practiced with echo reading, with the child repeating a portion of the text right after it is read to him. But if the poem is too difficult, look for easier ones. Favorite poems can be photocopied or typed and put into a collection the child can reread many times and eventually take home. Some children like to hear recordings of themselves reading poetry, and this can serve as an added incentive for practicing.

- *Readers' Theater.* In Readers' Theater, children read published or original plays, poems, or other text below or at their reading level while reading from a script. Readers' Theater subjects can include informational matter. Props are not necessary or are minimal, and there are no sets. The children do not have to move around the performance area while they are reading from the script.

While the Book Buddies format does not lend itself to longer plays with many characters, the coordinator can adapt poems, short books, and short plays for the Book Buddies child and tutor to perform together, taking more than one role each when there are many characters. If the text is on the child's reading level, it can be introduced in the reading and writing section of the lesson plan and then practiced several times in the reading for fluency section. As a shared activity, Readers' Theater is fun and motivating. Children can take home the material and practice, thereby increasing their accuracy, rate, and expressiveness. Some texts that lend themselves to Readers' Theater are the You Read to Me, I'll Read to You series by Mary Ann Hoberman, Mondo Publishing's *Reading Safari* magazines with short plays in the back, and folktales that can be easily adapted to a script format. You can also find Readers' Theater scripts online.

- *Familiar materials.* The most convenient source of easy reading material will be material the child has read before. From time to time the classroom teacher or another teacher who works with the student might share materials that the child has been reading. Also, the child can reread a book or a portion of a book that he enjoyed and read successfully in the last tutoring session. This might also be used for a timed repeated reading, described below. These materials can be sent home to read.

Timed Repeated Readings

Timed repeated reading (TRR) provides tangible evidence of progress in reading speed and accuracy, and many children respond well to this activity, which can be done regularly. The texts used for TRRs should be easier for the child than ones on his reading level and should be short—about 100 words. They can be books or selections from books the child has previously read, or they can be new, easy passages like those found in *QuickReads,* a leveled series of short nonfiction passages. The child reads and rereads aloud the short passage while the tutor keeps track of the time using a stopwatch or other timer. While the child reads, the tutor also tallies the number of errors.

If the child is reading a familiar book or passage, she can dive in with the first of three timed readings. If it's a new, easy passage, the child first reads the text silently and asks any questions she may have. Then the tutor models reading the same passage aloud with good expression and rate, taking care not to read too fast. Then the child reads the same text aloud three times. The three readings can be accomplished sequentially in one session or over two sessions. If spread over two lessons the child should read the text twice in a row in the first lesson and a third time in the next lesson.

Usually, reading rate will increase with each reading. It is very important that the child be told to do his best reading, attending to accuracy and expression. He should not be trying to read too fast. Assure him that increased speed will come with increases in accuracy and smoothness. There are three ways to do a TRR:

1. *Timed reading.* The easiest way is to count the number of seconds it takes to read the same text passage. This number should get smaller after each rereading.

2. *One-minute reading.* A second way is simply to have your child read for 1 minute and count up the number of words she read each time. This number should get bigger after each rereading.

3. *Words per minute.* The third way is actually to calculate words per minute (WPM). You will need to count the number of words in a selected text passage before

timing the reading. Sometimes the number of words in a book is supplied by the publisher on the last page or back cover. When you take the time to count the number of words in a book or passage, record it on the book for future reference. WPM is calculated by multiplying the number of words in the passage by 60 and then dividing by the number of seconds it took the child to read it. For example, if a child reads a 95-word passage in 1 minute and 54 seconds (or 114 seconds), her rate will be calculated as follows:

$$\frac{95 \text{ words} \times 60 \text{ seconds}}{114 \text{ (time spent reading in seconds)}} = 50 \text{ WPM}$$

Whichever way you choose to conduct your TRR, it is important that your child see tangible evidence of her progress. This can be in the form of a bar or line graph. An example of a TRR graph for WPM is shown in Figure 6.2, and forms are available in Appendix R. Circle *words, seconds,* or *WPM* on the form to indicate what you are counting and recording on the graph. You can also use the WPM progress charts in Appendix V.

Keep track of the number of errors the child makes during a TRR and record these as well. The number of errors should decrease over several readings. When your child makes an error during a TRR, do not correct it at the time, but revisit it after the reading. Ask the child to reread the sentence in which the error occurred. If a child pauses during reading and needs your help, supply the word but revisit it.

FIGURE 6.2. Timed Repeated Reading Chart

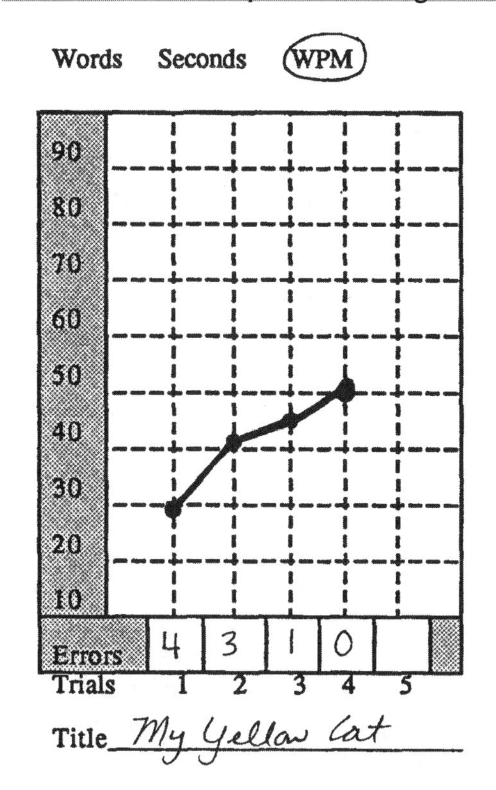

Transitional Reader Lesson Plan, Part 2: Word Study

The word study component of the transitional reader lesson plan focuses on phonics and is divided into three parts: (1) picture and word sorting, (2) writing sorts, and (3) word hunts. As described in Chapter 5, word sorts refer to the categorization of known words according to contrasting phonics features. For example, short *a* words such as *tap, fast, flat,* and *track* are sorted into one category, while long *a* words such as *game, plate, shake,* and *grade* are sorted into another. After the child sorts these words and describes how the words in each category are alike, he writes the words in a notebook under column headers. This is the writing sort. For the word hunt, the child looks through familiar reading material for words with the same features. These words are added to the word study notebook. The word hunt can also be done in the reading for fluency section of the lesson plan, as described below. The word study component of the lesson should last about 10 to 15 minutes.

Planning Word Study for the Transitional Reader

Transitional readers who are solidly representing consonants, short vowels in CVC words, blends, digraphs, some *r*-influenced vowels, and most preconsonantal nasals are ready to move into the within word pattern spelling stage. In the early part of the stage they will be studying common long vowel patterns in single-syllable words: CVCe, as in *trade,* and CVVC, as in *rain.* We also address a number of less common CVVC long vowel patterns from the middle within word pattern phase such as the long *a* pattern *ay* and the long *i* patterns *igh* and *y,* as well as *r*-influenced vowel sounds and patterns (see the phonics ladder in Chapter 2 and the suggested word study sequence in Appendix P).

Where you will start the word study sequence depends on your child's spelling efforts on the assessment. Refer to Table 3.2 in Chapter 3. Note that a child who solidly performs on the letter-name features on the assessment (consonants, short vowels, blends, and digraphs) will likely use but confuse the silent letters in words with long vowels (such as spelling *float* as FLOTE or *treat* as TREET). However, not all children who are ready to study long vowel patterns compared with short vowels will do this. Regardless, they should be placed in the transitional plan. The study of long vowel patterns includes a review of short vowels and uses words with blends and digraphs, providing additional practice for children who have occasional problems with any of those features.

Because the spelling assessment does not include words containing preconsonantal nasals or easy *r*-influenced vowel patterns, you may wish to dictate a few additional words with those patterns if a child has correctly spelled all or almost all the letter-name features. For example, you might call out *part, form, sing,* and *tank.* If the child misses any of the words you can go ahead and use the transitional plan, but briefly target for practice the missed feature(s) before you move into the study of long vowels (see Chapter 5).

As you move through word study instruction in this stage, observation of children's performance on writing sorts and free writing, as well as regular cumulative *spell checks,* will inform you of the students' progress and therefore guide you in planning continuing instruction.

Some Background Information on Vowels

The vowels are *a, e, i, o, u,* and sometimes *y*. Each of these letters has two basic sounds, long and short. Short vowel sounds are challenging for many young readers, because they do not sound like the name of the letter, as long vowels do. Say the words in the chart below to compare the short vowel sound and the long vowel sound:

Vowel	Short-vowel sound	Long-vowel sound
A	cat	cake
E	pet	feet
I	fix	kite
O	not	coat
U	rug	huge tune

Many children have difficulty hearing the difference between some of the short vowel sounds. Short *e* and short *i* are very similar in some words, and regional accents may make this difference even less. In central Virginia, the words *pen* and *pin* are said exactly the same. *Get* often rhymes with *it*. The short *o* in *dog* sounds more like *dawg* in many accents. Listen carefully as your child pronounces words and sorts them. It is a good idea to include an oddball category when sorting to accommodate words pronounced in ways that don't quite match the featured vowel sounds. But don't try to correct the child's accent. We all speak with an accent, and we learn to read and spell by matching our speech to the spelling patterns that represent it.

Long vowels are easier for children to hear, because the vowel almost always "says its name." The exception is the other sound for the long *u,* which is /oo/ as in *tune*. The hard part about long vowels is the silent letters that accompany them. For example, the long *i* sound can be spelled with *ie* as in *pie, i_e* as in *kite, igh* as in *light,* and *y* as in *my*. The study of long vowel patterns lasts a long time for most transitional readers, because there are multiple patterns for each long vowel sound.

Long and short vowel sounds are the most common vowel sounds, but there are others, such as the vowel sounds in *car* or *call,* which are neither long nor short. Some vowels are known as *r*-influenced (as in *car*) or *l*-influenced (as in *call*). Additional vowel sounds, known as ambiguous vowels, include diphthongs, such as the *ou* in *loud,* or the *oi* in *boil*. The study of *all* these vowel patterns extends beyond the scope of this book, which focuses on the earlier stages of reading development. For additional information on word study for vowel patterns, as well as other within word pattern features, see *Words Their Way: Word Study for Phonics, Vocabulary, and Spelling Instruction* (Bear et al., 2020). Also see *Words Their Way: Word Sorts for Within Word Pattern Spellers* (Invernizzi, Johnston, Bear, & Templeton, 2018), which offers a complete curriculum of ready-made sorts and guidelines for sorting.

Teaching the Long Vowel Sounds and Patterns

The study of long vowel patterns described below will also serve as a review of short vowels because short vowels are contrasted with long vowels in the first sorts. For example, a child's first long *a* word sort might look like the one in Figure 6.3.

FIGURE 6.3. Word Sort for Short and Long *a*

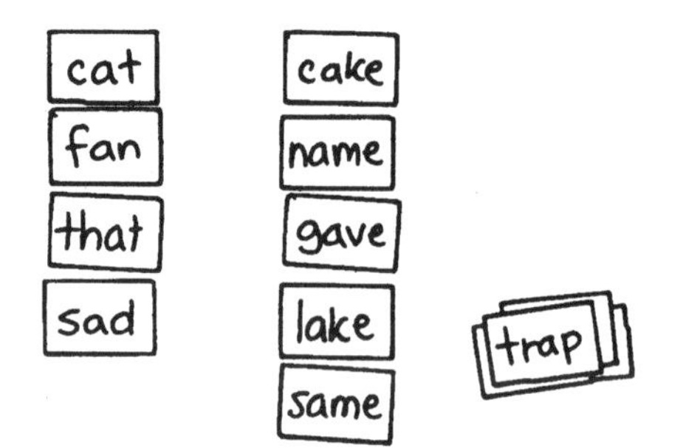

Additional sorts will contrast other long and short vowels as well as compare different spelling patterns for a particular long vowel sound. See the suggested sequence of vowel study with examples of the different long vowel patterns in the shaded box.

The word study for long vowels occurs at two levels: (1) sorting by sound and (2) sorting by pattern.

Picture Sort for Comparing Short and Long Vowel Sounds

When introducing each vowel for comparison of its short and long sounds, begin by sorting pictures. Gather about 15 picture cards with a mixture of short and long vowel sounds in the middle position (e.g., the pictures of a cat and a cake represent the short *a* and long *a* sounds, respectively). Choose one picture as a header for each sound along with a letter card identifying the vowel as short or long (e.g., "Short a" and "Long a"). Model sorting several pictures before turning the task over to the child. In order to isolate the vowel sound, the tutor should model the segmentation process by saying, "*Cake—ake—a,* this is the long *a* sound."

Sound sorts with pictures should prove fairly easy, so move on quickly to word sorts so your child can see how long vowels are spelled. Most words with a long vowel sound have a silent letter or letters that signal the long vowel sound. Only after word sorts can you expect the child to spell long vowel words correctly.

Suggested Sequence of Comparisons for Short and Long Vowel Study

1. **Sort by Sound: CVC versus CVCe**

   Short *a* vs. long *a__e* (*cat, cake*)
   Short *i* vs. long *i__e* (*fit, fine*)
   Short o vs. long *o__e* (*hot, home*)
   Short *u* vs. long *u__e* (*rug, huge/tune*)
   Note the two sounds for long *u:* /u/ as in *huge* and /oo/ as in *tune.*
   Short *e* vs. long *ee* (*pet, peek*)
   There are few CVCe words for long *e* so CVVC is introduced here.

2. **Sort by Pattern and Sound**

   Final *ck, ke, k* (*shack, shake, shook*)

   These ending /k/ sounds are spelled in relation to the vowel sound immediately preceding it. The words in the sort should be sorted first by the final *k* pattern in the words. Then the student should be asked what she notices about the vowel sounds in each column. She should realize all the words ending in *ck* have short vowel sounds, all those ending in *ke* have long vowel sounds, and all those ending in *k* alone have vowels that do not fit the short or long vowel sounds.

3. **Sort by Sound and Pattern: CVC versus Long Vowel Patterns (CVCe, CVVC, CV, CVV)**

   Short *a* vs. long *a__e, ai, ay* (*cat, cake, rain, play*)
   Short *o* vs. long *o__e, oa* (*hot, home, toad*)
   Short *u* vs. long *u__e, ui, oo* (*rug, huge/tune, fruit, room*)
   Short *e* vs. long *ee, ea* (*pet, peek, seat*)
   Short *e, ea* vs. long *ee, ea* (*pet, head, peek, seat*)
   Short *i* vs. long *i__e, igh, y* (*fit, fine, fight, fly*)

Word Sort for Comparing Short and Long Vowel Sounds

Most sorting at this stage is done with words, although a few pictures can be included. A word sort comparing CVC and CVCe words within a given vowel (*a, e, i, o,* or *u*) is described below.

1. *Prepare materials.* Gather a collection of words that the child can already read. Write the words on small cards or the template in Appendix G, which can be filled in and cut apart for sorting. You can add one to three words to be sorted in an *oddball* category, along with an oddball header. These are words that appear to fit the pattern but don't fit the sound, or vice versa. For example, *have* has the CVCe pattern but not the long *a* sound. *Was* is a CVC word but doesn't have the short *a* sound. Oddball words draw attention to sound and exemplify deviations from patterns.

2. *Introduce the sort.* Select a word or a picture labeled with a word to use as a header for each category, and lay it down to start the sort (e.g., *cat* and *cake*) as in Figure 6.3. Identify the header and its vowel sound. Model how to isolate the vowel in the middle by segmenting each word: "*Cat—at—a;* this is the short *a* sound. *Cake—ake—a;* this is the long *a* sound."

3. *Model.* If this is the first time the child has done a word sort with these particular features (short *a* vs. long *a__e*; short *o* vs. long *o__e*; etc.), model a few examples, including at least one oddball word. Discuss how the oddball word doesn't fit the other categories (e.g., *was* is pronounced *wuz,* not *waz*). Isolate the vowel as described in Step 2.

4. *Have the child sort.* Ask the child to do the next word. He should read the new word aloud and sort it under the correct header. Have the child sort the rest of

the words, reading each aloud. If he hesitates or makes a mistake in reading, model how to isolate the vowel. If he still can't read the word, set it aside and add it in later, after Step 6. Leave sorting errors to be corrected at the end, when you ask the child to read down each column to check the words.

5. *Check and discuss.* After all the words have been sorted, ask the child to read down from the top and listen for the vowel sound in each word. Ask the child how the words in each column are alike in both sound and pattern. In the case of the sort above, you want him to notice that the words under *cake* all have a long *a* sound in the middle and an *e* at the end, while the words under *cat* have a short *a* sound in the middle and only one vowel. If a child overlooks a mistake, say something like "There is a word in this column that needs to be moved. Let's read down the column and see if we can find it." Point out the pattern of consonants and vowels in the headers and write *C* or *V* over the letters on the header or create new headers to indicate the CVC and CVCe patterns.

6. *Re-sort.* Sort again immediately and ask the child to check the sort by reading down each column.

Two-Step Pattern Sort for Comparing Long Vowel Patterns

This sort differs slightly from the procedure described above. It begins with a two-step sort. Words are first sorted by sound and then by spelling patterns within categories of sound. The sort below using long and short *i* words is shown as two different sorts (see Figure 6.4).

FIGURE 6.4. Two-Step Word Sort with Short and Long *i*

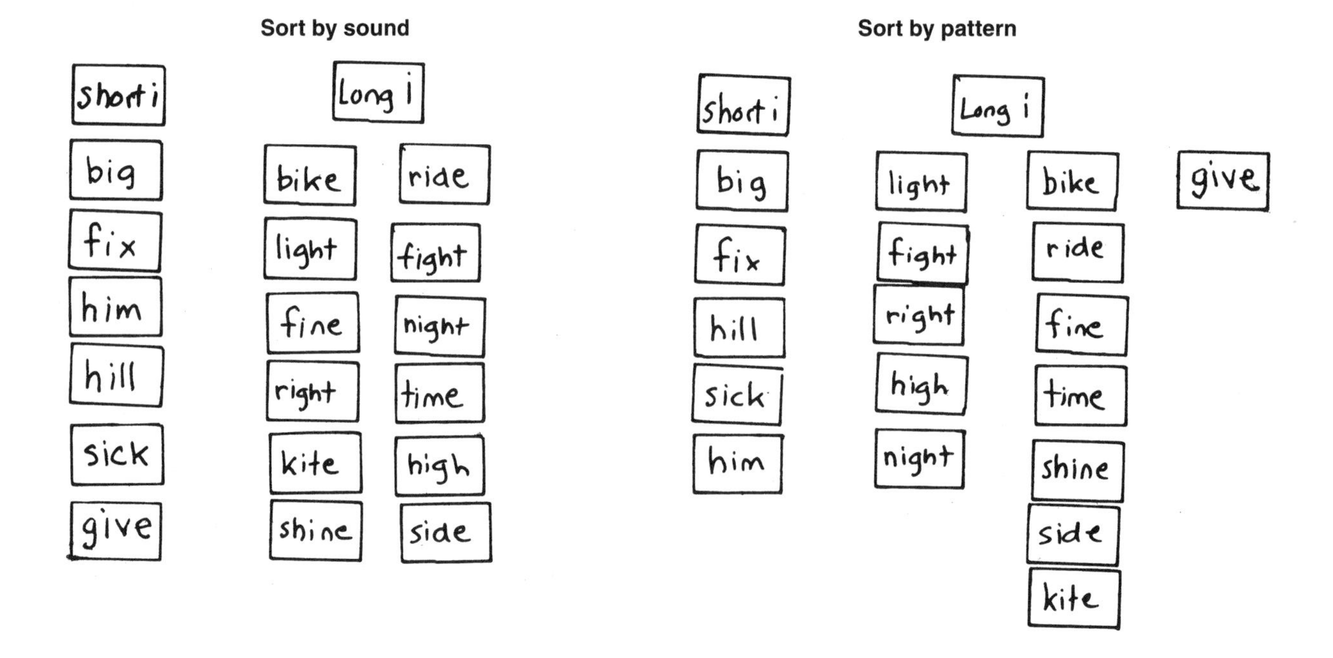

1. *Prepare materials.* Gather a collection of 15 to 20 words. Be sure to include words that have long and short vowel sounds as well as two different spelling patterns for the long vowel sound. The sort below has the two sounds for the letter *i* (short and long), as well as two patterns for the long *i* sound (*i_e* and *igh*). An oddball word like *give* can be included too. Prepare pictures or labels as headers.

2. *Introduce the sort.* Identify the headers and explain you will be sorting first by the vowel *sound* in the middle of the words, either short *i* or long *i*. Model several words if you think it is needed.

3. *Sort by sound.* Tell the child to read each word aloud and sort it by the vowel sound. Warn him to be on the lookout for an oddball word, or *oddball,* that has a pattern associated with a different vowel sound. Oddballs can be set aside and discussed later.

4. *Check.* After all the words have been sorted by vowel sound, ask the child to read down from the top of each column and check for the vowel sound in each word. If the child does not catch an error, say, "One of these does not sound quite right; let's read them again." Discuss any oddball words that have been set aside. In this sound sort, *give* would go under the "Short i" header, but what is odd about the word? (It has a silent *e* on the end, but the *i* makes the short vowel sound.)

5. *Sort by pattern.* To begin the second step of the sort (the pattern sort), ask the child whether he sees some words in a column that look as if they might "go together" or that are "spelled alike." Tell the child to make two columns out of the one long *i* column to create the second sort as shown on the right side of Figure 6.4. Warn him again to be on the lookout for oddballs.

6. *Check and discuss.* Ask the child to tell you how the words in each column are now alike: In the first column on the right side of Figure 6.4, there is only one vowel (the CVC pattern). In the second column, there is an *igh* pattern in each word. In the last column, we find a vowel and a silent *e* (the CVCe pattern). Then have the child read the words in each column, one column at a time, and state what they have in common—by sound as well as by spelling pattern.

Discuss any oddball words. In this pattern sort, the oddball *give* would go together with the *i_e* words. But does it fit there with the other words? Have the child explain why not and leave the oddball word aside. Next, hand the child pattern headers (*i, i_e, igh,* and *oddball*) for the sort below.

7. *Sort again by both sound and pattern.* Ask the child to sort the words again on his own, but start with four columns and sort by sound and pattern at the same time. Discuss and check as usual.

r-*Influenced Vowels*

Once you have worked through most of the long vowel patterns in this fashion, follow the same procedures for the *r*-influenced long vowel patterns, which work the same way. We presented some *r*-influenced word study in the last chapter, but transitional readers will run into many more of these patterns in their more extensive reading. Note that among the *r*-influenced vowels there are many *homophones*—words like *deer* and *dear* that sound the same but have different spelling patterns to represent their different meanings. We recommend systematically working though the sequence called out in the box below and then continuing the exploration of *r*-influenced vowel patterns through the study of homophones and other spelling-meaning connections described in the next section. Follow the same procedures for the two-step pattern sort for long vowel patterns except for *ir* versus *ire* and *ur* versus *ure,* in which we find only one long vowel pattern.

Suggested Sequence of Comparisons for *r*-Influenced Vowel Study:

ar, are, air (*star* vs. *stare* and *stair*)

ir, ire (*fir* vs. *fire*)

or, ore, oar (*for* vs. *more* and *roar*)

er, ear, eer (*her* vs. *hear* and *deer*)

ur, ure (*turn* vs. *sure* and *pure*)

Blind Sorts and Writing Sorts

In addition to the sorting described above, we recommend using blind sorts to reinforce the difference in sound between short and long vowels. We also suggest that writing sorts, including blind writing sorts, follow sorting activities.

Blind Sorts. After a child has worked on a particular short versus long vowel word sort a couple of times, plan a blind sort in the next lesson to practice attending to the vowel sound, or phoneme, and as a way to assess how well the child understands the difference. As described in Chapter 5, in a blind sort the tutor holds the word cards so the child can't see them. The tutor reads a word aloud, and the child points to the correct header under which it should go. Then the tutor hands the child the word card and asks, "Were you right?" The child answers and sorts the word card. After sorting, the child reads the words in each column and states what sound and pattern they have in common. If there's time, the child and tutor can trade places and repeat the procedure.

Writing Sorts for Short and Long Vowels. Writing sorts are a multisensory, tactile, kinesthetic activity that requires children's writing hands to function simultaneously with their eyes, ears, and voices to intentionally organize and preserve their learning. Asking the child to write these words into categories will further enforce the patterns that spell the long vowel sounds.

1. *Preparing for the writing sort.* At the top of the page (in a word study notebook or on a piece of paper), write the headers (e.g., *cat* and *cake*) for the categories you will need.

2. *Sorting.* When comparing only *one* type of long vowel pattern, like CVCe, to the short vowel, call out three or more words for each category in a mixed fashion for

the child to spell, saying the word slowly if needed. This is called a *blind writing sort,* because the child doesn't see the word before writing it. If you call out *mad,* the child should write it under the word *cat.* You can expect the child to spell the entire word correctly.

When comparing *more than one* type of long vowel pattern, such as CVCe and CVVC, to the short vowel, sound is not a clue to the long vowel spelling pattern (e.g., the long *o* vowel pattern *oa* sounds the same as the pattern *o__e*). In this case, have the child use the word sort to copy several words into the proper columns. After the child has sorted the words over a few sessions, try a blind writing sort.

3. *Checking the writing sort.* After finishing a blind writing sort comparing only *one* type of long vowel pattern, such as CVCe, to the short vowel, have the child read down each column, beginning with the header, and then state what the words have in common. With this she will likely catch any errors because she will hear the difference in sound between the short vowel pattern and the one long vowel pattern. If she fails to note an error in a column, have her read the header, then the first word, then the header, then the second word, and so on. If she still doesn't catch the error, show her the word card. If an error is made, simply ask the child to draw the line through it (no need to erase) and write it again in the correct column.

When a child engages in a blind writing sort comparing *more than one* vowel pattern, such as CVCe and CVVC, to the short vowel, the checking procedure is different. In this sort the sound isn't a clue as to which long vowel pattern represents the long vowel sound. Therefore, the feedback we provide is immediate: As soon as the child finishes writing each word, show the word card so she can check it. If an error is made, simply ask the child to draw a line through it (no need to erase) and write it in the correct column. After the sort is completed, the child should read down each column, beginning with the header, and state what the words have in common, identifying both sound and pattern.

Word Hunts for Short, Long, and r*-Influenced Vowels*

Word hunts do not have to be included in every lesson, but they are fun and valuable. Word hunts extend the application of phonics and spelling principles to other words found in text; they link spelling and writing to decoding and reading. As they hunt through books, stories, or poems they have already read, children learn that many other words have the same vowel sounds and spelling patterns they are studying. Words representing the targeted phonics feature should be read aloud and added to the writing sort in the word study notebook. After completing the word hunt the child should again read down the columns and state commonalities. Oddball words may turn up in word hunts and should be listed in their own column.

Word hunts can also occur in text-only copies of phonics-featured books that have been read several times. Have the child use a highlighter marker to highlight words that fit certain features (see Chapter 5 under "Other Word Study Activities").

If easy phonics-featured books (below the child's reading level but targeting the current word study) or text copies are read in the reading for fluency section, you can move the word hunt activity to occur immediately after the reading. Just indicate the move on the lesson plan as shown in the sample lesson plan in Figure 6.1.

Other Word Study Activities

Along with the sorting and writing sort activities described above, it is important that students work in other ways with the words/phonics features they are studying. Here we provide additional activities that are multisensory and engaging for children to extend their knowledge of the spelling principles they learn through the sorting.

Flip Books. A great way to reinforce long vowels with the CVCe pattern is with flip books. Staple together several cards or pieces of card stock, each displaying a CVC word. The bottom card is longer than the others, because it contains an *e* at the end of the CVC word and an extra inch of space that is folded over to hide the *e* (see Figure 6.5). The child reads the top CVC word and then opens up the flap to reveal the silent *e* and create a new word. The child reads the new word, folds over the *e* flap again, and flips to the next CVC word to repeat the process. You can make a book for each vowel: The short versus long *a* book would contain only *a* words. *Tap* becomes *tape, plan* becomes *plane,* and so on. The short versus long *u* book would contain only *u* words. *Tub* becomes *tube, cut* becomes *cute,* and so forth.

Flip books can also be created for beginning readers with manipulation of the onsets or rimes of short vowel words.

Push It Say It on a Dry-Erase Board. Like the flip book, this is a great instructional activity for comparing short vowels in CVC words to long vowels in CVCe words. Instead of pushing up letter cards to make a word called out by the tutor, the child uses a dry-erase marker to write the word on a dry-erase board. After writing, the child "pushes up" each sound from left to right, saying the sound /h/-/o/-/p/. Then she uses her finger to sweep beneath the word from left to right while saying the whole word aloud.

When the next word is called out by the tutor, the child determines how she must change the word to make the new word. To change *hop* to *hope,* the child must add an *e* at the end. When she "pushes up" each sound, she pushes the *p* and *e* at the same time, because the *e* is silent. To change *hope* to *rope,* she must erase the *h* and replace it with *r.* From *rope* to *robe,* the *p* is changed to *b,* and from *robe* to *rob,* the *e* is erased. Make sure to have the child say each sound as she's "pushing up" the letters, listening especially

FIGURE 6.5. Flip Book

for the vowel sound, and then read the whole word aloud. Push It Say It can also be done with letter cards, as described in the Word Study section of the previous chapter.

Word Study Games. The same games suggested for the beginning reader in Chapter 5 can be used for the transitional reader. They will simply reflect the features studied in the within word pattern stage of spelling. Bingo can be played using short and long vowel words and/or pictures. Concentration and board games can also feature short and long vowel patterns, or just long vowels in a review across vowels.

Tic-Tac-Toe boards can display CVC words to which the players add an *e* (with a dry-erase marker, a sticky note, or a small piece of card stock) to make a new, long vowel word. First the player reads aloud the CVC word, such as *tap* or *rip,* and then adds the *e* and reads aloud the word she made: *tape* or *ripe*. Or the board can be filled with long vowel word families, and the players can add onsets to the word families to make words, such as *tr* to *ain* to make *train*. In either case the new word created must be a real word in order for it to remain in play.

For more word study activities for transitional readers, see *Words Their Way* (Bear et al., 2020).

Further Exploration of Words: Spelling–Meaning Connections

Words related in meaning often share similar spelling patterns or, in the case of homophones, intentionally use a *different* spelling pattern to reflect the different meaning. Words like *act* and *actor* or *teach* and *teacher* share the same spelling of the base word because they share the same meaning. On the other hand, the word *pale* cannot be spelled *pail* because *pail* has a different meaning. These are just a few examples of many important connections among the spelling, grammar, and meaning of words. Understanding how spelling relates to pronunciations, meaning, and even parts of speech will extend children's vocabulary, deepen their awareness of syntax and grammar, and build an awareness of the multiple meanings of words, which is essential to reading comprehension.

Homophones. In the within word pattern stage, transitional readers encounter homophones, or words that sound the same but are spelled differently and mean different things. Examples are *road* and *rode, see* and *sea,* and *write* and *right*. There are also many *r*-influenced long vowel patterns among homophones (e.g., *stare, stair*; *hare, hair*; and *pare, pair*). We know the words' meaning by their spellings, and the words not only draw attention to different spelling patterns but also add wonderfully to a child's vocabulary. Include these words in sorts, but also ask students to draw and label them to include in a special vocabulary section of their notebooks or in homemade homophone books, or play games like Concentration (see Chapters 4 and 5 for a description of Concentration).

Irregular Verbs. Irregular verbs are verbs whose past tense is not formed by adding *-ed*. The spelling of irregular verbs also represents important spelling–meaning connections. When we ask children to compare and contrast the present and past tenses of verbs like *bend* and *send,* we are teaching them how the spelling of words represents meaning and even grammar, both important components of morphology and syntax.

Bend, send, and *lend* can be contrasted with *bent, sent,* and *lent*; *pay, lay,* and *say* can be contrasted with *paid, laid,* and *said*. Although *said* is an oddball because of its pronunciation, the spelling of the past tense of *say* is perfectly predictable from a grammatical point of view and will become more memorable once this connection has been made.

Multiple Meaning Words. Important interconnections among the spelling, grammar, and meaning of words are also made possible through a discussion of simple words that have multiple meanings—words like *jam,* which can have any number of meanings depending on whether you are using it as a noun or a verb. Consider the following: "I spread *jam* on my toast" (noun) versus "I *jam* everything into my desk" (verb). Sentences such as these can be sorted into categories of noun use versus verb use. The following list of common words can get you started, but be on the lookout for others in every word sort you do, and be sure to discuss them:

Words that Have Multiple Meanings Depending on Whether They Are Used as Nouns or Verbs:

act, back, bank, bend, block, brush, bump, call, camp, chip, cook, duck, dust, fish, fly, hand, kiss, land, lift, pack, play, rock, roll, run, step

Example: The *step* was very high (*noun*). *Step* up and take a bow! (*verb*).

Transitional Reader Lesson Plan, Part 3: Reading and Writing

Reading, reading comprehension, and writing are at the heart of the transitional reader tutorial. This section is divided into three parts: (1) before reading, (2) during reading, and (3) after reading. It should last approximately 20 to 30 minutes. If the child is reading at the end-of-first-grade level and above (numbered levels 15–17+; lettered levels I+), he should spend most of the time reading silently. The tutor should have a notebook so she can write along with the child. This can be fashioned from several pieces of folded paper stapled at the fold.

Selecting Books for Reading and Writing

Choosing books that the child can read with only an occasional problem is the first critical step in the reading and writing portion of the plan. Use the initial assessment and the chart in Table 3.1 as a guide. If the child read at the first- or second-grade level with good speed and quickly recognized at least 75% of the words on the corresponding word list, then put the child in a book at that level. If the child is reading between two levels, you'll have to try material at different levels. For instance, if the child read an end-of-first-grade passage with 98%–100% accuracy but could not quite read an end-of-second-grade passage, take materials from the range of levels in between (lettered levels J, K, and L), and conduct running records until you find a good match. You can find the 100 Word Chart for running records in Appendix V.

For transitional readers, you should capitalize not only on their individual interests but also on curricular topics that parallel those being covered in the classroom. Children who are poor readers often have great difficulty reading the content-area textbooks used in their classrooms. To help them out, find some books at their level on the topics they are studying.

Presenting New Material for Reading and Writing

New reading material is presented through the following steps. Each step is meant to enhance comprehension of the material.

Before Reading: Previewing the Material

Before reading, preview the new text by discussing the title and cover. The tutor might ask whether the book is fiction or nonfiction, and how the child knows that. The child should predict what will happen in the book or, in the case of a nonfiction book, what she thinks she'll learn. She can be asked what she knows about the topic. If the selection is an informational text with several unfamiliar vocabulary words, the tutor should briefly walk through the book, pointing out and discussing the meanings of those words. With an information book, it is also beneficial to draw the student's attention to the layout of the book—chapters, headings or subheadings, and graphics. If it is a fiction book with chapters listed on a "contents" page, the chapter names can be read, and another prediction can be made about the first chapter.

If children are reluctant or hesitant to make a prediction, explain that it's okay if the prediction isn't right. Good readers use clues in titles and illustrations to make predictions that will help us understand our reading, and we change our predictions as we get more information *during* reading. The tutor may need to model a think-aloud, saying something like "I notice that . . . and . . . , so I think . . . might happen."

Along with previewing the material, the coordinator may want to provide another activity to prepare the reader and invest her in the text:

- *Writing a prediction.* After making an oral prediction, the child can write it down. The written prediction can be revisited and revised during reading.

- *Anticipation guide.* One of our favorite pre-reading activities is the anticipation guide. True to its name, it is a vehicle for anticipating new reading material. Although it can be used with fiction, it best lends itself to nonfiction or fiction that includes factual information (e.g., the Magic Tree House series). Anticipation guides can take several forms. They can offer "true or false" questions or "agree or disagree" questions that can be revisited during and after reading (see Figures 6.6A and 6.6B), or they might offer open-ended questions. They can also take the form of a chart. For example, before starting *Frog and Toad Are Friends,* by Arnold Lobel (1970), the child can list the characteristics of good friends versus those of bad friends in columns on a prepared chart. Anticipation guides might also list vocabulary to be introduced, revisited in context, and studied through extension activities after reading.

Anticipation guides serve both to stimulate the reader's interest and to elicit and measure prior knowledge. It doesn't take long to create an anticipation guide, and you can quickly build a file of guides to use again and again.

FIGURE 6.6A. Anticipation Guide: Sea and Land Animals

Sea and Land Animals
by Sarah Dawson

Anticipation Guide

	True	False	**After reading:** Were you right (yes or no)?
Sea animals and land animals have nothing in common.			
Only sea animals have shells.			
Only land animals have claws.			
Some sea animals have fur.			

FIGURE 6.6B. Anticipation Guide: Owls

Owls
by Elizabeth Russell-Arnot

Anticipation Guide

Think about each statement and check *True* or *False*. Then, after you read, go back to see whether you were right!

	True	False	**After reading**: Were you right (yes or no)?
Nocturnal animals hunt at night.			
Owls are very noisy when they fly.			
Owls chew their food.			
Most owls do not build nests.			
All owls make the same sound.			

Vocabulary:

nocturnal

clumsy

owlet

owl pellet

camouflage

• *K-W-L chart.* This chart is for informational material and is completed before, during, and after reading. It is divided into three columns: What I **K**now, What I Think I **W**ill Learn, and What I **L**earned. The first two columns are filled out before reading. During reading the child revisits the *K* column to confirm or correct items and adds to the *L* column. After reading, any other new information is added to the *L* column, and all three columns are reviewed and discussed.

• *List, Group, and Label.* Similar to the K-W-L, this before-reading activity starts with what the child already knows about the topic, genre, theme, or author. The child and tutor (with the child taking the lead) brainstorm what they know in the form of a list and then group into categories the items or phrases that go together. These groups are then labeled. For example, before reading *It's a Mammal,* by Sharon Stewart (2005), the child and tutor would brainstorm what they know about mammals. Their resulting list, grouped and labeled, might look like this:

Facts about mammals: warm-blooded, babies drink milk, soft, furry

Kinds of mammals: bear, dogs, mice, cows, whales

Where they live: on land, in the water

These categories should be changed and expanded during reading.

During Reading: Discussing the Material and New Vocabulary

Transitional readers should be encouraged to read silently. Children in the earliest part of this stage might spend more time reading aloud than silently, but as they progress through the stage, the amount of silent reading should increase. The tutor can ask her child to read a certain amount of text silently and then stop to discuss. Of course, the tutor is right there to help with unknown words (see "What to Do When a Reader Needs Help with Words" in Appendix W). If you can't provide an extra copy of the book for the tutor so she can read along, the tutor can read over her child's shoulder. It is important for the tutor to read silently *with* the child to emphasize the importance of reading *every* word, and to make sure the tutor can help the child if she gets stuck.

As the child continues to read, the tutor should encourage him to react to new events or information and discuss them in an informal way. The tutor should also discuss new vocabulary and ideas. Along with these discussions, the reader can engage in other activities:

• *Writing a new prediction.* This can be one that alters the first prediction, or it can be a whole new one.

• *Listing new vocabulary.* The child can list new vocabulary in his notebook in a special vocabulary section. These words should be revisited several times and can be used in spelling sorts as appropriate.

• *Taking notes.* This is a valuable skill for children to practice in this stage. The coordinator should choose a relevant topic—within fiction or nonfiction material—on which the note-taking should occur. Or the student can choose the topic. The tutor should be ready to model note-taking several times before expecting the child to do it.

• *Fact chart.* The child might read a series of texts on one subject and create a fact chart, to which he adds over several sessions as he reads. For example, he might read several books about different mammals and collect various facts. By dividing a piece of paper into columns labeled with categories such as "Where They Live" and "What They Eat," the child can take notes as he reads the books (see Figure 6.7).

- *Stick-on note questions.* On previewing the text to be read, the coordinator can strategically place stick-on notes with questions throughout the text. These provide good stopping points for reflection and discussion and model the kind of questioning good readers do automatically as they read. Don't overdo the number of questions though—we don't want the reader to have to stop *too* often, as it may detract from overall comprehension and interest.

- Add to, revise, and refine the K-W-L Chart or List, Group, and Label started before reading.

After Reading: More Discussion

At the end of the book or at the day's stopping point, the tutor should engage the child in further discussion of the reading. If the child has not yet finished the book, he can be asked to write another prediction, change a previous prediction, write about how the previous prediction was correct or incorrect, or answer in writing a question you've posed about the book. You might write the question in the child's notebook or on the lesson plan.

When the child finishes the text, he can engage in one of several writing activities designed to deepen concepts and vocabulary, and foster critical thinking and comprehension:

- *Response to a question.* We want children to stretch their comprehension of text to the highest levels and to be able to back up their responses with examples from the text. Questions like "What are three ingredients Ned put into the stone soup?" do not represent higher-level thinking. But "Who was smarter—Ned or the innkeeper—and why?" forces the reader to attend to the big idea of the story.

After reading an informational book, the child can respond to an open question like "What did you learn?" Or he can answer a more focused question that forces him

FIGURE 6.7. Fact Chart

Mammals

Name	Live	E~~e~~at	Enimes	Babes
Blak ~~Bare~~ Bear	Woods	roots bares	man	cubs
Kiler Wales	Osun	Seels fish	man	caf
Frut	rain	frute	?	baby

to draw information from various places in the text, such as "How is a spider's silk very important to its survival?"

Paragraph-length responses should be planned first with a web, notes, or other strategy.

- *Complete an after-reading chart.* In completing a chart after reading a nonfiction book, the child must go back to find specific, requested information from the text. This effort not only reinforces comprehension of the big picture but also gives the child practice in retrieving information from text.

Figures 6.8A and 6.8B present after-reading charts for two nonfiction books.

- *Book chart.* Similar to the fact chart described earlier, a book chart is often used in author studies to compare narrative elements of fiction titles by the same

FIGURE 6.8A. After-Reading Chart: Sea and Land Animals

Sea and Land Animals
by Sarah Dawson

How are these animals alike?

Sea	Land	What is alike?
Otter	Rabbit	
Shark	Lion	
Sea urchin	Hedgehog	
Lobster	Bear	
Crab	Tortoise	
Clownfish	Tiger	

Can you think of any other examples?

Sea	Land	What is alike?

FIGURE 6.8B. After-Reading Chart: River Life

River Life
by Kate McGough

The Mississippi River: Where does it start? ______________________

Where does it end? ______________________

	Northern Mississippi River	Central Mississippi River	Southern Mississippi River
What kind of terrain (land) does it flow through?			
What is the weather like?			
What is the water like?			
What grows along the banks?			
What animals live here?			

author. These elements include character, plot, setting, and theme. Fiction by different authors on the same subject also lends itself to book charts.

• *Revisit and revise the List, Group, and Label* started and refined before and during reading.

• *Extension writing.* A motivating, creative post-reading activity for fiction books is writing a different ending, adding a chapter, or writing a paragraph or two about events that might occur in a sequel. The child first plans for writing by brainstorming ideas with a web, notes, or other strategy. After some basic editing with the child, the coordinator can type up the writing and add it to the tutoring box for rereading. Because the piece will be reread, the coordinator would correct spelling. A copy can be sent home, and one can go to the classroom teacher. The children are proud of their published work!

• *Summarizing.* The child can summarize a paragraph, section, or chapter of a book—or even a whole book. Summarizing is a complex skill that requires modeling and explanation. The tutor will likely have to model how we figure out what is most important in the piece of text—the big idea—and boil it down to just a few sentences (or even one sentence in the case of a paragraph).

• *Concept sorts.* The child can sort pictures, objects, or words into conceptual categories based on the content or theme of the book. For example, after reading a book about beekeeping, the child might sort the following words into groups related to the physical hive parts (e.g., *brood box, super, wax frames, bottom board*) versus the types of bees in a colony (e.g., *queen, worker bees, nurse bees, drones*). Other categories might include bee-made products (e.g., *wax, honey*) and beekeeping equipment (e.g., *smoker, hive tool, veil*). After sorting, the child creates a chart or reference book that can be extended as additional books about the topic or theme are read.

- *Vocabulary extension.* Vocabulary from the text that has been targeted for explicit instruction can be reinforced through various activities ranging from the child's writing his own sentences to acting out the words. For great vocabulary instruction activities, see *Bringing Words to Life: Robust Vocabulary Instruction* (Beck, McKeown, & Kucan, 2013).

As with the anticipation guides, copies of any prepared post-reading charts can be kept in folders and used each time a text is assigned.

More Writing Activities

The writing done in this part of the lesson plan is structured and limited, but there may be occasions that warrant a change of pace. Sometimes, creating personal materials can motivate a child who otherwise may dislike writing. Two forms of more personalized writing are described below.

1. *Writing little books.* Create your own little books that reflect a particular theme (holidays, likes and dislikes, things I can do, etc.), or model a pattern from something that has been read. Little books can be easily made by folding two sheets of 8″ × 11″ paper in half and stapling them in the middle to create an eight-page book. The Book Buddies pair can work together on the composing, writing, and illustrating, maybe adding a page at each tutoring session. Because these books will be reread, the tutor should help with spellings the child can't do on her own.

Here is a simple pattern you might adapt for any holiday or season:

At Halloween you see . . .
red apples
orange pumpkins
white ghosts
green witches
black bats

In winter I love to see . . .
snow falling in the night sky
icicles hanging from the roof
bright lights in the window
my friends making giant snowmen
smiles on people's faces

2. *Messages and cards.* Children enjoy writing messages and making cards for each other and for family. Creating seasonal cards (Halloween, Valentine's Day) is popular and need not involve a lot of time. Sometimes, children become interested in writing short notes back and forth to other children in the room, and this becomes a highly motivating writing activity. The tutor might be able to work out a way that he and the child can write notes to each other. Whenever a student is absent, the tutor can write the child a simple, short note in neat block letters that he leaves with the teacher, and he can invite the child to write back.

Questions Tutors Often Ask about Reading and Writing

As in the previous two chapters, we offer questions tutors have consistently asked us over the years, along with the answers.

"What Do I Do When My Child Makes a Mistake or Turns to Me for Help While Reading?" You can expect your child to make errors and encounter words she does not know when she is reading new materials. These problems are really opportunities to grow and should be left up to the child to solve as much as possible, putting to use what she is learning. If you just supply the missing or miscalled word every time, your child will grow dependent on you instead of learning how to handle problems independently. The first thing you do when your child needs help is *nothing*. Stop and think, and give the child time to think as well. See if you can determine the source of the problem and think of questions you can ask to guide your child to solve the problem. An often-used response to an error is simply "Try that again."

If the word contains a phonics or spelling feature that you have examined in the word study section of the lesson plan, prompt your child to decode the word by calling attention to that feature. Sometimes it helps to cover up part of the word to expose the chunk that contains the spelling pattern you want her to decode. Sometimes if the word is a difficult one and does not contain phonics or spelling features the child has learned, there may be nothing better to do than just tell her what the word is (e.g., *enough* or *height*). As a reading tutor, your skill in making decisions about how to intervene appropriately is important and will grow with experience. Use "What to Do When a Reader Needs Help with Words," in Appendix W, as a reference when reading with transitional readers.

"How Accurate Does Children's Spelling Need to Be When They Write?" In general, accept your child's spelling efforts but hold him accountable for what he has been taught during the word study portion of your lessons. *Wait until the child has finished writing to review any errors*—we want the child to apply what he knows, feel confident, and maintain momentum. After writing, the child should reread his writing. He may catch his own spelling errors. If not, you might remind your child of any features you've studied. Or you can remind him of similar words that he knows how to spell. For example, if he spells *bike* as BIK, you could remind him that *bike* is spelled the same way as *like,* a word most transitional readers know. Your child's efforts on the spelling assessment and your ongoing word study will serve as a guide to what you can expect your child to handle when he writes.

"How Should I Teach High-Frequency Words?" High-frequency words show up often in reading materials and are needed when we write; however, many are hard to sound out and spell phonetically. By this point children should know how to spell some of these words, such as *of* and *come,* because they've read and written them so frequently. For the high-frequency words your child spells incorrectly, try prompting him with cues to make an analogy to another known word with the same spelling pattern. For example, if he is stuck on *could* but knows *should* or *would,* point out how *could* rhymes with *should* and is spelled the same way. Or remind him of a spelling-meaning connection he has learned. For example, if he is stuck on how to spell *said,* remind him

of the spelling–meaning connections you discussed when examining the present and past tenses of irregular verbs: *pay, paid*; *lay, laid*; and *say, said*.

If these strategies don't work, you may want to write the word for your child to copy or correct on his own paper, but don't overdo this. At this stage, too much time spent on spelling correction may discourage your child from writing or problem solving on her own.

"What If My Child Wants Help with Spelling?" Tell her to say the word and listen for the sounds, and do the best she can. Say you'll check the writing together when she's finished. Just as we want to build independent and confident readers, we want to build independent and confident writers. When you do go over misspelled words later, always begin by pointing out what a child got right, and when possible offer some strategies for figuring out a spelling: "You have the first blend and the final sound in *clown,* but that vowel in the middle is tricky. Do you remember the words *cow* or *now*? That /ow/ sound is spelled with *ow* in *clown* too."

If the child won't continue without getting help with a word, you can offer help—but you can say, "Just this once!" If you remain consistent with telling the child to do her best and assure her you'll check the spelling together when she's finished, she will quickly adopt a more independent attitude. It will help if you are writing at the same time.

"What about Punctuation, Capitalization, and Sentence Structure?" Once your child has finished writing, remind him about common conventions such as capitals, space between words, and ending punctuation if needed. Prompt with questions like "What goes at the end of a sentence?" As a child moves through the transitional stage, attention to these conventions should become more automatic. However, some children will continue to need reminders.

You'll also want to prompt the child if, after he finishes writing and rereading, he doesn't realize he's missed a word or his sentence doesn't make sense. We want the child to attend to sentence structure and meaning, building their awareness of syntax and semantics.

"What If My Child Refuses to Write?" Writing is hard work, and many children are reluctant to write, especially those who also find reading difficult. Deemphasizing spelling and writing conventions will be important for reluctant writers until they develop some confidence. Getting one's idea firmly in place by brainstorming what to write about before trying to write it down may be helpful. Ask your child to tell you what she wants to write, and be ready to repeat it for her as she starts to write. You might want to jot down some keywords to refer to as she writes, or work with her to create a list or a web as preparation for writing. Sometimes, a special pencil, pen, paper, or notebook that is only used during writing can provide an incentive. As the child becomes more confident, your level of support will decrease, and the child can prepare ideas for writing and write more independently. Writing yourself while the child writes can be helpful, too.

"Why Should I Be Writing with My Child While He's Writing?" When you write, you're modeling the writing process—and motivating the child to write. For example, if the

child is reluctant to write down his predictions, you can model the process by writing your own predictions on your own sheet of paper. You might make a game of this, hiding your prediction until your child has written his. You can then compare predictions. You and your child can both read on to see whose prediction was closest (you may want to deliberately make a wrong prediction).

When you plan to share your writing with one another, you're adding an engaging, social aspect to the activity. You are an enthusiastic partner in this reading/writing process, not a taskmaster. While the child reads, you read. While he writes, you write. Together you elevate reading and writing to a shared intellectual and *fun* pursuit!

English Language Learners

English language learners have much to negotiate in the transitional reading stage. The more complex text they are now reading requires them to understand more English vocabulary and sentence structure. Word study, too, has become more complex, introducing more than one pattern to spell sounds. The English learner must now move one step beyond identifying the sound in a word to figure out which pattern to use to spell it. And homophones confuse things further.

English learners in the transitional stage need additional fluency practice; explicit, systematic, and cumulative word study; and extra writing and reading instruction. Wide reading on their level helps English learners with English vocabulary, background knowledge of words and concepts, and familiarity with high-frequency words. Along with wide reading, word study at this stage increases understanding of English words and improves pronunciation.

As was true for English learners at the emergent and beginning reading stages, the Book Buddies framework offers an excellent intervention opportunity for the English learner at the transitional stage. Book Buddies coordinators and tutors must be aware that explicit vocabulary instruction will be necessary not only during reading but also with words used in sorting during word study. The one-on-one nature of the tutorial opens up possibilities for discussion that can engage even a reluctant learner and build confidence.

Remember that English language learners have much to teach us—about their lives, what their parents may read in their native language, and what traditions they may have for communicating in writing. Building an awareness of these cultural differences benefits everyone and allows us to celebrate children's heritage and faith, even though they are different from our own. For more information on word study for English learners, see *Words Their Way with English Learners: Word Study for Phonics, Vocabulary, and Spelling Instruction* (Helman et al., 2012).

Learners with Challenges, Including Dyslexia

It is commonly accepted that learners dealing with reading challenges such as dyslexia require explicit, systematic, cumulative, and multisensory instruction based on diagnostic assessment. The lesson plan for the transitional reader does exactly that. The content of the lesson plan is based on the diagnostic assessment presented in Chapter 3. The tutor's instruction is intentional and explicit. Phonics instruction progresses in a methodical way, with each new skill building on previous skills.

Children see spelling patterns (visual), while simultaneously saying (phonological) and writing them (kinesthetic–tactile), which enhances their memory and learning. For example, children simultaneously see a vowel pattern, say the speech sound it represents, and write it—and vice versa. The hands-on process of categorizing printed words and pictures targeting specific vowel sounds requires students to pay attention to the look and feel of words and their vowel sounds as they pronounce them. They compare and contrast the words and pictures according to the way they sound (phonology) and the way they are spelled (phonics and spelling). They also compare and contrast words by the way they mean (morphology and semantics), and the way they are used in a sentence (syntax).

These aspects of word knowledge are applied in identifying words in context and in isolation in all sections of the lesson plan, and are harnessed in the tutors' efforts to prompt students to decode words they are not sure of. Because Book Buddies lessons are based on diagnosed individual needs, this structured approach is magnified in a one-on-one setting.

Positive Reinforcement

We've said this at the ends of the emergent and beginning reader chapters, and we say it again here: Praise, praise, and more praise is important at every turn in all the Book Buddies lesson plans. Tutors should be instructed to be generous and explicit with specific praise that describes exactly what the student did correctly, such as "That prediction shows good thinking" and "I like how you wrote that without any help." We are building confident readers and writers, and there's no such thing as too much praise.

Best Wishes!

We wish you the best of luck in starting up and moving forward with your Book Buddies program. By recognizing where children are in their literacy abilities and building on what they know in the context of personalized, one-on-one instruction, you are helping to propel them on their journey toward becoming fluent readers and writers. The attention and caring of a special tutor and the student's own burgeoning confidence and motivation complete the formula for success. Have fun!

Appendices

Materials for Coordinators and Tutors

APPENDIX A.1. Emergent Reader Lesson Plan

Student: ______________ Tutor: ______________ Date: __________ Lesson #: _____

Lesson Plan	*Description of Planned Activities*	*Comments*
Rereading and Concept of Word (10–15 minutes)		
Alphabet and Word Study ***Word Bank** ***Letter Recognition** ***Picture Sort/Writing Sort** ***Glue and Label** **Writing** (15–20 minutes)		
Language Play ***Rhyme** ***Syllable Awareness** ***Beginning Sounds** ***Phoneme Awareness** (5–7 minutes)		
New Reading (8–10 minutes)	**Book:** ______________ 1. **Read title to student and look at cover.** 2. **Student makes a prediction.** 3. **Discuss pictures, words, and patterns in the story.** 4. **Read to the student.** 5. **Choral, echo, independent reading.**	
Take-Home Book	**Book:** ______________	

APPENDIX A.2. Beginning Reader Lesson Plan

Student: ____________ Tutor: ____________ Date: ________ Lesson #: ____

Lesson Plan	*Description of Planned Activities*	*Comments*
Rereading (10–12 minutes)		
Word Bank and Word Study (15–20 minutes)	**Word Bank:** **Push It Say It:** **Picture/Word Sort:** **Writing Sort:** **FastRead:**	**Score: ___/___ (# read correctly in 1:00)**
Writing (8–10 minutes)		
New Reading (8–10 minutes)	**Book:** ____________ **1. Read title to student and look at cover.** **2. Student makes a prediction.** **3. Discuss pictures, words, and patterns in the story.** **4. Student reads the book to you.**	
Take-Home Book	**Book:** ____________	

APPENDIX A.3. Transitional Reader Lesson Plan

Student: ______ **Tutor:** ______ **Date:** ______ **Lesson #:** ______		
Lesson Plan	*Description of Planned Activities*	*Comments*
Reading for Fluency (5–10 minutes)		
Word Study (10–15 minutes)	**Picture/Word Sort:** **Writing Sort:** **Word Hunt:**	
Reading and Writing (20–30 minutes)	**Book:** ______ **Before Reading:** **During Reading:** **After Reading:**	
Take-Home Book	**Book:** ______	

APPENDIX B. Sample Permission Letter

Any Elementary School
1600 Washington Street
Yourtown, State

September 1, 20____

Dear ________________________,

Your child, ________________________________, has been selected to receive one-on-one tutoring in reading ______ times a week through the Book Buddies program. Each tutor will work under the direction of ________________________________, the Book Buddies Coordinator, who will work closely with your child's classroom teacher to provide the help your child needs to make good progress in reading. We are very pleased to have this reading tutorial at our school.

We may want to videotape your child working with his or her tutor as a way to train other tutors or to interest people in our program. We also ask that you give us permission to videotape or take a picture of your child.

Once we have received your permission, we will let you know the name of your child's tutor. We encourage you to come and visit a tutoring session any time to observe or to meet your child's tutor.

If you have any questions about the tutoring program, please contact me, *name of the Book Buddies Coordinator (email address)*, or your child's classroom teacher.

Sincerely,

________________________________, Principal

(Contact information)

I give permission for ________________________________ to participate in the Book Buddies reading tutoring program at Any Elementary School. I understand that my child may be photographed or videotaped.

____

Parent or Guardian's Signature

APPENDIX C. Phonics Book Sets

Bob Books
Scholastic Inc.
www.scholastic.com

Dr. Maggie's Phonics Readers
Creative Teaching Press
www.creativeteaching.com

Dr. Seuss: Beginner Books
Penguin Random House
www.penguinrandomhouse.com

Green Light Readers
Houghton Mifflin Harcourt
www.hmhbooks.com

Foundations Word Family Books
McGraw Hill
www.mheducation.com

Reading A-Z
www.readinga-z.com

Ready Readers
Modern Curriculum Press/Pearson Learning
www.teachchildren.com

Real Kids Readers
Lerner Publishing Group
www.lernerbooks.com

Start to Read!
School Zone
www.schoolzone.com

Wonder Books Nonfiction Phonics Readers
Sundance/Newbridge
www.sundancenewbridge.com

APPENDIX D. Leveled List of Trade Books by Individual Authors *(p. 1 of 7)*

Author	Title of Book	Numbered (Reading Recovery) Level
Carle, Eric	*Do You Want to Be My Friend*	1
Hoban, Tana	*Count and See*	1
Hutchins, Pat	*1 Hunter*	1
MacMillan, Bruce	*Growing Colors*	1
Ormerod, Jan	*Sunshine*	1
Wildsmith, Brian	*Applebird*	1
Wildsmith, Brian	*Cat on the Mat*	1
Carle, Eric	*Have You Seen My Cat?*	2
Pienkowsky, Jan	*Colors*	2
Tafuri, Nancy	*Have You Seen My Duckling?*	2
Steptoe, John	*Baby Says*	3
Wildsmith, Brian	*What a Tale*	3
Wildsmith, Brian	*Toot, Toot*	3
Wildsmith, Brian	*All Fall Down*	3
Kalan, Robert	*Rain*	4
Martin, Bill	*Brown Bear, Brown Bear*	4
Mueller, Virginia	*Halloween Mask for Monster*	4
Mueller, Virginia	*Playhouse for Monster*	4
Peek, Merle	*Roll Over*	4
Tafuri, Nancy	*Spots, Feathers, and Curly Tails*	4
Tuchman, G., & Dieterichs, S.	*Swing, Swing, Swing*	4
Williams, Sue	*I Went Walking*	4
Aruego, Jose	*Look What I Can Do*	5
Brown, R., & Carey, S.	*Hide and Seek*	5
Mueller, Virginia	*Monster and the Baby*	5
Wildsmith, Brian	*Animal Shapes*	5
Barton, Byron	*Where's Al?*	6
Carle, Eric	*From Head to Toe*	6
Carter, David	*How Many Bugs in a Box?*	6
Crews, Donald	*School Bus*	6
Ginsburg, Mirra	*The Chick and the Duckling*	6
Jones, Carol	*Old MacDonald Had a Farm*	6
Lindgren, Barbro	*Sam's Ball*	6
Lindgren, Barbro	*Sam's Cookie*	6
Lindgren, Barbro	*Sam's Teddy Bear*	6
Lindgren, Barbro	*Sam's Wagon*	6
Moncure, J.	*Stop! Go! Word Bird*	6
Peek, Merle	*Math Is Everywhere*	6

Author	Title of Book	Numbered (Reading Recovery) Level
Rounds, Glen	*Old MacDonald Had a Farm*	6
Salem, L., & Stewart, J.	*The Cat Who Loved Red*	6
Salem, L., & Stewart, J.	*It's Game Day*	6
Adams, Pam	*There Were Ten in the Bed*	7
Crews, Donald	*Flying*	7
Moncure, J.	*No, No, Word Bird*	7
Poulet, Virginia	*Blue Bug's Book of Colours*	7
Salem, L., & Stewart, J.	*What's for Dinner?*	7
Shaw, Charles	*It Looked Like Spilt Milk*	7
Berenstain, Stan & Jan	*Inside, Outside, Upside Down*	8
Christelow, Eileen	*Five Little Monkeys Jumping On . . .*	8
Cummings, Pat	*Show and Tell*	8
Eastman, P. D.	*Go, Dog, Go!*	8
Hill, Eric	*Where's Spot?*	8
Jonas, Ann	*Where Can It Be?*	8
Kraus, Robert	*Herman the Helper*	8
Langstaff, John	*Oh, A-Hunting We Will Go*	8
Mayer, Mercer	*All By Myself*	8
Perkins, Al	*Ear Book*	8
Perkins, Al	*Nose Book*	8
Adams, Pam	*This Old Man*	9
Asch, Frank	*Just Like Daddy*	9
Campbell, Rod	*Dear Zoo*	9
Galdone, Paul	*Cat Goes Fiddle-i-fee*	9
Henkes, Kevin	*Shhhh*	9
Hutchins, Pat	*Rosie's Walk*	9
Lilgard, D., & Zimmerman, J.	*Frog's Lunch*	9
Medearis, A., & Keeter, S.	*Harry's House*	9
Moncure, J.	*Hide and Seek, Word Bird*	9
Moncure, J.	*Watch Out, Word Bird*	9
Raffi	*Wheels on the Bus*	9
West, Colin	*Pardon?*	9
Westcott, Nadine	*The Lady with the Alligator Purse*	9
Ziefert, Harriet	*Wheels on the Bus*	9
Ziefert, Harriet	*Here Comes the Bus*	9
Brown, Ruth	*Dark, Dark Tale*	10
Gernstein, Nordicai	*Roll Over!*	10
Ginsburg, Mirra	*Across the Stream*	10
Hall, N., & Robinson, A.	*My Holiday Diary*	10
Hurd, Edith Thatcher	*Johnny Lion's Rubber Boots*	10

Author	Title of Book	Numbered (Reading Recovery) Level
Krauss, Ruth	*Is This You?*	10
Moncure, J.	*Word Bird Builds a City*	10
Rockwell, Anne	*Cars*	10
Rockwell, Harlow	*My Kitchen*	10
Salem, L., & Stewart, J.	*Notes from Mom*	10
Seuss, Dr.	*Foot Book*	10
Stadler, John	*Hooray for Snail*	10
Ward, Cindy	*Cookie's Week*	10
Ziefert, Harriet	*Harry Takes a Bath*	10
Ziefert, Harriet	*Thank You, Nicky!*	10
Ahlberg, A., & Ahlberg, J.	*Each Peach Pear Plum*	11
Barton, Byron	*Dinosaurs, Dinosaurs*	11
Dorros, Arthur	*Alligator Shoes*	11
Hill, Eric	*Spot's First Walk*	11
Jonas, Ann	*When You Were a Baby*	11
Mack, Stan	*Ten Bears in My Bed*	11
Mayer, Mercer	*Just for You*	11
Mayer, Mercer	*Just Me and My Babysitter*	11
Minarik, E. H.	*Cat and Dog*	11
Reese, Bob	*Tweedledee, Tumbleweed*	11
Rockwell, Anne	*Boats*	11
Shaw, Nancy	*Sheep in a Jeep*	11
Bonsall, Crosby	*The Day I Had to Play with My Sister*	12
Bonsall, Crosby	*Mine's the Best*	12
Bunting, E., & Sloan-Childers, E.	*Rabbit's Party*	12
Crews, Donald	*Ten Black Dots*	12
Gelman, Rita	*More Spaghetti, I Say!*	11
Gelman, Rita	*Why Can't I Fly?*	12
Hutchins, Pat	*Titch*	12
Keller, Holly	*Ten Sleepy Sheep*	12
Kline, Suzy	*Shine Sun*	12
Krauss, Ruth	*Carrot Seed*	12
Long, Erlene	*Gone Fishing*	12
Shulevitz, Uri	*One Monday Morning*	12
Taylor, Judy	*My Dog*	12
Wescott, Nadine	*Peanut Butter and Jelly*	12
Ziefert, Harriet	*New House for Mole and Mouse*	12
Ziefert, Harriet	*Nicky Upstairs and Downstairs*	12
Barton, Byron	*Buzz, Buzz, Buzz*	13
Berenstain, Stan & Jan	*Old Hat, New Hat*	13

Author	Title of Book	Numbered (Reading Recovery) Level
Jonas, Ann	*Two Bear Cubs*	13
Joyce, William	*George Shrinks*	13
Kraus, Robert	*Whose Mouse Are You?*	13
Reese, Bob	*Rapid Robert, Road Runner*	13
Rockwell, Anne	*Tool Box*	13
Sendak, Maurice	*Seven Little Monsters*	13
Ziefert, Harriet	*No Ball Games Here*	13
Adams, Pam	*There Was an Old Lady*	14
Aliki	*We Are Best Friends*	14
Barchas, Sarah	*I Was Walking Down the Road*	14
Barton, Byron	*Building a House*	14
Brown, Margaret Wise	*Goodnight Moon*	14
Butler, Dorothy	*My Brown Bear Barney*	14
Hutchins, Pat	*You'll Soon Grow into Them, Titch*	14
Hutchins, Pat	*What Game Shall We Play?*	14
Johnson, Crockett	*Picture for Harold's Room*	14
Kraus, Robert	*Come Out and Play, Little Mouse*	14
Kraus, Robert	*Where Are You Going, Little Mouse?*	14
Seuling, Barbara	*Teeny, Tiny Woman*	14
Taylor, Judy	*My Cat*	14
Wildsmith, Brian	*Animal Tricks*	14
Ziefert, Harriet	*Clean House for Mole and Mouse*	14
Barton, Bryon	*Airport*	15
Brown, Marc	*Spooky Riddles*	15
Cebulash, M., & Ford, G.	*Willie's Wonderful Pet*	15
Eastman, P. D.	*Are You My Mother?*	15
Eastman, P. D.	*Big Dog, Little Dog*	15
Fox, Mem	*Hattie and the Fox*	15
Gibson, A., & Meyer, K.	*Nana's Place*	15
Hayes, Sara, & Craig, H.	*This Is the Bear*	15
Jonas, Ann	*Reflections*	15
Mayer, Mercer	*Just a Mess*	15
Mayer, Mercer	*Just Grandma and Me*	15
McPhail, David	*Fix-it*	15
Nodset, Joan	*Who Took the Farmer's Hat?*	15
Rosen, Michael	*We're Going on a Bear Hunt*	15
Sendak, Maurice	*Alligators All Around*	15
Seuss, Dr.	*Great Day for Up*	15
Seuss, Dr.	*Hop on Pop*	15
Seuss, Dr.	*I Can Read with My Eyes Shut*	15

Author	Title of Book	Numbered (Reading Recovery) Level
Wood, Don, & Wood, Audrey	*The Napping House*	15
Wood, Don, & Wood, Audrey	*The Little Mouse, the Red Ripe Strawberry and the Big Hungry Bear*	15
Bennett, Jill	*Teeny Tiny*	16
Berenstain, Stan, & Berenstain, Jan	*Bike Lesson*	16
Brown, Marcia	*Three Billy Goats Gruff*	16
Carle, Eric	*The Very Busy Spider*	16
Cook, Barnadine	*The Little Fish That Got Away*	16
Freeman, Don	*Rainbow of My Own*	16
Galdone, Paul	*Little Yellow Chicken*	16
Galdone, Paul	*Henny Penny*	16
Heilbroner, Joan	*Robert the Rose Horse*	16
Hill, Eric	*Spot's Birthday*	16
Hoff, Syd	*Albert the Albatross*	16
Hutchins, Pat	*Happy Birthday Sam*	16
Hutchins, Pat	*Tidy Titch*	16
Hutchins, Pat	*Goodnight Owl*	16
Jonas, Ann	*The Quilt*	16
Jonas, Ann	*Triceratops on the Farm*	16
Kent, Jack	*Fat and Thin*	16
Kovalski, Mary Ann	*Wheels on the Bus*	16
Kraus, Robert	*Leo the Late Bloomer*	16
Mayer, Mercer	*Just Me and My Dad*	16
Mayer, Mercer	*Just Me and My Puppy*	16
Mayer, Mercer	*There's a Nightmare in My Closet*	16
McLeod, Emilie	*Bears' Bicycle*	16
Rockwell, Anne	*Trucks*	16
Wells, Rosemary	*Noisy Nora*	16
Wood, Don, & Wood, Audrey	*The Big Kick*	16
Ahlberg, A., & Ahlberg, J.	*Funny Bones*	17
Asch, Frank	*The Lost Puppy*	17
Bonsall, Crosby	*And I Mean It, Stanley*	17
Bornstein, Ruth	*Little Gorilla*	17
Flack, Marjorie	*Ask Mr. Bear*	17
Galdone, Paul	*Three Billy Goats Gruff*	17
Hoff, Syd	*Horse in Harry's Room*	17
Hurd, Edith Thatcher	*Johnny Lion's Book*	17
Hutchins, Pat	*The Doorbell Rang*	17
Hutchins, Pat	*Clocks and More Clocks*	17

APPENDIX D. Leveled List of Trade Books by Individual Authors *(p. 6 of 7)*

Author	Title of Book	Numbered (Reading Recovery) Level
Isadora, Rachel	*Max*	17
Johnson, Crockett	*Harold and the Purple Crayon*	17
Kraus, Robert	*Milton the Early Riser*	17
LeSeig, Theo	*Ten Apples Up on Top*	17
Mayer, Mercer	*There's an Alligator under My Bed*	17
McGovern, Ann	*Stone Soup*	17
Parkinson, Kathy	*Farmer in the Dell*	17
Perkins, Al	*Hand, Hand, Fingers, Thumb*	17
Roy, Ron	*Three Ducks Went Wandering*	17
Udry, Janice May	*Let's Be Enemies*	17
Alexander, Martha	*Blackboard Bear*	18
Asch, Frank	*Bear Shadow*	18
Bridwell, Norman	*Clifford the Big Red Dog*	18
Carle, Eric	*The Very Hungry Caterpillar*	18
Degen, Bruce	*Jamberry*	18
DePaola, Tomie	*Charlie Needs a Cloak*	18
Eastman, P. D.	*Sam and the Firefly*	18
Eastman, P. D.	*Best Nest*	18
Emberly, Barbara, & Emberly, Ed	*Drummer Hoff*	18
Farley, Walter	*Little Black, a Pony*	18
Keats, Ezra Jack	*The Snowy Day*	18
Lear, Edward	*Owl and the Pussycat*	18
Lionni, Leo	*Little Blue and Little Yellow*	18
Littledale, Freya	*The Boy Who Cried Wolf*	18
Lobel, Arnold	*Owl at Home*	18
Mayer, Mercer	*I Was So Mad*	18
Nims, Bonnie	*Where Is the Bear?*	18
Numeroff, L. J.	*If You Give a Mouse a Cookie*	18
Preller, J., & Scherer, J.	*Wake Me in Spring!*	18
Seuss, Dr.	*Cat in the Hat*	18
Wallner, John	*City Mouse—Country Mouse*	18
Bogart, J., & Wilson, J.	*Daniel's Dog*	19
Bonsall, Crosby	*Piggle*	19
Burningham, John	*Mr. Gumpy's Outing*	19
Byars, Betsy	*The Golly Sisters Go West*	19
Cole, Joanna	*Bony-Legs*	19
Cronin, Doreen	*Giggle, Giggle, Quack*	19
Elkin, Benjamin	*Six Foolish Fishermen*	19
Hutchins, Pat	*Don't Forget the Bacon*	19

Author	Title of Book	Numbered (Reading Recovery) Level
Hutchins, Pat	*Surprise Party*	19
Slobodkina, Esphyr	*Caps for Sale*	19
Stevens, Janet	*Three Billy Goats Gruff*	19
Zolotow, Charlotte	*I Know a Lady*	19
Allen, Pamela	*Who Sank the Boat?*	20
Asch, Frank	*Happy Birthday, Moon*	20
Cole, Joanna	*Hungry, Hungry Sharks*	20
DePaola, Tomie	*The Art Lesson*	20
Galdone, Paul	*The Gingerbread Boy*	20
Galdone, Paul	*Three Little Pigs*	20
Hall, N., & Robinson, A.	*What a Funny Thing to Do*	20
Hurd, Edith Thatcher	*Stop, Stop*	20
Hutchins, Pat	*The Wind Blew*	20
Keats, Ezra Jack	*Whistle for Willie*	20
Lewis, Thomas P.	*Hill of Fire*	20
Littledale, Freya	*Magic Fish*	20
Bloom, Judy	*Freckle Juice*	21
Davidson, Margaret	*Five True Dog Stories*	21
Gibbons, Gail	*Dogs*	21
Giff, Patricia Reilly	*Fish Face*	21
Henkes, Kevin	*Chrysanthemum*	21
Jordan, Deloris	*Dream Big: Michael Jordan and the Pursuit of Excellence*	21
Lobel, Arnold	*Uncle Elephant*	21
Monjo, F. N.	*The Drinking Gourd*	21
Richardson, Charisse K.	*The Real Slam Dunk*	21
Sendak, Maurice	*Chicken Soup with Rice*	21
Soto, Gary	*Too Many Tamales*	21
Viorst, Judith	*Alexander and the Terrible, Horrible, No Good, Very Bad Day*	21
Aardema, Verna	*Why Mosquitoes Buzz in People's Ears: A West African Tale*	22
Bulla, Clyde Robert	*The Chalk Box Kid*	22
Bulla, Clyde Robert	*Shoeshine Girl*	22
Cannon, Janell	*Stellaluna*	22
Dahl, Roald	*The Magic Finger*	22
Henkes, Kevin	*Lilly's Purple Plastic Purse*	22
Polacco, Patricia	*Chicken Sunday*	22
Steptoe, John	*Mufaro's Beautiful Daughters*	22

APPENDIX E. Controlled Literature for Transitional Readers by Series *(p. 1 of 2)*

Trade Series by Individual Authors

Series	Author
Amanda Pig/Oliver Pig	Jean Van Leeuwen
Amber Brown	Paula Danziger
Amelia Bedelia	Peggy Parish
Arthur	Marc Brown
Ballpark Mysteries	David A. Kelly
The Black Lagoon	Mike Thaler
Cam Jansen/Young Cam Jansen	David Adler
The Chicken Squad	Doreen Cronin
The Critter Club	Callie Barkley
Commander Toad	Jane Yolen
Danny and the Dinosaur	Syd Hoff
Dragon	Dav Pilkey
Fly Guy	Tedd Arnold
Fox	Edward Marshall and James Marshall
Frog and Toad	Arnold Lobel
Galaxy Zack	Ray O'Ryan
George and Martha	James Marshall
Heidi Heckelbeck	Wanda Coven
Henry and Mudge	Cynthia Rylant
Ivy and Bean	Annie Barrows
Julian	Ann Cameron
Junie B. Jones	Barbara Park
Keena Ford	Melissa Thomson
Little Bear	Else Holmelund Minarik
Magic Treehouse	Mary Pope Osborne
Miss Nelson	Harry Allard
Mouse Tales	Arnold Lobel
Mr. Putter and Tabby	Cynthia Rylant
Nate the Great	Marjorie Weinman Sharmat
Pets to the Rescue	Andrew Clements
Pinky and Rex	James Howe
Princess in Black	Shannon Hale & Dean Hale
Ruby and the Booker Boys	Derrick Barnes

Leveled Trade Series: Fiction and Nonfiction

Discovery Links Science & Social Studies, Early Science
Sundance/Newbridge
www.sundancenewbridge.com

DK Readers
Penguin Random House
www.penguinrandomhouse.com

Hello Reader
Scholastic Inc.
www.scholastic.com

I Can Read!
HarperCollins
www.harpercollins.com

Just for You!
Scholastic Inc.
www.scholastic.com

Let's-Read-and-Find-Out Science
HarperCollins
www.harpercollins.com

National Geographic Kids Readers
Scholastic Inc.
www.scholastic.com

National Geographic Windows on Literacy
National Geographic
https://ngl.cengage.com

Penguin Young Readers
Penguin Random House
www.penguinrandomhouse.com

Reading Safari Magazine
Mondo Publishing
www.mondopub.com
(nonfiction, fiction, poetry, plays)

Ready-to-Read
Simon & Schuster
www.readytoread.com

Rigby PM Photo Stories/Rigby PM Plus Starters
Houghton Mifflin Harcourt
www.hmhco.com

Scholastic Reader and Scholastic News Nonfiction Reader
Scholastic Inc.
www.scholastic.com

Step Into Reading
Penguin Random House
www.penguinrandomhouse.com

TIME for Kids (books)
HarperCollins
www.harpercollins.com

TWiG Books
McGraw Hill
www.mheducation.com

Wonder Books Nonfiction Readers
Sundance/Newbridge
www.sundancenewbridge.com

APPENDIX F. Alphabetized Word-Bank List

A	F	M	S
	G		
B		N	T
	H		
		O	
C			U
	I	P	
			V
			W
	J		
D			
	K	Q	
	L	R	X
			Y
E			
			Z

APPENDIX G. Template for Word Cards

APPENDIX H. Common Word Families

Short *a* (and *-all* and *-ar*)

-AT: bat, cat, fat, hat, mat, pat, rat, sat, that, flat, brat, chat
-AN: can, fan, man, pan, ran, tan, van, plan, than
-ACK: back, pack, jack, rack, sack, tack, black, quack, crack, track, shack, snack, stack
-AB: cab, dab, jab, nab, lab, tab, blab, crab, scab, stab, grab
-AD: bad, dad, had, mad, pad, sad, rad, glad
-AG: bag, rag, sag, wag, nag, flag, brag, drag, shag, snag
-AM: am, dam, ham, ram, jam, clam, slam, cram, wham, swam
-AP: cap, lap, map, nap, rap, tap, zap, clap, flap, slap, trap, chap, snap
-ASH: bash, cash, dash, hash, mash, rash, sash, flash, trash, crash, smash
-AND: band, hand, land, sand, brand, grand, stand
-ANK: bank, sank, tank, yank, blank, plank, crank, drank, prank, spank, thank
-ALL: ball, call, fall, hall, mall, tall, wall, small, stall
-ANG: bang, fang, hang, sang, rang, clang
-AR: bar, car, far, jar, par, star
-ART: art, cart, dart, mart, part, tart, start, chart, smart

Short *i*

-IT: bit, kit, fit, hit, lit, pit, sit, quit, skit, spit
-IG: big, dig, fig, pig, rig, wig, zig
-ILL: bill, dill, fill, hill, kill, mill, pill, will, drill, grill, chill, skill, spill, still
-IN: bin, fin, pin, tin, win, grin, thin, twin, chin, shin, skin, spin
-ICK: lick, kick, pick, sick, tick, click, slick, quick, trick, chick, flick, brick, stick, thick
-IP: dip, hip, lip, nip, rip, sip, tip, zip, whip, flip, slip, skip, drip, trip, chip, ship,
-INK: ink, link, mink, pink, sink, rink, wink, blink, drink, stink, think
-ING: king, sing, ring, wing, sling, bring, sting, swing, thing

Short *o*

-OT: cot, dot, got, hot, jot, lot, not, pot, rot, blot, slot, plot, shot, spot
-OG: dog, bog, fog, hog, jog, log, clog, frog
-OCK: dock, lock, rock, sock, tock, block, clock, flock, smock, shock
-OB: cob, job, rob, gob, mob, sob, snob, blob, glob
-OP: cop, hop, pop, mop, top, clop, flop, slop, drop, chop, shop, stop

Short *e*

-ET: bet, get, jet, let, met, net, pet, set, wet, vet, fret
-EN: den, hen, men, ten, pen, then, when
-ED: bed, fed, led, red, wed, bled, fled, sled, shed
-ELL: bell, fell, jell, sell, tell, well, shell, smell, spell
-EG: beg, peg, leg, keg
-ECK: deck, neck, peck, wreck, speck, check

Short *u*

-UT: but, cut, gut, hut, nut, rut, shut
-UB: cub, sub, rub, tub, club, grub, snub, stub
-UG: bug, dug, hug, jug, mug, rug, tug, slug, plug, drug, snug
-UCK: buck, duck, luck, suck, tuck, yuck, pluck, cluck, truck, stuck
-UFF: buff, cuff, huff, muff, puff, fluff
-UM: bum, gum, hum, drum, plum, slum, glum, scum, chum
-UN: bun, fun, gun, run, sun, spun, stun
-UP: up, cup, pup
-UMP: bump, jump, dump, hump, lump, pump, rump, plump, stump, thump

APPENDIX I. Letter Cards *(p. 1 of 3)*

a	b	c	d	e	f
g	h	j	k	l	m
n	o	p	q	r	s
t	u	v	w	x	y
z	a	e	i	o	u

sh	ch	wh	th	ck
sn	sp	sm	sw	st

qu	bl	cl	fl	sl
gl	pl	br	cr	dr
fr	gr	pr	tr	at
am	ab	ad	ag	an
ap	it	ig	in	id
ip	ot	og	ob	op
et	en	ed	eg	ut

ub	ug	um	un	up

ack	ick	ock	uck
eck	ink	ank	unk
ang	ing	ung	ong
all	ill	ell	and
ump	ish	ush	ash
ast	est	ust	uff

APPENDIX J. Book Buddies Book List

For ____

Date	Title	# Times Read	Text Copy?

APPENDIX K. Small Alphabet Chart and Consonant Sound Chart

Aa Bb Cc Dd Ee Ff Gg Hh Ii Jj
Kk Ll Mm Nn Oo Pp Qq Rr Ss
Tt Uu Vv Ww Xx Yy Zz

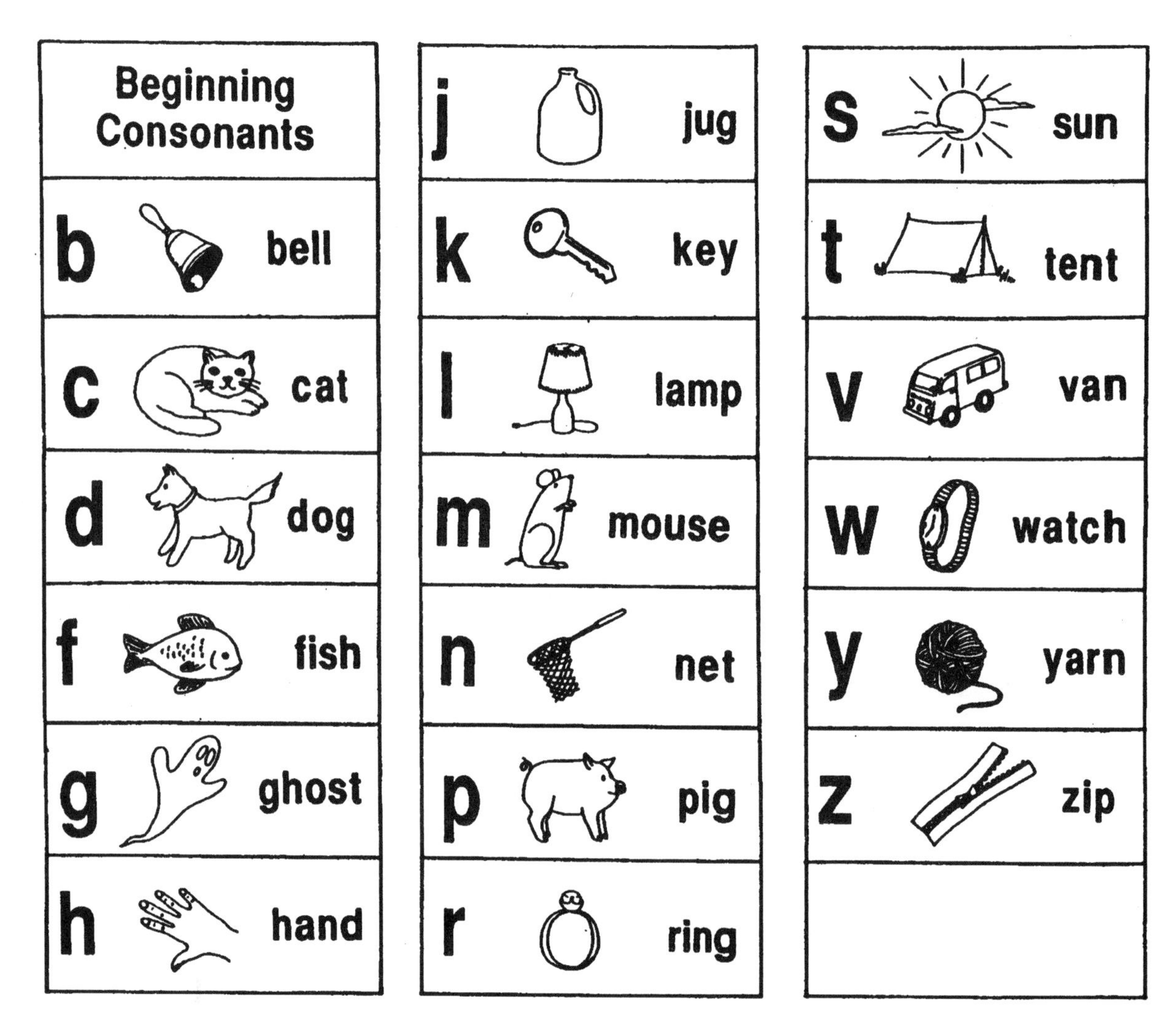

APPENDIX L. Sound Chart for Blends and Digraphs

Beginning Blends and Digraphs	br  broom	sc  scooter
bl  block	cr  crab	sk  skate
cl  cloud	dr  drum	sm  smile
fl  flag	fr  frog	sn  snail
gl  glasses	gr  grapes	sp  spider
sl  slide	pr  present	st  star
pl 2+1=3 plus	tr  tree	sw  swing
tw  twins	ch  chair	th  thumb
qu  quilt	sh  shovel	wh  wheel

APPENDIX M. Handwriting Chart for Lowercase Letters

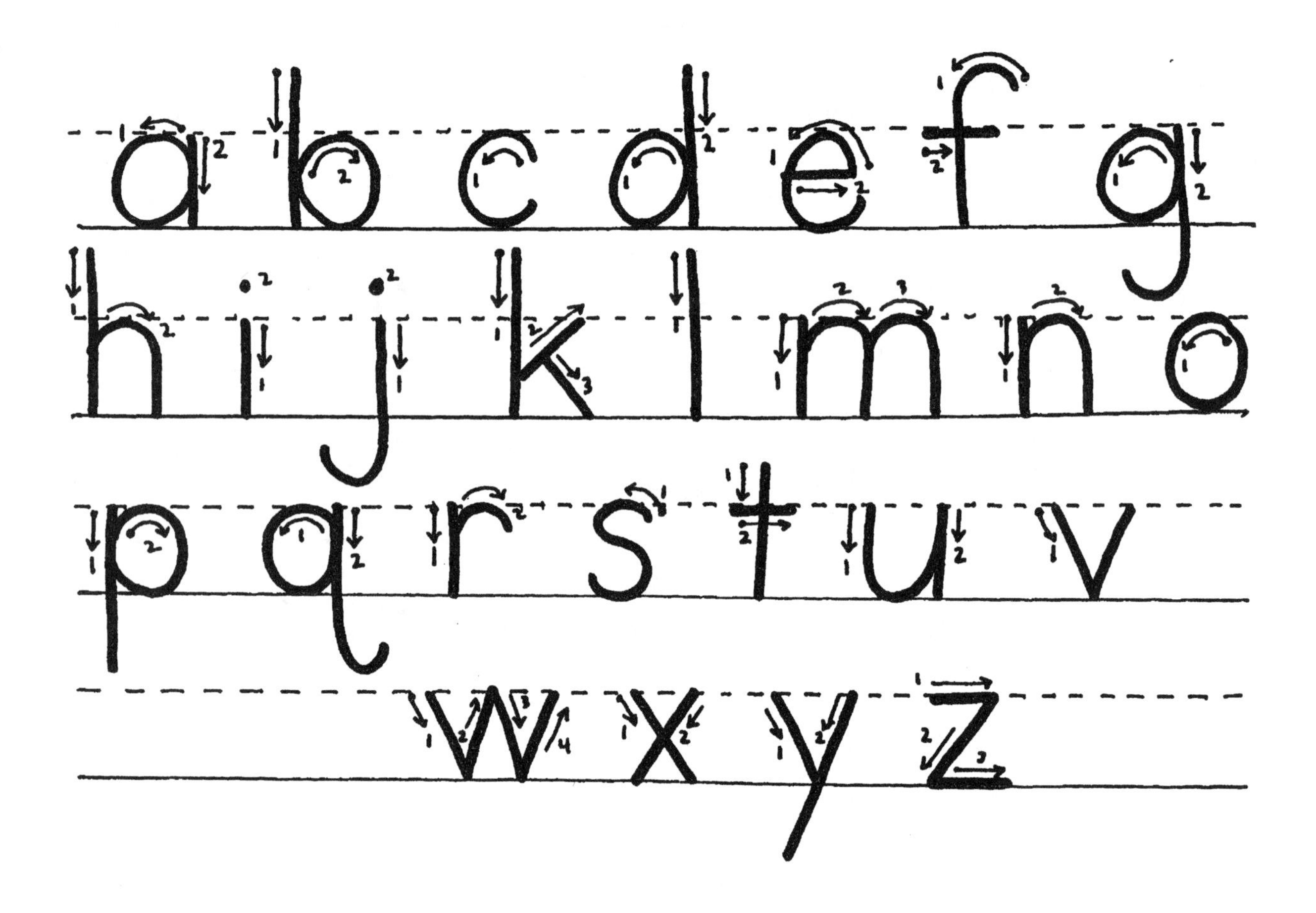

APPENDIX N. Book Buddies Take-Home Sheet

Rereading familiar books builds your child's confidence and knowledge of words. Please help your child become a better reader by listening to the enclosed book. Then please sign the form and return the book to school. Thanks for your support!

Name: ______________________________

Title of book	Date sent home	Parent/guardian signature

APPENDIX O. Alphabet Chart with Lions

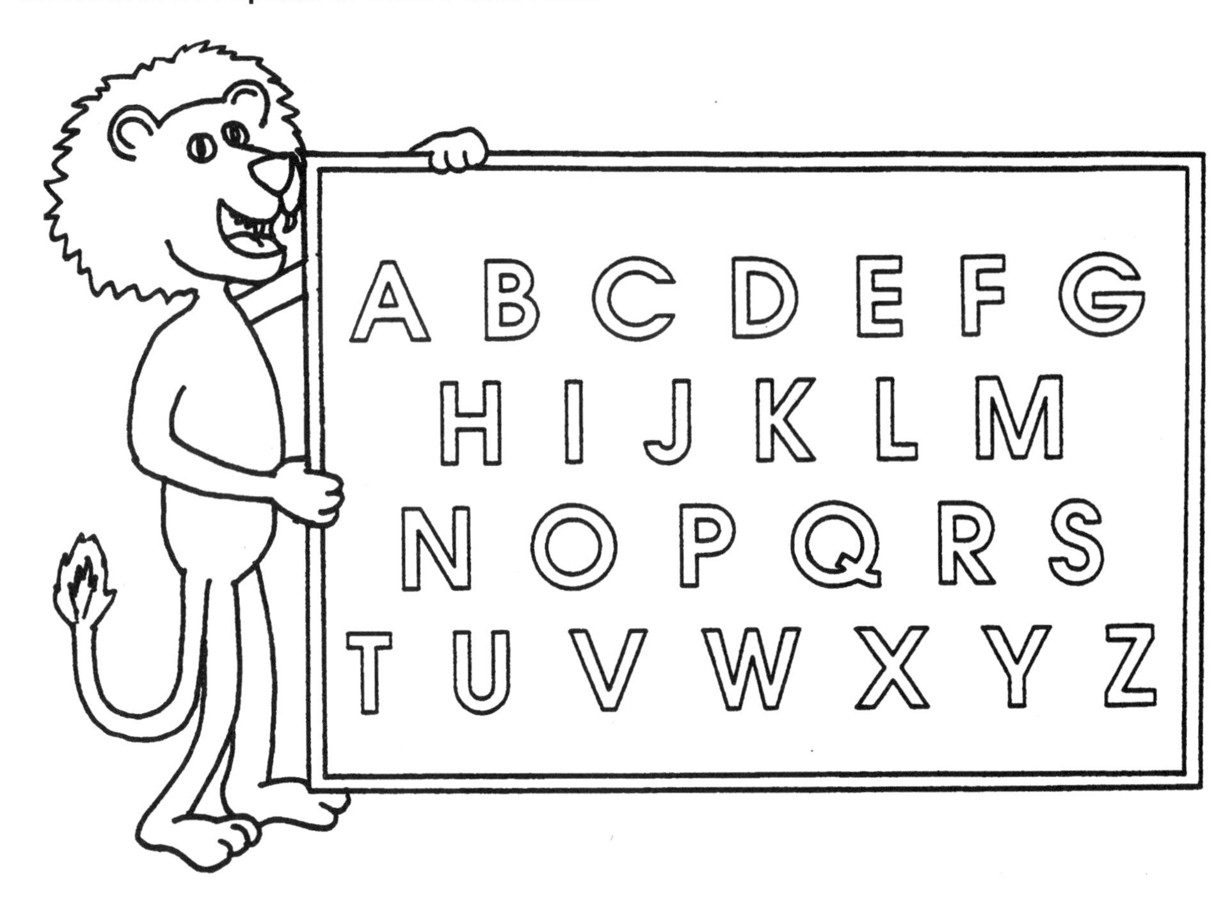

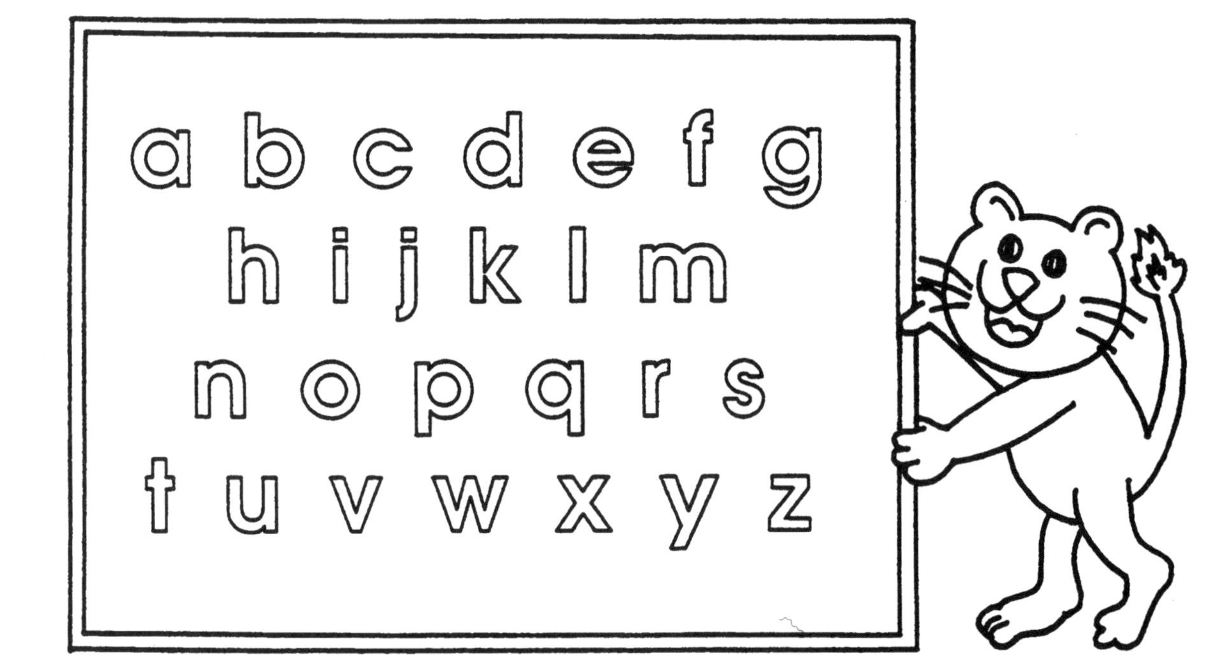

APPENDIX P. Suggested Word Study Sequence

The following is an approximate order of the sounds and patterns your child will learn this year. I will check off the sounds as they are introduced. Please hold your child accountable for the *introduced* sounds whenever you are spelling and writing.

Beginning Sounds m s b r t g n p c h f d l k j w y z v sh th ch a o e u i

Beginning Digraphs (2 letters that make 1 sound)—*pictures only* ch sh th
Beginning Blends—*pictures only* (3 types: *S*, *L*, and *R* blends) st sn sm sk bl br

Word Families (CVC)	it in ip ig ill ick	un ug um ut ud
at an ad ap ag ack	op ot og ock	et ed en eg ell

Beginning Digraphs ch sh th wh	**Beginning *s*-Blends** st sp sn sm sk sl sc sw

Short Vowels in Mixed-Vowel Word Families (with digraphs and blends) o/u/a/e/i words

Beginning *l*-Blends bl gl pl cl fl	**Beginning *r*-Blends** fr gr br cr pr tr dr

Short Vowels Outside Word Families (with digraphs and blends) o/u/a/e/i	**Affricates (type of speech sound)** dr j tr ch

---Cut here---

APPENDIX P. Suggested Word Study Sequence

The following is an approximate order of the sounds and patterns your child will learn this year. I will check off the sounds as they are introduced. Please hold your child accountable for the *introduced* sounds whenever you are spelling and writing.

Final Digraphs and Blends -ch -sh -th -st -sk -ft -lt	***r*-Influenced Vowels** Short *a* vs. *ar* Short *o* vs. *or*

Preconsonantal Nasals ing ang ong ung ink ank unk amp ump end and ent

Short and Long Vowels (CVCe)	o, o_e u, u_e e, ee (CVVC)
a, a_e i, i_e	CVC vs. VCe review across vowels

Final *k* -ck -ke -k

Short, Long, and *r*-Influenced Vowel Sounds and Patterns (CVVC, other)		
a, a_e, ai, ay	u, u_e, ui, oo	i, i_e, igh, -y
o, o_e, oa	e, ee, ea, short ea	Review patterns across vowels

ar, are, air	or, ore, oar	ur, ure
ir, ire	er, ear, eer	

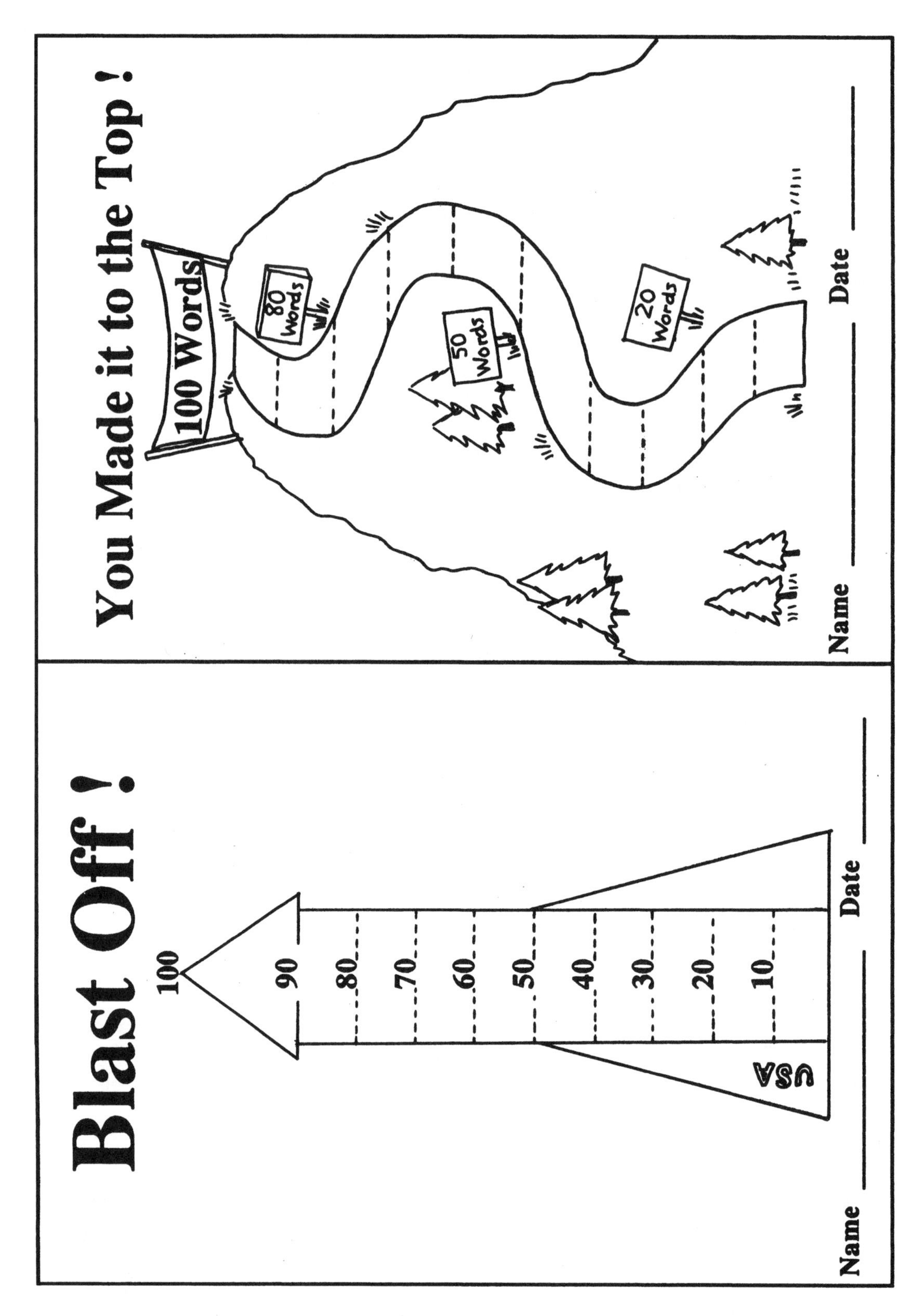
You Made it to the Top !
100 Words
80 Words
50 Words
20 Words
Name
Date
Blast Off !
100
90
80
70
60
50
40
30
20
10
USA
Name
Date

APPENDIX R. Timed Repeated Reading Charts

Words	Seconds				WPM
130					
120					
110					
100					
90					
80					
70					
60					
50					
40					
30					
20					
Errors					
Trials	1	2	3	4	5

Title ____________________

Words	Seconds				WPM
130					
120					
110					
100					
90					
80					
70					
60					
50					
40					
30					
20					
Errors					
Trials	1	2	3	4	5

Title ____________________

FastRead

at	an	ap
__at cat	__an pan	__ap map

cap	sat	man
fan	pat	rap
bat	nap	ran
fat	can	tap
pan	lap	rat

FastRead

ig	it	ip
__ig pig	__it sit	__ip lip

pit	big	sip
wig	dip	hit
dig	kit	tip
rip	fit	pig
hip	jig	bit

FastRead

ch	sh	th
 ch__ chip	 sh__ shell	 th__ think

shed	chop	thin
chick	that	ship
this	chug	shop
shell	chat	them
chill	shut	chin

FastRead

ot	ut	et
__ot pot	__ut nut	__et net

spot	let	but
cut	hot	met
set	shut	rut
not	pet	slot
wet	hut	got

FastRead

gr	br	fr	cr
gr- grill	br- brush	fr- frog	cr- crab

brick	frill	crush	grab
crack	grip	brim	frog
grim	fresh	crop	brush
brat	grill	crab	frill

FastRead

short *a*   short *i*   short *o*

short *a*	short *i*	short *o*

short *a* cat	short *i* pig	short *o* pot

stop   grab   trip   slim

flock   ship   brag   twig

crab   chick   blot   flap

frog   skip   clock   that

FastRead

short *e*	short *o*	short *u*

short *e* bed	short *o* pot	short *u* bug

stop	sled	tub	crush
clock	plug	shop	then
fresh	trot	stuck	bet
drum	step	frog	check

FastRead

short *i* short *e*

stem net drip sled

shell thick chip vet

slim crib check flip

web skip step click

FastRead

tr	ch
tr__ trash	ch__ chin

trap	chip	check	trot
chat	track	chum	trip
chest	trick	trim	chick
chop	trash	chill	truck

FastRead

short *a*	ar	short *o*	or
			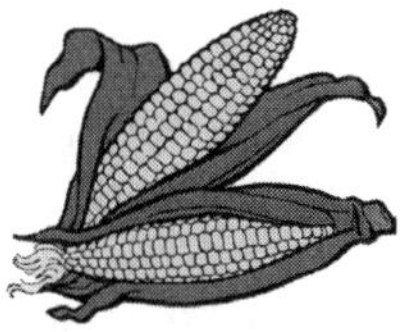
short *a* cat	__ar car	short *o* pot	__or corn

clap	star	job	port
smart	for	black	lost
grasp	flop	harm	born
harsh	cord	task	crop

FastRead

ank	ink	unk
 __ank tank	 __ink sink	 __unk skunk

yank	wink	dunk	pink
clunk	link	sank	bunk
blank	stink	trunk	plank
chunk	think	hunk	drank

APPENDIX T. Video Companion Materials for Tutor Training *(p. 1 of 11)*

The online videos accompanying this book present two Book Buddies lessons in action—one for a beginning reader and one for a late beginning reader. The materials in this appendix are meant to be used along with the videos for training tutors. Book Buddies coordinators should also find them valuable, together with the videos, for extending their own familiarity with the Book Buddies lesson. Purchasers of this book can access the two video lessons online, one for Beginning Readers and one for Late Beginning Readers (for more information on where to find the video lessons, see the box at the end of the table of contents).

For each of the two video lessons we offer background notes on the lesson plan so coordinators will understand the basis for the instructional choices. We suggest the lesson plans, provided with blank tutor comment boxes, be reproduced for the trainees so they can follow along as they view the lessons and add comments *they* would write if they were the tutor. We've also included for each video lesson a list of tutor behaviors to note. These should benefit coordinators as they prepare for group training. Before viewing a lesson, coordinators can ask the trainees to watch out for things the tutor does to engage, instruct, and support her or his Book Buddy, which should lead to productive discussion after viewing. Following discussion, the "Notes on Tutor Behaviors: What to Look For" might be handed out to tutors for review.

Enjoy!

Video: Beginning Reader Lesson—Minuette and Ms. Flory

Background Notes on the Lesson Plan

Minuette's reading level is numbered (Reading Recovery) level 7, or lettered (Guided Reading) level E. She has been studying short *o* word families.

Rereading

- The book *Little Green Frog*, targeting short *o* word families, has been read over several previous lessons. Minuette is now ready for the text-only copy. A word hunt for *op* and *og* words follows immediately. The book will now be retired from the box.
- *Who Can Be a Friend?* is a book introduced in a previous lesson.
- *My Clock Is Sick*, targeting the *ock* word family, was introduced in the previous lesson.
- "Chili in a Pot" is a new poem for Minuette, featuring the *ot* word family. It not only offers practice with expression, pacing, and accurate reading, but supports her current phonics instruction.

Word Bank and Word Study

- **Word bank**—Word cards from *Little Green Frog* are presented.
- **Push It Say It**—The word family *ock* was introduced in the previous lesson. Today's activity focuses on the families *ock* and the previously introduced *og*. In the last lesson Minuette had trouble discriminating between the ending sounds of the two families, so this is a perfect Push It Say It activity for her today. Both families are included in the sort that follows.
- **Picture/word sort**—Minuette has worked on *op*, *ot*, and *og* over previous lessons. In her last lesson, she sorted words and pictures with the families *ot*, *og*, and the newly introduced *ock*. Because she struggled with *og* versus *ock*, she is repeating the sort today. Although her coordinator could have had Minuette sort *op* as well, the coordinator felt three categories were enough for Minuette at this time.
- **Writing sort**—Words from the picture/word sort are called out.
- **FastRead**—This FastRead sheet offers practice to increase automaticity with previously studied short *a* and short *i* word families. This is the first time Minuette has read this particular sheet, so the tutor will model it.

Writing

The dictated sentence, which includes the short *o* word families Minuette is studying, offers an opportunity for her to apply her learning.

New Reading

The book *Polly's Shop* is on Minuette's reading level. It was chosen for its level and its featuring of short *o* words, again allowing Minuette to apply what she's learned.

Student: *Minuette* **Tutor:** *Ms. Flory* **Date:** *12/3* **Lesson #:** *14*

Lesson Plan	*Description of Planned Activities*	*Comments*
Rereading (10–12 minutes)	• *Little Green Frog — text copy* *1) read* *2) highlight -og words* *3) underline -op words* *(Highlight while saying words aloud)* • *Who Can Be a Friend?* • *My Clock Is Sick* • *"Chili in a Pot" poem 1) Model 2) Choral read 3) M. reads*	
Word Bank and Word Study (15–20 minutes)	**Word Bank:** *Add words from Little Green Frog* **Push It Say It:** *#32 Make these words: d-og, d-ock, l-ock, l-og, cl-og, cl-ock* **Picture/Word Sort:** *-ot, -og, -ock* **Writing Sort:** *Call out 2-3 words for each header: -ot, -og, -ock* **FastRead:** *Word Families #5 1) Model 2) Time for 1:00*	
Writing (8–10 minutes)	*Dictate this sentence:* *Minuette and the frog can hop on the hot rock.*	
New Reading (8–10 minutes)	**Book:** *Polly's Shop* **1. Read title to student and look at cover.** **2. Student makes a prediction.** **3. Discuss pictures, words, and patterns in the story.** **4. Student reads the book to you.** *Read 2x if time*	
Take-Home Book	**Book:**	

Video: Beginning Reader Lesson—Minuette and Ms. Flory

Notes on Tutor Behaviors: What to Look For

Throughout the lesson, notice the praise and encouragement the tutor gives to her student.

Rereading

Ms. Flory reminds Minuette to point to each word as she reads. As a beginning reader, Minuette needs this support.

- *Little Green Frog* text copy—Ms. Flory tells Minuette to say each word as she highlights it. By doing this, Minuette must read the word instead of simply looking for the word family, reinforcing the sound–print connection and supporting automatic word recognition.
- Ms. Flory gives Minuette her choice between the two books to read next.
- *My Clock Is Sick*—When Minuette mixes up *tick* and *tock,* and doesn't self-correct, Ms. Flory points to the first word and says, "Look carefully at your vowel. Look at this word." Minuette rereads the sentence, correcting herself. After Minuette has finished reading the book, successfully reading *tick* and *tock* on another page, Ms. Flory reinforces that word recognition by saying, "I like the way you paid attention to the vowels on that second page with *tock* and *tick.*"
- *Who Can Be a Friend?*—When Minuette struggles with the word *send,* Ms. Flory does nothing. When she reads the word incorrectly and is about to continue without self-correcting, Ms. Flory points to the word, says, "Sound this word out," and allows her to fix the error herself. Ms. Flory then has Minuette reread the sentence.
- "Chili in a Pot"—Ms. Flory explains that they're going to read a poem and the procedure they'll follow. She introduces the poem by reading the title and discussing the subject, sparking Minuette's interest. She models a fluent reading of the poem, pointing to each word. Note that she has slowed her pace a bit for this first reading to support the beginning reader. Next Ms. Flory supports Minuette in a choral reading. Finally, Minuette reads the poem alone.

Word Bank and Word Study

- **Word bank**—Ms. Flory keeps in a pile the words Minuette identifies automatically and will deal with these after the lesson.
- **Push It Say It**—Ms. Flory introduces the word-family letter tiles and has Minuette identify the sounds of the onset tiles, supporting her with *cl.*
  - Ms. Flory makes sure Minuette matches her pronunciation of each tile with her manipulation of it, so she is aware of the segmentation of the word before she blends the chunks.
  - Ms. Flory takes the time to make sure Minuette identifies the blend *cl*. To further reinforce this, she could have brought out the previously read *My Clock Is Sick* and connected the *cl* to the word *clock* in the text.
- **Picture/word sort**—Ms. Flory establishes the headers before beginning and asks Minuette what's the same about each (short *o*). She reviews the sound /k/ in *ock* and the use of *ck* to make the /k/ sound immediately following a short vowel.

- Ms. Flory has Minuette sort the pictures first. Some coordinators like to start a sort in this manner to reinforce the sound–letter relationship. Others mix up the words and pictures.
- Usually the tutor should allow the student to finish the sort and catch any errors herself as she checks each column. However, when Minuette sorts the picture of a sock beneath the header *og*, it is the first card she has placed under the header (and is, in fact, the very first card to be sorted). Ms. Flory knows Minuette struggled in the last lesson with discriminating between the ending sounds in *ock* and *og*, and that in making this error at the beginning she will probably be thrown off completely. Therefore, Ms. Flory immediately asks Minuette, "You have *sock*; what family does *sock* belong to?" Minuette says the name of the family and, recognizing her error, moves the picture to the correct column. Ms. Flory then has Minuette state what family *sock* goes with.
- Ms. Flory sees that Minuette needs the support of orally matching the picture cards to the word-family headers and instructs her to do so.
- After the sorting is completed, Ms. Flory makes sure Minuette reads the cards in each column and states the common feature.

- **Writing sort**—Ms. Flory establishes each word family header and has Minuette identify the matching picture glued beside the word family.
  - Minuette begins to spell *jog* with a g instead of a *j*. Ms. Flory says nothing, and Minuette discovers her own error without prompting.
  - On completion of the writing sort, Ms. Flory makes sure Minuette reads the words she's written in each column, first reading the header and afterward stating the common feature.
  - As she reads her words, Minuette cannot read *not* because the *t* looks like an *x*. Ms. Flory allows her to discover the problem and fix it.
- **FastRead**—Ms. Flory explains to Minuette what they're going to do.
  - Ms. Flory lends support with *ig*, which Minuette reads as *ick* and *ack* in the Practice Box, and reinforces that g says /g/.
  - Ms. Flory models clearly with a slow, consistent pace.
  - Minuette uses a piece of card stock as a guide so she won't lose her place.
  - After Minuette is finished, Ms. Flory announces, with praise, Minuette's score, and she takes Minuette back to review and correct her errors.

Writing

- Ms. Flory explains the procedure for the dictated sentence up front. She reads the full sentence, then dictates slowly, word by word.
- Ms. Flory reminds Minuette to leave spaces between her words.
- Ms. Flory has Minuette read her sentence after she has finished writing. Finally, Ms. Flory goes back and points out the words containing short *o* families, asking Minuette to identify the families.

New Reading

Introducing the New Book: Polly's Shop

- Ms. Flory reads the title, draws attention to the cover picture, and asks Minuette what she sees.
- Ms. Flory conducts a picture walk, leaving the last page as a surprise. In the picture walk she talks about the word *dock,* a concept with which she thinks Minuette might be unfamiliar. As she proceeds she also uses the word *mixed,* which appears in the text and might be hard for Minuette to decode. She asks Minuette questions about the pictures and what she thinks is happening.
- *Polly's Shop* features short *u* words, too. While Minuette knows the sound of short *u,* she has not studied the vowel in word families. To further support her in her upcoming reading, Ms. Flory has Minuette name some of the objects in the pictures, which include both short *u* and short *o* words.
- Finally, Ms. Flory asks Minuette for a prediction about what will happen on the last page.

Reading the New Book

- Ms. Flory gives Minuette time to fix her own errors, and when she doesn't, Ms. Flory prompts her to read the word correctly. Examples:
  - With *were,* Ms. Flory redirects Minuette, draws attention to the first letter, tells her to get her mouth ready, and gives her a chance to figure out the word. However, Minuette struggles, and Ms. Flory finally gives her the word. Minuette rereads the sentence now that she knows the word.
  - When Minuette reads *there* for *here* and continues without correcting herself, Ms. Flory points to the word and asks, "Is this word *there*? Look at your first sound." Minuette corrects herself.
  - When Minuette reads *there* for *where* and moves on without discovering her error, despite a question mark, Ms. Flory asks, "Does that make sense? I see a question mark so I know he's asking a question." When Minuette says *there* again, Ms. Flory draws her attention to the beginning of the word. Minuette figures it out and rereads the sentence.
  - In the second reading of the book Ms. Flory praises Minuette for getting "that tricky word *were*" and revisits the word after Minuette finishes reading.

Take-Home Book

Minuette chooses the book she will take home.

After the lesson, Ms. Flory:

- Finishes writing her comments on the lesson plan
- Checks the new word-bank words against an alphabetized word-bank record
- Creates cards to add to Minuette's word-bank ring
- Updates the "Books I Have Read" list

Video: Late Beginning Reader Lesson—Ashley and Donna

Background Notes on the Lesson Plan

Ashley's reading level is numbered (Reading Recovery) level 12, or lettered (Guided Reading) level G. She is studying consonant blends and digraphs that produce an affricate sound.

Rereading

This section is usually a bit shorter for the late beginning reader: Not only is the New Reading book getting longer, but the New Reading and Writing sections are generally becoming more complex, and they take more time.

- The book *Dragon's Lunch*, at Guided Reading level F, is an easy book incorporated into Ashley's rereading list several lessons earlier, when she was studying the affricate blend *dr*. Ashley is now ready for the text copy. A word hunt follows immediately. The book will now be retired from the box.
- "See You Later, Alligator" is a new poem for Ashley, offering practice with expression, pacing, and accurate reading.
- Ashley will choose a book from her box and read her favorite part.

Word Bank and Word Study

- **Word bank**—Ashley has at least 100 words in her word bank by this time, so she skips the word-bank section.
- **Push It Say It**—This is the second lesson in which Ashley is studying the affricate blend *tr* and the affricate digraph *ch*, which are often confused. She'll sort these affricates next.
- **Picture/word sort**—Ashley did well with the TR, CH word sort in the last lesson. In this lesson she'll participate in a blind sort, in which she'll identify the affricate by its sound before seeing the word.
- **Writing sort**—Words from the sort are called out.
- **FastRead**—This FastRead sheet offers practice to increase automaticity with the previously studied *fr*, *gr*, and *br* blends. This is the first time Ashley will read this particular sheet, so the tutor will model it for her.

New Reading

The book *Animal Armor* is on Ashley's reading level.

Writing

Writing follows the New Reading section of the Beginning Reader Lesson Plan when the writing activity emanates from the completed book. Often this is an activity designed to enhance comprehension.

Student: *Ashley*	**Tutor:** *Donna*	**Date:** *12/16* **Lesson #:** *16*
Lesson Plan	*Description of Planned Activities*	*Comments*
Rereading (10–12 minutes)	• *Dragon's Lunch—text copy* *1) Read 2) Highlight dr- words while saying words aloud.* • *"See You Later, Alligator" poem* *1) Model 2) Choral read 3) A. reads* • *Choice—A. reads her favorite part*	
Word Bank and Word Study (15–20 minutes)	~~**Word Bank:**~~ **Push It Say It:** *tr-, ch-* **Picture/Word Sort:** *tr-, ch- blind sort* **Writing Sort:** *Call out 3-4 words for each header: tr-, ch-* **FastRead:** *r-blends #2 1) Model 2) Time for 1:00*	
Writing (8–10 minutes)	*After new book, answer questions on sheet about armor for people.*	
New Reading (8–10 minutes)	**Book:** *Animal Armor* 1. **Read title to student and look at cover.** *—Discuss "armor."* 2. **Student makes a prediction.** 3. **Discuss pictures, words, and patterns in the story.** *—Animal names* 4. **Student reads the book to you.**	
Take-Home Book	**Book:** ____________	

Video: Late Beginning Reader Lesson—Ashley and Donna

Notes on Tutor Behaviors: What to Look For

Throughout the lesson, note the praise and encouragement the tutor gives to her student.

Rereading

- *Dragon's Lunch* text copy—When Ashley reads a word incorrectly, Donna waits for her to discover the error herself. When she's about to move on to the next sentence without doing so, Donna points to the word and asks, "Is that *sandwich*?" Ashley reads the word correctly.
  - In the word hunt, Donna tells Ashley to say each word as she highlights it. This way, Ashley must read the word instead of simply looking for the *dr* at the beginning, reinforcing the sound–print connection and supporting automatic word recognition.
- "See You Later, Alligator"—Donna introduces the poem by reading the title and discussing the subject. She reviews with Ashley the various animal names, which may not be easily recognized. Donna explains she'll read first, then they'll read together. She models a fluent reading of the poem, supports Ashley in a choral reading, and then assists her with a couple of difficult words as Ashley reads the poem alone.

Word Study

- **Push It Say It**—Donna explains they'll be doing this activity with *tr* and *ch*. She has Ashley identify the short vowels and the *tr* and *ch* tiles.
  - Donna makes sure Ashley matches her pronunciation of each tile with her manipulation of it, so she is aware of the segmentation of the word before she blends the sounds.
- **Picture/word sort**—Donna tells Ashley that they'll be doing a blind sort, with which Ashley is familiar, and reminds her of the procedure. Before the sort Donna has Ashley identify the headers: *tr* with a key word/picture and *ch* with a key word/picture.
  - By this time in the word study sequence, sorts are mostly comprised of words. A blind sort will always be done with words, so that after a student has identified the targeted sound, she can check her accuracy with the printed word.
- **Writing sort**—Donna makes sure Ashley establishes the *tr*/picture and the *ch*/picture headers.
  - After Ashley has finished, Donna asks her to read down each column, beginning with the header and has her state the feature the words have in common.
  - When Ashley reads the correctly spelled *chop* as *trop*, Donna suggests they look at the word again and points to the onset, *ch*. When Ashley identifies it correctly, Donna points to the rime, *op*. Ashley reads the rime, and Donna prompts her to blend the chunks.
- **FastRead**—Donna explains the procedure to Ashley.
  - Donna clearly models the words with a slow, consistent pace.
  - Ashley uses a word finder to focus on each word individually and to help her keep her place.

– After Ashley is finished, Donna reviews with her the words *brand,* which she'd read as *bran,* and *grip,* which she'd read as *drip.* Ashley identifies both words correctly this time. Because confusion between *gr* and *dr* is fairly common, Donna takes the time to make sure Ashley knows how she would spell the word *drip.*

New Reading

Introducing the New Book: Animal Armor

- This is an informational book introducing some difficult words, including animal names. Donna spends some time discussing the title, the cover, and the concept of "armor," using the words *protect* and *covering,* which appear in the text. She asks Ashley to predict what she might learn. When Ashley says she doesn't know, Donna asks a question, leading her into investing in a prediction.
- With fiction books at this level, a brief, partial walk-through is usually all that is necessary. However, with informational books, which often offer less familiar formats, concepts, and vocabulary, a more thorough walk-through may be needed. Donna goes through the book with Ashley, pointing out animal names and mentioning *spines,* a word in the text that Ashley may have trouble reading.

Reading the New Book

The interactive nature of the book, with its question-and-answer format, invites discussion as the book is read.

- At the beginning of the book Donna realizes she'd failed to point out the difficult word *layers* during the introduction, so she does it before Ashley reads the page.
- Donna gives Ashley time to figure out words and discover and fix her own errors. If Ashley can't get a word and fails to self-correct an error, Donna offers prompts. Examples:
  - Throughout the book when Ashley struggles with the word *armor,* Donna gives her time to recall the word. When Ashley doesn't come up with the word the first time she encounters it, Donna draws her attention to the title on the cover. When Ashley can't get the word once more, later in the book, Donna asks, "What's the word we've been reading all along?"
  - With *enemies,* Donna prompts Ashley to sound out as much as she can, then helps her with the rest. She has Ashley reread the sentence.
  - When Ashley reads *thick* as *chick* and doesn't correct herself before moving on to the next page, Donna asks her, "Did that make sense?" and repeats the sentence the way Ashley read it. Ashley fixes the error.
  - When Ashley reads *spines* as *spins,* Donna, knowing that Ashley has not yet studied long-vowel patterns, acknowledges that the word would be *spins* if not for the silent *e,* which makes the *i* say its own name. Donna doesn't dwell on this, but helps to lay a foundation for Ashley's awareness of the VCe spelling pattern.

Writing

The coordinator has prepared the question sheet for *Animal Armor* and keeps copies in a file so she can use it for each child who reads the book. The questions extend the concept of armor to humans.

- Donna introduces the activity, explaining that Ashley is going to answer questions about *human* armor now that she's read about animal armor.
- Donna uses the opportunity presented by the word *protect* on the sheet to praise Ashley for getting the word so quickly. She also goes back to the book to revisit another word with which Ashley had trouble, *enemies.*
- When Ashley has trouble thinking of responses, Donna asks leading questions and gives Ashley time to think. She resorts to suggestions when Ashley does not appear to be coming up with any response.
- If Ashley were writing sentences, Donna would wait for her to finish writing before prompting her for any corrections. However, Ashley is making a list. Donna waits for her to finish writing an item, then asks if she's represented all the sounds she hears. Donna repeats the word, supporting Ashley by dragging out the sounds.
- Donna holds Ashley accountable for the features Ashley has learned. She doesn't worry about correct spelling for any word except *pads,* a CVC word Ashley should know how to spell.
- After prompting her to hear the *r* and *d* in *swords,* Donna draws Ashley's attention to the little word she knows, *or.*
- Because Ashley has not yet studied preconsonantal nasals, like *ank*, Donna does not correct Ashley when she spells *tanks* as *tacks.* But when Ashley reads back the word—correctly—as *tacks,* Donna acknowledges that and asks her how she can make the word into *tanks,* assisting her by saying the word slowly, stressing the /n/.
- Donna writes, too.
- Donna has Ashley reread her writing.

Take-Home Book

When Ashley wants to take home *Animal Armor*, Donna suggests she wait until she's read it a second time, because it contains some hard words.

After the lesson, Donna:

- Finishes writing her comments on the lesson plan
- Updates the "Books I Have Read" list

General

- I followed the lesson plan.
- I monitored my time on each section of the lesson plan.
- I wrote comments for each activity.
- I generously praised my student throughout the lesson, offering specific praise that described her accomplishments.
- I updated the book list and word-bank record as needed.

Rereading

- I gave the student a structured choice in selecting the first book for the session.
- During digressions, I suggested we save the discussion for our walk back to the room or directed the student's attention back to rereading.
- I assisted the student to use appropriate strategies when he had difficulty with a word.
- I gave the student time to think when he made an error.
- *For emergent and beginning readers*: I encouraged the student to point to each word while reading.
- *For emergent readers*: I adjusted my level of support depending on the familiarity with the material.

Word Study

Word Bank

- I laid the word cards from the designated book on the table.
- I asked the student to read the words she knew right away.
- I chose only a couple of unknown words and asked the student to find them on the page.
- I recorded the words she knew and made word cards for her word bank *after* the tutorial session.
- I reviewed the word-bank words using the activity provided by the coordinator.
- I quietly discarded unknown words after several reviews.

Phonics

- I introduced the key words/headers and, if needed, modeled several cards.
- I handed the shuffled cards to the student.
- When the student did not recognize a picture, I immediately told him what it was.
- I made sure the student said each word aloud during sorting.
- I remained silent and allowed my student to make mistakes.
- At the conclusion of the sort, I
  - Had the student read down each column
  - Helped my student find and correct his mistakes
  - Asked what the words in each column have in common: Sounds? Letters? Patterns?

Writing

- I gave clear directions about what the child should do.
- For dictated sentences, I enunciated words clearly, and I encouraged the student to say the words slowly to listen for sounds when writing.
- If the student asked me how to spell a word, I gave the student just enough information to discover the answer on her own, encouraging her to do her best. I told her we would check the spelling together when she finished.
- I did not correct what had not been taught.
- I supported the student as needed in planning for any original writing.

Introduction and Reading of New Book

Note: The transitional reader lesson plan provides specific instructions from the coordinator for before, during, and after reading. The following guidelines are generic ones.

Before Reading

- I read the title to my student, and we looked at the cover.
- I asked my student what she thought the book might be about based on the title and cover illustration (prediction).
- I pointed out some difficult words.
- *For emergent and beginning readers*: We looked at the illustrations on some pages (more pages for the emergent and earlier beginning reader), and I asked her what she saw (I modeled a think-aloud if needed).
- *For beginning and transitional readers*:
  - I gave my student just enough prereading support so that she could read by herself, but not so much that I became the reader.
  - I handed the book to my student and asked her to read it.

During Reading

- I gave my student time to discover his own errors and attempt to correct them himself.
- I intervened with strategies to help the student figure out words when necessary (see the "What to Do When a Reader Needs Help with Words" strategy sheet).
- *For emergent readers*: I used choral and echo reading to support my student.

After Reading

- We revisited original predictions and compared them to how the text actually unfolded.
- We looked back at problem words or pages.
- *For emergent and beginning readers*: We read the book a second time.

Oral Reading in Context: 100 Word Chart

____

Student *Date*

____

Passage Title ❑ *expository* ❑ *narrative* *Passage Level*

Directions: Mark words read correctly with a check in each box. Mark errors by leaving the box blank or note the error. Record the number of errors and the total time below. Use the equations below to determine WPM and accuracy.

1. Number of errors: ____________ Total Time: ______:______ (*min* *sec*) WPM:____________

2. Accuracy if 100 word passage: 100 (*# of words*) – ________ (*# of errors*) = ________% (*accuracy*)

OR

Accuracy if passage less than 100 words: ________ (*# of words*) – ________ (*# of errors*) = ________ / ________ (*# of words*) = ________% (*accuracy*)

3. WPM: ________ (*# min*) x 60 (*60 sec/min*) = ________ + ________ (*# sec*) = ____________ (*total time in seconds*)

AND

WPM: ________ (*# words*) x 60 (*60 sec/min*) = ________ / ____________ (*total time in seconds*) = ________ (*WPM*)

Oral Reading in Context: Accuracy Progress Chart

Student ______________________ *Grade Level* ______________________

Level of Passages ______________ ❑ *expository* ❑ *narrative*

Accuracy (%)					
100					
95					
90					
85					
80					
75					
70					
65					
60					
55					
50					
45					
40					
35					
30					
25					
20					
15					
10					
5					
0					
Date	______	______	______	______	______

Date: ____________ Passage Title: ______________________________ Accuracy %: ____________

Date: ____________ Passage Title: ______________________________ Accuracy %: ____________

Date: ____________ Passage Title: ______________________________ Accuracy %: ____________

Date: ____________ Passage Title: ______________________________ Accuracy %: ____________

Date: ____________ Passage Title: ______________________________ Accuracy %: ____________

Oral Reading in Context: WPM Progress Chart

____
Student *Grade Level*

____
Level of Passages ❑ *expository* ❑ *narrative*

Words Per Minute

100
95
90
85
80
75
70
65
60 — 1st Grade Goal
55
50
45 — Primer Goal
40
35
30
25
20
15
10
5
0

________ ________ ________ ________ ________

Date

Date: ____________ Passage Title: ______________________________ Accuracy %: ____________

Date: ____________ Passage Title: ______________________________ Accuracy %: ____________

Date: ____________ Passage Title: ______________________________ Accuracy %: ____________

Date: ____________ Passage Title: ______________________________ Accuracy %: ____________

Date: ____________ Passage Title: ______________________________ Accuracy %: ____________

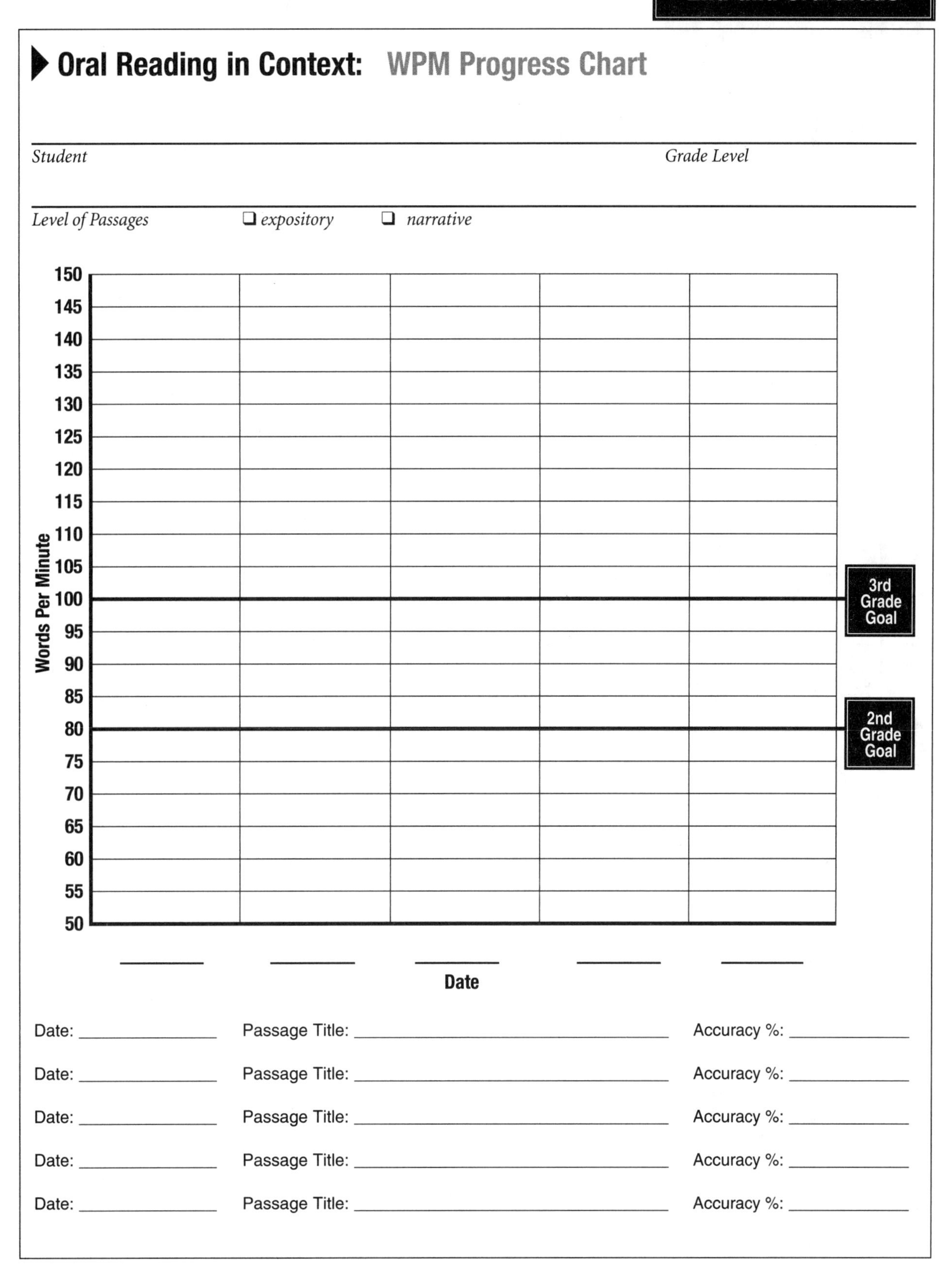
Oral Reading in Context: WPM Progress Chart
Student
Grade Level
Level of Passages
❑ expository
❑ narrative
150
145
140
135
130
125
120
115
110
105
100
95
90
85
80
75
70
65
60
55
50
Words Per Minute
3rd Grade Goal
2nd Grade Goal
Date
Date: ______ Passage Title: ______ Accuracy %: ______
Date: ______ Passage Title: ______ Accuracy %: ______
Date: ______ Passage Title: ______ Accuracy %: ______
Date: ______ Passage Title: ______ Accuracy %: ______
Date: ______ Passage Title: ______ Accuracy %: ______

APPENDIX W. What to Do When a Reader Needs Help with Words

1. **DON'T SAY ANYTHING!** Give the child time to think or to self-correct. Praise briefly if the child self-corrects. If the error does not change the meaning revisit it later. Do not interrupt any more than is necessary.

2. **PROMPT:** Say *Try that again! Did that make sense?* Or, *Something isn't right. Can you fix it?* (Sometimes you can simply point to the sentence or word.) Praise a correction or consider the following prompts depending on developmental level, the word, and support from context. Give only a few prompts before moving on, but revisit the word later. Sometimes you just need to tell the word.

EMERGENT	*BEGINNING*	*TRANSITIONAL*
3. **DRAW ATTENTION TO THE FIRST LETTER** *Look at the first letter.* *Reread the sentence and get your mouth ready to say this sound.* *Could that word be ____________? Why not?* (Repeat the child's error.) *What would you expect to see at the beginning of ____________?* **CONTEXT** *What would make sense?* *What would sound right?* *Look at the picture.* *Read the sentence and try that word again.* **GIVE THE WORD** Say, *Would that word be ____________ or ____________?* (Include correct word in choice.) *That is a hard word. It is ____________.* *Watch me* (slide your finger under the word as you sound it out).	3. **DRAW ATTENTION TO LETTERS** *Look at the first letter(s).* *Reread the sentence and get your mouth ready to say this (these) sound(s).* *Could that word be ____________? Why not?* (Repeat the child's error.) *Does that word match what you see?* *Sound it out. Start here (point to first letter).* **CONTEXT** *Reread the sentence up to here and use the first few letters to start to say the word.* *What would make sense?* *What would sound right?* *Read the sentence and try that word again.* **GIVE THE WORD** Say, *Could that word be ____________ or ____________?* (Include correct word in choice.) *That is a hard word. It is ____________.* *Watch me* (slide your finger under the word as you sound it out).	3. **DRAW ATTENTION TO EVERYTHING STUDENT KNOWS ABOUT LETTERS** *Slide your finger under this word and look at all the letters.* *Sound it out.* *Do you see a part of that word you know?* *Does that look like another word you know?* *Cover up ____________ and try it* (cover beginning blends, endings, or prefixes). **CONTEXT** *Reread the sentence and try that word again.* *Skip the word, read to the end, and then come back and try it.* *What would make sense?* *What would sound right?* **GIVE THE WORD** *That is a hard word. It is ____________.* *Watch me* (slide your finger under the word as you sound it out).

4. **REVISIT THE WORD AFTER READING**
Let's look at this word again. (Revisit in text or write it down. Then use the prompts above.) *Do you remember what you did here? Do you remember this word? How did you figure it out?*

5. **PRAISE**
You did something really smart here when you ____________ (name what they did). *You worked hard to figure that out. I like the way you went back and fixed that word. That's what good readers do!*

APPENDIX X. Alphabet Cards (p. 1 of 2)

A	a	ɑ	B	b
C	c	D	d	E
e	F	f	G	g
g	H	h	I	i
J	j	K	k	L
l	M	m	N	n

O	o	P	p	Q
q	R	r	S	s
T	t	t	U	u
V	v	W	w	X
x	Y	y	Z	z

Glossary

Affricate. This is a speech sound produced with a stop in the breath stream followed immediately by a release of air creating friction, usually where the tip of the tongue touches the roof of the mouth just behind the teeth. The /ch/ sound at the end of *coach,* the /tr/ sound at the beginning of *trap,* and the /j/ sound at the beginning of *jam* are examples of affricates and may be confused by young spellers.

Alphabetic Principle. The understanding that spoken language is made up of individual sounds (phonemes) and that letters represent them in a systematic way. The alphabetic principle allows children to spell phonetically and begin to decode words.

Anchored Word Instruction. A strategy for teaching vocabulary that includes introducing a new word in context, showing the printed form of the word and asking students to pronounce it, giving a definition of the word and then providing additional examples using the word in other contexts.

Beginning Reader. This is a reader in the beginning stage of literacy who has a concept of word in text and knows most or all of the alphabet letters and most letter sounds. Because beginning readers are just beginning to build a sight-word or automatic reading vocabulary, they read and write very slowly.

Blend. A blend is two or three consonants that are blended together to make a sound that retains the identities of each letter. For example, the word *stop* begins with the *st* blend. When you say *stop,* you hear both the *s* and the *t* sounds blended together. Blends occur at the beginning of words, as in *stop,* and also at the end of words, as in *fast.* Other blends include the *bl* in *blend,* the *br* in *brown,* and the *str* in *string.*

Blind Sort. This is a word sort in which the person sorting is given words verbally by a partner and must identify the correct category by sound or by visualizing the spelling pattern (depending on the categories) before seeing each word.

Choral Reading. When two or more people read the same text at the same time, it is called choral reading.

Chunk. A structural part of a word associated with certain phonics or spelling patterns, such as the spellings of consonant blends in the onset or the spellings of vowel patterns in the rime. See onset and rime.

Concept of Word in Text. The ability to match spoken words to printed words in a one-to-one correspondence. This is demonstrated when children can accurately point with their finger as they read memorized text. If they get "off track" and point to a word or part of a word that doesn't match what they're saying, they don't have a full concept of word. Emergent readers and early beginning readers frequently get off track on two-syllable words.

Consonants. The consonant letters are all the letters that are not vowels (see below). Consonants can usually be "felt" as we interrupt the flow of air through our vocal cords and mouth with our lips, tongue, teeth, and palate. Each of these words begins and ends with a consonant: *bed, map, fig, lot.*

Decodable Books. Books that contain words that can be sounded out. Decodable books contain letter sounds and phonics features the reader has been taught and provides an opportunity for the reader to apply phonics knowledge to reading in context.

Decoding. The ability to apply knowledge of letter–sound correspondences and letter patterns to figure out and correctly pronounce written words. Multiple opportunities to decode words leads to the ability to recognize them automatically and to figure out new words not previously seen.

Digraph. A digraph is a pair of letters that creates a single and unique sound. The new sound does not retain the identities of the individual letters. In this book, when we use the term *digraph,* we are usually referring to the most common consonant digraphs that occur at the beginning of words: *sh* (*ship*), *th* (*the* and *thin*), *wh* (*when*), and *ch* (*chip*). Consonant digraphs also occur at the end of words (as in *dish* and *each*).

Dyslexia. A reading disability characterized by difficulty with word recognition, spelling, and decoding, typically stemming from a weakness in the phonological component of language. These difficulties are often said to be "unexpected" in relation to other cognitive abilities and the provision of appropriate classroom instruction. In the absence of early intervention, early word-level difficulties often lead to an overall reduction in reading experience and ultimately to secondary problems in reading comprehension, vocabulary, and knowledge development.

Echo Reading. When readers reread or *echo* what has just been read to them, it is called echo reading.

Emergent Reader. This is a reader in the emergent stage of literacy. The stage begins around age 1 and ends when the reader has attained the *alphabetic principle* and has developed a rudimentary concept of word in text, meaning she is matching spoken words to printed words as she reads and points to words in text.

FastRead. This is an activity designed to help beginning readers build automatic word recognition. In FastRead children read, as quickly as they can, a series of randomly ordered words or word families representing phonics features they are currently studying or have previously studied.

High-Frequency Words. There are a small number of words that occur over and over in English such as *the, of, is,* and *were.* High-frequency words provide the "glue" for putting other words together in a meaningful sentence and have little meaning by themselves. In the past, these words were sometimes called Dolch words. They are often not spelled completely phonetically (e.g., *from*), and for this reason, they may be difficult to remember.

Inflectional Morphemes. An inflectional morpheme is a suffix that is added to a word to indicate its grammatical role. Inflectional morphemes include *-ed,* which indicates that a verb is past tense; *-s,* which indicates whether a noun is singular or plural; and *-er,* which indicates whether an adjective is comparative.

Irregular Verbs. Irregular verbs are verbs whose past tense is not formed by adding the usual inflectional morpheme -ed to the end of the word. Examples of irregular verbs include *bend (bent), go (went), pay (paid).*

Letter Name–Alphabetic Spelling Stage. Corresponding to the beginning stage of reading, this stage of spelling development is characterized by representation of beginning, middle, and ending sounds of words with letter choices that are phonetically accurate.

Leveled Texts. A hierarchy of books arranged from easiest to hardest according to a set of criteria for each level. Assigning books to levels assists tutors in selecting texts that match children's reading skill to the supports and challenges of the text.

Long Vowels. There are five common long vowel sounds. Long vowels usually "say their names," as in *cake, feet, pride, road,* and *cute.*

Morphemes. Morphemes refer to the spelling of meaning units in words that cannot be further divided into smaller units of meaning. For example, the word *reheated* has three morphemes: *re-*, *heat,* and *-ed*. Morphemes in written English include base words, roots, and affixes.

Morphology. Morphology is the study of word parts or morphemes related to syntax and meaning. Morphological knowledge helps learners read and understand the meaning of words. See *morphemes*.

Multisensory. Multisensory refers to teaching that presents information simultaneously in visual, auditory, and kinesthetic-tactile modalities. Early literacy instruction that asks children to see, say, feel, and write sounds, letters, letter patterns, and words is said to enhance memory and learning.

Oddballs. Words that do not fit the targeted feature in a phonics or spelling sort because they are spelled with a pattern associated with another sound. Words like *give* and *have* are oddballs.

Onset. This is the initial consonant or consonant blend or digraph before the vowel in a syllable or single-syllable word. The onset of *back* is *b*. The onset of *black* is *bl*. See *rime*.

Phoneme. This is the smallest unit of speech sound in a language system. The /c/ in *cat* and the /sh/ in *ship* are phonemes.

Phonemic Awareness. Under the umbrella of phonological awareness, this is the ability to hear, say, and manipulate individual phonemes, such as segmenting a word into phonemes (*bag* is *b-a-g*) or blending phonemes to make a word (*p-o-t* is *pot*). Although phonemic awareness primarily relates to speech sounds, its development is enhanced by simultaneous exposure to the printed units (letters) that correspond to those speech sounds.

Phonics. Phonics refers to the systematic correspondence between letters and sounds. Phonics is not a method of teaching reading but refers to the knowledge of these letter–sound correspondences.

Phonological Awareness. This is the awareness of the sounds in speech including rhyme, syllables, onset and rime, and phonemes. See *phonemic awareness*.

Phonology. The study of speech sounds. The word *phonology* is used to refer to the innate but subconscious knowledge that underlies our ability to speak, including how to pronounce words and the syllables within them, and how to use expression within and across phrases and sentences.

Picture Sort. A picture sort is one strategy for teaching phonics. Pictures can be sorted into categories on the basis of particular speech sounds.

Preconsonantal Nasal. Nasals that occur before final consonants in words or syllables, such as the *m* in *bump* or the *n* in *sink*. The nasal is not fully articulated in the mouth and passes through the nose, making it difficult to detect.

Preprimer. In the traditional leveling system used by basal readers, the preprimer level corresponds to the first third of the first-grade year. There are three traditional preprimer levels. In the basal system they are PP1[A], PP2[B], and PP3[C]. In the Guided Reading (lettered) system, level C corresponds roughly to PP1, level D to PP2, and level E to PP3. In the Reading Recovery (numbered) system, levels 3–4 correspond roughly to PP1, levels 5–6 to PP2, and levels 7–8 to PP3.

Primer. In the traditional leveling system used by basal readers, the primer (pronounced with a short *i*) level corresponds to the middle of first grade and is labeled 1.1 (first grade, first semester). Guided Reading (lettered) levels F and G and Reading Recovery (numbered) levels 9–12 correspond roughly to the primer level.

Push It Say It. This phonemic blending activity involves the use of small cards that children push forward as they say the sound represented by the letter or letters on the card. The activity helps learners blend sound chunks together to say words, an essential strategy for decoding.

Readiness. In the traditional leveling system used by basal readers, this is a term used to refer to the earliest reading level. Guided Reading (lettered) levels A and B and Reading Recovery (numbered) levels 1 and 2 correspond roughly to the readiness level.

Reading Level. An individual's reading level is the level at which he or she can read the words in a text and understand them with instructional support.

Rime. This is the part, or unit, of a syllable constituted by the vowel and the letters that follow. The rime unit of *black* is *ack*. The rime unit of *goat* is *oat*. See *onset*.

***r*-Influenced Vowels.** Refers to the spelling of words that include an *r* immediately following the vowel in words such as *cart, bird,* or *hurt*. In such words, the *r* takes over the sound of the preceding vowel and makes it difficult to detect the vowel sound apart from the *r* sound.

Running Record. This is a record of oral reading accuracy taken as the student reads aloud. Accuracy can be marked atop a copy of the passage that is being read or on a blank chart such as the 100 Word Chart in Appendix V. When a student is reading late primer text and beyond, the running record is timed, and the number of words read per minute can be calculated.

Semantics. A branch of linguistics concerned with the meaning underlying words, phrases, sentences, or texts.

Short Vowels. Each vowel (*a, e, i, o, u*) represents two major sounds: a long vowel and a short vowel. Short vowels do not mimic the name of the letter, as do the long vowels. Each of the short sounds is represented by the beginning letter in these words: *ax, Ed, igloo, octopus,* and *umbrella*.

Sight Words. Words that can be read instantly—"at first sight"—without having to be sounded out. Sight words become sight words by having had many previous opportunities to sound them out.

Spell Check. This is a spelling assessment of features that have been taught and practiced. A *cumulative* spell check, more specifically, is one covering different features that have been taught usually over two or more weeks.

Spelling Patterns. Certain combinations of letters work as a unit to represent sounds and meaning in words. We can see the *at* pattern in these words: *cat, mat, sat*. There are also spelling patterns that contain silent letters, which serve to "mark" the particular vowel sound of that letter. The silent *e* at the end of *cake, home,* and *tribe* has no sound of its own but in conjunction with the vowel in the middle forms a pattern: vowel, consonant, silent *e* (VCe). English has many such patterns, especially for the long vowels, which can also signal different meanings in words that otherwise sound the same, as in the homophones *male* and *mail*.

Syllable. Syllables are units of speech sounds set off by breaths or air flow. A syllable consists of a vowel that may be preceded and/or followed by one or more consonants.

Syntax. The structure of sentences including word order, parts of speech and grammar, and other mechanics of written language. Knowledge of syntax helps learners make sense of reading and writing.

Timed Repeated Readings (TRR). This technique requires the child to read and reread the same passage of text three to five times. Each reading is timed, and errors are tallied. Progress can be charted on a graph.

Tracking. The process of pointing to each word in a text as it is read. Accurate tracking demonstrates the reader's development of a concept of word in text.

Transitional Reader. This is a reader in the transitional stage of literacy. The reader is *transitioning* between the beginning stage, in which readers are just developing their literacy skills, and the intermediate stage, in which readers are reading and writing fluently. Transitional readers are beginning to read in phrases with more expression, and they build speed. They are beginning to read silently.

Vowels. Vowels are speech sounds that are created by an unobstructed flow of air through the vocal cords and mouth. The vowel sounds are represented by the letters *a, e, i, o, u,* and sometimes *y* (as in *my* and *myth*). The other letters of the alphabet represent consonant sounds.

Within Word Pattern Spelling Stage. Corresponding to the transitional stage of reading, this stage of spelling development is characterized by the study of patterns, especially long vowel patterns, in single-syllable words. The *ai* in *chain* and the *ea* in *cream* are examples of within word patterns.

Word Bank. This is a collection of words the child recognizes automatically out of context. Word-bank words are written on cards or small slips of paper and form a corpus for review and phonics study. They are *known* words comprising a growing reading vocabulary.

Word Families. All the words in a "family" rhyme and are spelled with the same pattern of letters also known as *rimes.* The *ed* family would include *bed, red, led,* and *sled,* but not *head.* See *rime.*

Word Hunt. This is an activity in which children look through texts they have already read to find words that have particular sounds or spelling patterns.

Word Sort. A word sort is a phonics teaching activity. In a word sort, words on cards are categorized by a particular sound or by a particular spelling pattern that goes with that sound.

Writing Sort. A word study activity in which students write the words they have sorted into categories of sounds and spelling patterns.

Resources Cited in Text

Children's Books

Barrett, J. (1970). *Animals should definitely* not *wear clothing.* New York: Aladdin Paperbacks.
Carle, E. (1997). *From head to toe.* New York: HarperCollins.
Casey, A. J. (1997). *Can you find it?* Parsippany, NJ: Modern Curriculum Press.
Grout, B. J. (1996). *Polly's shop.* Parsippany, NJ: Modern Curriculum Press.
Hoberman, M. A. (2001). *You read to me, I'll read to you: Very short stories to read together.* New York: Little, Brown.
Hoberman, M. A. (2004). *You read to me, I'll read to you: Very short fairy tales to read together.* New York: Little, Brown.
Hoberman, M. A. (2005). *You read to me, I'll read to you: Very short Mother Goose tales to read together.* New York: Little, Brown.
Hoberman, M. A. (2007). *You read to me, I'll read to you: Very short scary tales to read together.* New York: Little, Brown.
Lobel, A. (1970). *Frog and toad are friends.* New York: HarperCollins.
McGovern, K. L. (2000). *Let's move!* Parsippany, NJ: Modern Curriculum Press.
Parkes, B. (1998). *A pond.* New York: Newbridge.
Pernick, G. (1996). *As fast as a fox.* Parsippany, NJ: Modern Curriculum Press.
Raffi. (1988). *Down by the bay.* New York: Crown.
Smith, C. (2001). *Animal armor.* Washington, DC: National Geographic.
Stewart, S. (2005). *It's a mammal.* Parsippany, NJ: Celebration Press.
Williams, R. L. (1994). *All through the week with cat and dog.* Cypress, CA: Creative Teaching Press.
Williams, S. (1992). *I went walking.* New York: Houghton Mifflin Harcourt.

Professional Resources

Adams, M. J., Foorman, B. R., Lunberg, I., & Beeler, T. (1998). *Phonemic awareness in young children.* Baltimore: Brookes.
Bear, D. R., Invernizzi, M., Johnston, F., & Templeton, S. (2019). *Words their way: Letter and picture sorts for emergent spellers* (3rd ed.). New York: Pearson Education.
Bear, D. R., Invernizzi, M., Templeton, S., & Johnston, F. (2020). *Words their way: Word study for phonics, vocabulary, and spelling instruction* (7th ed.). Hoboken, NJ: Pearson Education.
Beck, I. L., McKeown, M. G., & Kucan, L. (2013). *Bringing words to life: Robust vocabulary instruction* (2nd ed.). New York: Guilford Press.

Blevins, W. (2017). *Phonics from A to Z* (3rd ed.). New York: Scholastic.

Helman, L., Bear, D. R., Invernizzi, M., Templeton, S., & Johnston, F. (2009a). *Words their way: Emergent sorts for Spanish-speaking English learners.* Boston: Pearson Education.

Helman, L., Bear, D. R., Invernizzi, M., Templeton, S., & Johnston, F. (2009b). *Words their way: Letter name–alphabetic sorts for Spanish-speaking English learners.* Boston: Pearson Education.

Helman, L., Bear, D. R., Templeton, S., Invernizzi, M., & Johnston, F. (2012). *Words their way with English learners: Word study for phonics, vocabulary, and spelling instruction* (2nd ed.). Boston: Pearson Education.

Hiebert, E. H. (2012). *QuickReads* (Levels A–F). Paramus, NJ: Savvas.

Invernizzi, M., Johnston, F., Bear, D. R., & Templeton, S. (2018). *Words their way: Word sorts for within word pattern spellers* (3rd ed.). New York: Pearson Education.

Johnston, F., Bear, D. R., Invernizzi, M., & Templeton, S. (2018). *Words their way: Word sorts for letter name–alphabetic spellers* (3rd ed.). New York: Pearson Education.

Johnston, F., Invernizzi, M., Helman, L., Bear, D. R., & Templeton, S. (2014). *Words their way for PreK–K.* New York: Pearson Education.

References

Aaron, P. G. (2012). *Dyslexia and hyperlexia: Diagnosis and management of developmental reading disabilities* (Vol. 1). Berlin: Springer Science & Business Media.

Bear, D. R., Invernizzi, M., Johnston, F., & Templeton, S. (2019). *Words their way: Letter and picture sorts for emergent spellers* (3rd ed.). Hoboken, NJ: Pearson Education.

Bear, D. R., Invernizzi, M., Templeton, S., & Johnston, F. (2020). *Words their way: Word study for phonics, vocabulary, and spelling instruction* (7th ed.). Hoboken, NJ: Pearson Education.

Beck, I. L., McKeown, M. G., & Kucan, L. (2013). *Bringing words to life: Robust vocabulary instruction* (2nd ed.). New York: Guilford Press.

Berninger, V. W. (2008). Defining and differentiating dysgraphia, dyslexia, and language learning disability within a working memory model. In M. Mody & E. R. Silliman (Eds.), *Brain, behavior, and learning in language and reading disorders* (pp. 103–134). New York: Guilford Press.

Berninger, V. W., Lester, K., Sohlberg, M. M., & Mateer, C. (1991). Interventions based on the multiple connections model of reading for developmental dyslexia and acquired deep dyslexia. *Archives of Clinical Neuropsychology, 6*(4), 375–391.

Blachman, B. A., Ball, E., Black, S., & Tangle, O. (1994). Kindergarten teachers develop phonemic awareness in low-income, inner-city classrooms: Does it make a difference? *Reading and Writing: An Interdisciplinary Journal, 6,* 1–17.

Blevins, W. (2017). *Phonics from A–Z: A practical guide* (3rd ed.). New York: Scholastic.

Brady, S. A. (2011). Efficacy of phonics teaching for reading outcomes. In S. A. Brady, D. Braze, & C. A. Fowler (Eds.), *Explaining individual differences in reading: Theory and evidence* (pp. 69–96). New York: Psychology Press.

Brown, K., Morris, D., & Fields, M. (2005). Intervention after grade one: Serving maximum numbers of struggling readers effectively. *Journal of Literacy Research, 37*(1), 61–94.

Bryant, P. E., Bradley, L., MacLean, M., & Crossland, J. (1990). Rhyme and alliteration, phoneme detection, and learning to read. *Developmental Psychology, 26,* 429–438.

Christensen, C., & Bowey, J. (2005). The efficacy of orthographic rime, grapheme-phoneme correspondence, and implicit phonics approaches to teaching decoding skills. *Scientific Studies of Reading, 9,* 327–349.

Clay, M. M. (1985). *The early detection of reading difficulties.* Portsmouth, NH: Heinemann.

Cowen, C. D. (2016, Summer). What is structured literacy? Retrieved from *https://dyslexiaida.org/what-is-structured-literacy.*

de Graaff, S., Bosman, A., Hasselman, F., & Verhoeven, L. (2009). Benefits of systematic phonics instruction. *Scientific Studies of Reading, 13,* 318–333.

Ehri, L. C. (2014). Orthographic mapping in the acquisition of sight word reading, spelling memory, and vocabulary learning. *Scientific Studies of Reading, 18*(1), 5–21.

Ehri, L. C., & McCormick, S. (1998). Phases of word learning: Implications for instruction with delayed and disabled readers. *Reading and Writing Quarterly, 14,* 135–163.

Elliott, J. G., & Grigorenko, E. L. (2014). *The dyslexia debate.* New York: Cambridge University Press.

Flanigan, K. (2007). A concept of word in text: A pivotal event in early reading acquisition. *Journal of Literacy Research, 39*(1), 37–70.

Francis, D. J., Shaywitz, S. E., Stuebing, K. K., Shaywitz, B. A., & Fletcher, J. M. (1996). Developmental lag versus deficit models of reading disability: A longitudinal, individual growth curves analysis. *Journal of Educational Psychology, 88,* 3–17.

Gattis, M. N., Morrow-Howell, N., McCrary, S., Lee, M., Jonson-Reid, M., McCoy, H., . . . Invernizzi, M. (2010). Examining the effects of New York Experience Corps® Program on young readers. *Literacy Research and Instruction, 49*(4), 299–314.

Helman, L., Bear, D. R., Invernizzi, M., Templeton, S., & Johnston, F. (2009a). *Words their way: Emergent sorts for Spanish-speaking English learners.* Boston: Pearson Education.

Helman, L., Bear, D. R., Invernizzi, M., Templeton, S., & Johnston, F. (2009b). *Words their way: Letter name–alphabetic sorts for Spanish-speaking English learners.* Boston: Pearson Education.

Helman, L., Bear, D. R., Templeton, S., Invernizzi, M., & Johnston, F. (2012). *Words their way with English learners: Word study for phonics, vocabulary, and spelling instruction* (2nd ed.). Boston: Pearson Education.

Huang, F. L., & Invernizzi, M. A. (2014). Factors associated with lowercase alphabet naming in kindergarteners. *Applied Psycholinguistics, 35*(6), 943–968.

Huang, F. L., Tortorelli, L. S., & Invernizzi, M. A. (2014). An investigation of factors associated with letter-sound knowledge at kindergarten entry. *Early Childhood Research Quarterly, 29*(2), 182-192.

International Dyslexia Association. (2000). Multisensory teaching. Retrieved from *http://in.dyslexiaida.org/wp-content/uploads/sites/34/2016/10/MSL-Teaching.pdf.*

Invernizzi, M. (2014, October 9). Should we teach 100 sight words to kindergartners? [Web log post]. Retrieved from *www.literacyworldwide.org/blog/2014/10/09.*

Invernizzi, M., Johnston, F., Bear, D. R., & Templeton, S. (2018). *Words their way: Word sorts for within word pattern spellers* (3rd ed.). New York: Pearson Education.

Invernizzi, M., Juel, C., & Rosemary, C. A. (1996). A community volunteer tutorial that works. *The Reading Teacher, 50,* 304–311.

Invernizzi, M., Juel, C., Swank, L., & Meier, J. (2007). *PALS-K: Phonological awareness literacy screening for kindergarten* (6th ed.). Charlottesville, VA: University Printing Services.

Invernizzi, M., Meier, J., & Juel, C. (2007). *PALS 1–3: Phonological awareness literacy screening* (6th ed.). Charlottesville, VA: University Printing Services.

Invernizzi, M., Rosemary, C., Juel, C., & Richards, H. C. (1997). At-risk readers and community volunteers: A 3-year perspective. *Scientific Studies of Reading, 1*(3), 277–300.

Invernizzi, M., & Tortorelli, L. (2013). Phonological awareness and alphabet knowledge: The foundations of early reading. In D. M. Barone & M. H. Mallette (Eds.), *Best practices in early literacy instruction* (pp. 155–174). New York: Guilford Press.

Johnston, F., Bear, D. R., Invernizzi, M., & Templeton, S. (2018). *Words their way: Word sorts for letter name–alphabetic spellers* (3rd ed.). New York: Pearson Education.

Johnston, F. R., Invernizzi, M., Helman, L., Bear, D. R., & Templeton, S. (2014). *Words their way for PreK–K.* New York: Pearson Higher Education.

Johnston, R. S., Watson, J. E., & Logan, S. (2009). Enhancing word reading, spelling and reading comprehension skills with synthetic phonics teaching. In C. Wood & V. Connelly (Eds.), *Contemporary perspectives on reading and spelling* (pp. 221–238). New York: Routledge.

Joshi, R. M., Treiman, R., Carreker, S., & Moats, L. C. (2008). How words cast their spell. *American Educator, 32*(4), 6–16.

Juel, C. (1988). Learning to read and write: A longitudinal study of 54 children from first through fourth grades. *Journal of Educational Psychology, 80*(4), 437.

Juel, C. (1991). Cross-age tutoring between student athletes and at-risk children. *The Reading Teacher, 45*(3), 178–186.

Juel, C. (1996). What makes literacy tutoring effective? *Reading Research Quarterly, 31*(3), 268–289.

Juel, C., & Deffes, R. (2004). Making words stick. *Educational Leadership, 61*(6), 30–34.

McNamara, J. K., Scissons, M., & Gutknetch, N. (2011). A longitudinal study of kindergarten children at risk for reading disabilities: The poor are really getting poorer. *Journal of Learning Disabilities, 44*(5), 421–430.

Meier, J. D., & Invernizzi, M. (2001). Book Buddies in the Bronx: Testing a model for America Reads. *Journal of Education for Students Placed at Risk, 6*(4), 319–333.

Mesmer, H. A. E., & Williams, T. O. (2015). Examining the role of syllable awareness in a model of concept of word: Findings from preschoolers. *Reading Research Quarterly, 50*(4), 483–497.

Metsala, J. L., & Ehri, L. C. (2013). *Word recognition in beginning literacy*. New York: Routledge.

Miller, S. (2003). Partners-in-Reading: Using classroom assistants to provide tutorial assistance to struggling first-grade readers. *Journal of Education for Students Placed at Risk, 8,* 333–349.

Morris, D. (2006). Using noncertified tutors to work with at-risk readers: An evidence-based model. *The Elementary School Journal, 106*(4), 351–362.

Morris, D., Bloodgood, J. W., Lomax, R. G., & Perney, J. (2003). Developmental steps in learning to read: A longitudinal study in kindergarten and first grade. *Reading Research Quarterly, 38*(3), 302–328.

Morris, D., Shaw, B., & Perney, J. (1990). Helping low readers in grades 2 and 3: An after-school volunteer tutoring program. *Elementary School Journal, 91,* 133–150.

National Center on Intensive Intervention. (2020). Intensive intervention and multi-tiered system of supports (MTSS). Retrieved from *https://intensiveintervention.org/intensive-intervention/multi-tiered-systems-support.*

National Reading Panel. (2000, December). *Report of the National Reading Panel: Teaching children to read* (NIH Publication No. 00-4769). Bethesda, MD: National Institute of Child Health and Human Development, National Institutes of Health.

Post, Y. V., & Carreker, S. (2002). Orthographic similarity and phonological transparency in spelling. *Reading and Writing, 15*(3–4), 317–340.

Rawlins, A., & Invernizzi. M. (2019). Reconceptualizing sight words: Building an early reading vocabulary. *The Reading Teacher, 72*(6), 711–719.

Shaywitz, S. E., Morris, R., & Shaywitz, B. A. (2008). The education of dyslexic children from childhood to young adulthood. *Annual Review of Psychology, 59,* 451–475.

Spear-Swerling, L. (2019). Structured literacy and typical literacy practices: Understanding differences to create instructional opportunities. *Teaching Exceptional Children, 51*(3), 201–211.

Vellutino, F. R., Fletcher, J. M., Snowling, M. J., & Scanlon, D. M. (2004). Specific reading disability (dyslexia): What have we learned in the past four decades? *Journal of Child Psychology and Psychiatry, 45*(1), 2–40.

Vellutino, F. R., & Scanlon, D. M. (2002). The interactive strategies approach to reading intervention. *Contemporary Educational Psychology, 27*(4), 573–635.

Vellutino, F. R., Scanlon, D. M., Sipay, E. R., Small, S. G., Chen, R., Pratt, A., & Denckla, M. B. (1996). Cognitive profiles of difficult-to-remediate and readily remediated poor readers: Early intervention as a vehicle for distinguishing between cognitive and experimental deficits as basic causes of specific reading disability. *Journal of Educational Psychology, 88,* 601–638.

Vellutino, F. R., Scanlon, D. M., Small, S., & Fanuele, D. P. (2006). Response to intervention as a vehicle for distinguishing between children with and without disabilities: Evidence for the role of kindergarten and first-grade interventions. *Journal of Learning Disabilities, 39*(2), 157-169.

Walton, P., & Walton, L. M. (2002). Beginning reading by teaching in rime analogy: Effects on phonological skills, letter-sound knowledge, working memory, and word-reading strategies. *Scientific Studies of Reading, 6* (1), 79–115.

Wanzek, J., Stevens, E. A., Williams, K. J., Scammacca, N., Vaughn, S., & Sargent, K. (2018). Current evidence on the effects of intensive early reading interventions. *Journal of Learning Disabilities, 51*(6), 612–624.

Wanzek, J., & Vaughn, S. (2007). Research-based implications from extensive early reading interventions. *School Psychology Review, 36*(4), 541–561.

Warley, H. P., Invernizzi, M. A., & Drake, E. A. (2015). Sight word learning: There's more to it than meets the eye. *Journal of the Virginia State Reading Association, 37,* 40–45.

Wasik, B. (1997). Volunteer tutoring programs: Do we know what works? *Phi Delta Kappan, 79*(4), 282-288.

Wasik, B. (1998). Using volunteers as reading tutors: Guidelines for successful practices. *The Reading Teacher, 51*(7), 562–570.

Index

Note. **Boldface** indicates the term appears in the Glossary; *f* = figure; *t* = table.

F

G

H

I

J

K

L

M

N

O

P

R

S

V

W